The climate of workplace relations

The climate of workplace relations

Ali Dastmalchian,
Paul Blyton
and Raymond Adamson

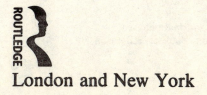

London and New York

First published 1991
by Routledge
11 New Fetter Lane, London EC4P 4EE

Simultaneously published in the USA and Canada
by Routledge
a division of Routledge, Chapman and Hall, Inc.
29 West 35th Street, New York, NY 10001

© 1991 Ali Dastmalchian, Paul Blyton, Ray Adamson

Typeset by J&L Composition Ltd, Filey, North Yorkshire
Printed and bound in Great Britain by
Biddles Ltd, Guildford and King's Lynn

British Library Cataloguing in Publication Data
Dastmalchian, Ali *1954–*
    The climate of workplace relations.
    1. Organisations. Organisation climate
    I. Title II. Blyton *1953–* III. Adamson, Ray *1934–*
302.35

    ISBN 0–415–03738–7

Library of Congress Cataloging in Publication Data
Dastmalchian, Ali, 1954–
    The climate of workplace relations / Ali Dastmalchian, Paul
    Blyton, and Raymond Adamson.
    p.   cm.
      Includes bibliographical references and index.
      ISBN 0–415–03738–7
      1. Industrial relations. 2. Organizational behavior.
    3. Personnel management. I. Blyton, Paul. II. Adamson,
    Raymond, 1934–. III. Title.
      HD6971.D29 1991
      658.3′145 — dc20   90–24430
                                                           CIP

For Ann, Ticky and Marg,
who are just glad to
see it finished

Contents

List of figures

List of tables

Preface

With hindsight, the questions which led to the work described in this book appear deceptively simple: what constitutes the 'climate' or 'atmosphere' in which industrial relations take place? What accounts for the variation in climate from one context to another? How and to what degree does the prevailing climate impact upon industrial relations outcomes? Designing a model, establishing a reliable measure of climate and charting its influence within diverse work contexts has proved complicated and time-consuming. It is for others to judge if this endeavour was worthwhile. For the authors, the effort feels productively spent. Pursuing climate and its relationships has given us a fresh approach to industrial relations enquiry and confirmed the value of greater integration of organizational and industrial relations research. In addition, it has provided us with an opportunity to re-examine the notion of climate and its implications for organizational change and human resource management, and to contribute to the current theoretical debates on climate and related subjects such as organizational culture.

For those readers less interested in our measures and calculations and more concerned with the general findings and their significance, we have tried to write the book in such a way that the sense of the overall findings can be gained from the summaries (especially in chapter 5), without the need for a detailed understanding of the statistical techniques employed. These findings are then extended by case-study analysis in chapter 6.

The process of concept development, model building, and measurement is a long one and we are the first to recognize that many shortcomings remain in the present work, partly due to our failings and partly due to occasional problems of achieving the depth of access and co-operation needed for the full enquiry to proceed.

However, if the findings prompt further discussion and investigation we shall be satisfied. This satisfaction will be all the greater if the present work encourages further bridges to be constructed between organizational and industrial relations research.

Trying to complete this work while based in different continents had its difficulties (as well as some welcome benefits). In overcoming these we are grateful to a number of institutions and individuals who have made the work possible. The Strategic Grants Division of The Social Sciences and Humanities Research Council of Canada and the Saskatchewan Health Research Board provided funding for the main data collection, while the British Council generously contributed to our transatlantic travel costs. We would also like to acknowledge the assistance of the Canadian High Commission, the Foundation for Canadian Studies in the UK, and Wardair/ Canadian Airlines International for making our meetings possible. The University of Saskatchewan provided Ali Dastmalchian with sabbatical leave in 1989–90 to work on the text, which he spent as a Visiting Fellow at Cardiff Business School, University of Wales, Cardiff, and as a Visiting Professor at the Department of Organizational Analysis, Faculty of Business, University of Alberta in Edmonton. Our thanks go to these institutions for providing support for our work. Our sincere thanks too to many managers of participating organizations, their union representatives and the union organizations involved, the many employees who gave generously of their time, and to our research assistants Ellen Gunn (whose excellent work and admirable dedication to the project was key to both stages of the data collection), Shawn Poisson, Lynn McNally, Bryan Acton, Ralph Troschke, Lorraine Fortier, Mark Trowell, and Marie Ty who worked so conscientiously on the project. Our appreciation goes also to Nigel Nicholson for the initial ideas and for supporting the project from a distance, Bob House for helping us formulate the research ideas at a workshop in the Faculty of Management Studies, University of Toronto, Bob Hinings for his helpful comments on the direction of our work throughout the whole process, Steve McShane, Barbara Townley, Basu Sharma, John Hassard, Mansour Javidan, and our colleagues at the University of Saskatchewan: Richard Long, Ignace Ng, Ron Edmonds, and Kurt Wetzel, and at Cardiff Business School: Roger Mansfield, Michael Poole, and Andy Thompson for their helpful and much needed comments on various parts of the project and on the manuscript. Various anonymous Social Sciences and Humanities Research Council of Canada (SSHRC) reviewers also set us straight on a number of issues and problems early on in the process. John Brennan provided the computer resources, and Calvin Barnes helped in software installation and the statistical packages. A special thanks to Louise Jones for typing the manuscript so proficiently.

1 Setting the stage

A leading industrial relations academic in Britain subtitled a recent book 'Theory and Practice in a Cold Climate' (Hyman 1989). The phrase is apt: the 1980s was at best an inclement decade in which to pursue many aspects of industrial relations enquiry. During that decade, several factors achieved prominence in many of the leading industrial countries which significantly altered the context in which industrial relations take place. Among the most important of these were: general economic recession in the early 1980s and persistently high levels of unemployment; the contraction of manufacturing and extractive industries which formerly represented trade union strongholds; the growth of production and service activities often employing workforces with little or no previous experience of union representation; the reassertion of managerial power over labour issues; and the implementation of state policies variously designed to reduce state monopolies and to deliver a less protected labour force to the market-place.

Though many of these trends were present long before the 1980s, a number became increasingly salient in latter years and, by coinciding, have collectively exerted a substantial impact on the nature of industrial relations, undermining a broad pattern which had been developing in several industrial market economies since 1945. Indeed, one view of these developments is that they are prefacing a fundamental shift in power relationships within industrial relations, thereby allowing an increasing management withdrawal from reliance on 'union–management' relations based on collective bargaining and the substituting of a more 'employee relations' orientation with a greater emphasis on individualized negotiation and contract determination.

Yet, while it is clear from various studies that in many work organizations the character of industrial relations has changed significantly during the 1980s, the argument here (and developed in more detail in chapter 2) is that those relations – and the enquiry which seeks greater insight into them – remains no less important today than in any previous period. Indeed, as we discuss below, several of the paths along which managers have been initiating changes in recent years (for example, the pursuit of higher quality standards, lower staffing levels, and the procurement and creation of goods and services 'just-in-time' to satisfy a demand) can act as much to enhance labour power as to diminish it.

More generally, the continued emphasis both by practitioners and academics on the *social* organization of work – the importance given to worker attitudes, motivation and commitment, the acquisition of skills and training, and the design of work tasks and work teams, for example – all attest to a recognition of the continued significance of the work-force in contemporary work organizations. It is this attestation which underpins our belief in the continued importance of both the practice and the study of industrial relations. Moreover, while it is the changes taking place in the field of employment relations which have attracted most attention in the academic and management literature, there is also considerable evidence of important continuities in the attitudes and behaviours comprising those relations. While some aspects of industrial relations have altered markedly in the last decade, others have shown themselves surprisingly impervious to change.

THE STUDY OF INDUSTRIAL RELATIONS

If industrial relations remain an important area for future enquiry, the question this still begs is, what sort of enquiry? The corpus of industrial relations knowledge is not of sufficient standing to encourage a simple extension of past practice. One lacuna, for example, which various writers have alluded to at different times, is that of theory and concept development. According to Hyman, this lack of theory has led to undue prominence being given to systems theory in North America and to pluralism in the UK, despite the significant shortcomings in each (Hyman 1989). Recent advances in theorizing, such as those emerging from the labour process debate (Knights and Willmott 1990), have improved the situation but have not yet been sufficient to rectify the inadequacy of theoretical development in industrial relations, including the development of 'middle range' theories which seek to draw the links between general theories and particular patterns, strategies and practices of industrial relations, and thereby seek explanations for why the character of industrial relations differs from one context to another.

Another shortcoming evident in past British and, particularly, North American industrial relations enquiry has been a widespread tendency among researchers to limit the field of enquiry to the processes of collective bargaining and related institutions, rather than adopting a broader definition of influences on, arenas for, and outcomes of, industrial relations. In the US in particular, this can be seen to have had important consequences for the general health of the subject and was one reason why the changing fortunes of trade unionism in the US from the mid-1950s onwards also marked the end of what has been termed a 'golden age' of industrial relations research in that country. As we have written elsewhere, and in part echoing an earlier argument by Strauss and Feuille (1978), 'it is partly due to its development as an "institutionally oriented field centred on collected bargaining" that industrial relations research did not develop the theoretical base and intellectual breadth and excitement sufficient to prevent some academic drift away from this field of enquiry in the 1960s' (Blyton *et al.* 1987: 207).

Yet one of the continuing strengths of industrial relations is its ability to draw upon and draw together several relevant disciplines (sociology, psychology, law, economics, politics, history, etc.) to inform its analysis of particular industrial relations situations and events. Where this has been translated into a cross-fertilization of concepts, the results have often been fruitful in providing industrial relations researchers with additional tools and frameworks of analysis. For example, sociological concepts such as role, orientation, control, power, dependence, and the institutionalization of conflict have provided valuable insights into the behaviour of particular industrial relations actors and the functioning of industrial relations processes as a whole (Nicholson 1976; Lockwood 1966; Hyman 1975; Ursell and Blyton 1988; Coser 1956). Similar claims can be made on behalf of political science (which has informed industrial relations on concepts such as pluralism) and economics (offering insights into such areas as pay, productivity, and performance).

INDUSTRIAL RELATIONS AND ORGANIZATION THEORY

The present study was partly based on a belief that this process of cross-fertilization could usefully be taken further. It seems logical to expect that just as the dynamics of work organizations do not neatly compartmentalize into the subject areas traditionally taught separately in most business schools and university departments, so too, many of the major concepts developed in one area will potentially have a bearing on, and an application in, related subject areas. The background of the authors – organization theory (Dastmalchian), industrial relations (Blyton) and organizational behaviour (Adamson) – encouraged particular attention to the potential of organizational research for informing industrial relations enquiry (and vice versa). Despite the continued advocacy of greater cross-boundary activity, and the illustration of its utility in the work of a small number of academics primarily working in the United States, most notably George Strauss (Strauss and Feuille 1978; Strauss 1987; also Brett 1980; Kochan 1980; Thomson and Warner 1981; Lewin and Feuille 1983; Beaumont 1990), the organizational and industrial relations areas have not been as closely connected in the past as their overlapping subject matter might suggest. There are many possible reasons for this, over and above the general problems of academic over-specialization.

One hindrance may have been the tendency for organizational research to be more 'managerial' in orientation compared to industrial relations research, which has often in the past been more informed by an analysis of trade union activity. This managerialism has been much more typical of what is defined (particularly by North Americans) as organizational behaviour, which focuses primarily on individuals and examines concepts such as motivation and leadership, compared to organization theory (OT) which principally addresses the structure and behaviour of groups within organizations, rather than that of individuals. For Daft, OT is the sociology of organizations, concentrating on the social system, while organizational behaviour (OB) is the psychology of organizations, concentrating on the individual person (Daft 1988: 26). As will become clear, our own work is rather more informed by OT than OB. Our climate construct, level of analysis, choice of methods, identification of dependent and independent variables, etc. are more closely aligned with OT. In recent years, OT has entered into a considerable amount of rethinking and self-questioning with regard to the identity of the field, its methodologies, and its relations with other branches of enquiry (*Organization Studies* 1988; Donaldson 1985), as well as theory-building and development (*Academy of Management Review* 1989). With this, and with the emergence of organizational culture as a new paradigm for understanding organizations, OT appears as ripe for greater cross-fertilization as industrial relations (IR) would seem to be. While the emphasis in this book tends to be mainly on the potential for industrial relations to gain from closer association with organization theory, we try not to lose sight of the value of the traffic moving in the other direction.

One area for possible cross-fertilization which appeared worthy of closer investigation was the concept of 'climate'. In general, the formal, structural aspects of industrial relations have been studied more extensively than the processes of those relations, particularly the informal processes. Further, while particular studies have considered the attitudes of different groups to aspects of industrial relations, less attention has been paid to the general attitudinal context or atmosphere in which industrial relations is conducted. This is not the case in organizational research, however. Since first discussed in the late 1950s (e.g. Argyris 1958), the concept of organizational climate has attracted considerable attention, and not a little debate on how it might be satisfactorily measured. There is widespread agreement, however, that climate comprises the norms, feelings and attitudes – the 'atmosphere' – prevailing in an organization. More recently, the literature on organizational climate has been supplemented by a growing attention paid to organizational 'cultures'. The distinction between climate and culture remains ill-defined, and has not been assisted either by those commentators who have used the terms interchangeably or by enquirers into aspects of culture often neglecting the existing body of research on climate (Rousseau 1988: 140). However, the concept of organizational culture generally refers to an overarching set of beliefs, norms, expectations, and ways of working that is usually generated over a long period by a combination of factors, and remains relatively impervious to short-term fluctuations. One of the contributing factors to this culture is the attitudinal *climate* in which employees function, and which is susceptible to a greater degree of volatility (the effect of volatility in any one contributor to culture is diminished by the presence of several other contributing factors). We return to this relationship of climate and culture at a number of points in subsequent chapters.

Over time, the organizational climate concept has been refined and as part of this a number of studies have investigated the validity of viewing organizations not as characterized by a single, all-encompassing climate, but rather as several distinct climates attaching to different aspects of the organization (Schneider *et al.* 1980; Zohar 1980). Within this development, a small number of researchers had begun, by the late 1970s, to explore the concept of industrial relations climate (Nicholson 1979; Warr *et al.* 1978; Kelly and

Nicholson 1980). Coupled with the findings from a small climate study of our own (Dastmalchian *et al.* 1982) this early work was sufficiently encouraging to suggest that the efforts involved in a more detailed study would be repaid by clarifying what many involved in the practice and study of industrial relations view as critical – the general atmosphere in which industrial relations are conducted.

THE STUDY

Our intention, therefore, was to create a working model of how climate might be related to industrial relations structures and processes and outcomes at the establishment level, and then to proceed to devise a reliable measure of climate and apply this to a range of industrial relations contexts. While always aware of the need to take into account the influences of head offices and other centralizing aspects of industrial relations, it was our aim to focus on workplace arenas where union representatives met management on a day to day basis to conduct industrial relations. By establishing the links between climate and the other elements of workplace industrial relations (inputs, processes, and outcomes) our aim was to shed light not only on what factors influenced climate but also on the dynamics of workplace industrial relations and the organizational factors outside the immediate union–management context which influenced the conduct and outcomes of those relations.

The choice of research design was guided by a desire to gain benefits from a combination of quantitative and qualitative approaches. In a discussion of changing fashions in methods of enquiry in industrial relations research, Lewin and Strauss contrast the predominantly micro-level case-study approach undertaken in the 1950s with more recent research relying increasingly on complex data manipulation techniques made available through access to computer technology (Lewin and Strauss 1988).

However, in some, if not in many cases, this availability of sophisticated number-crunching capability has been a mixed blessing. What has been gained in being able to handle a large range of variables and unearth subtle relationships within large samples, has often been at the cost of losing some of the 'reality' of industrial relations. That reality is *people* – people making decisions, interacting with one another, adjusting (or not) to each other's expectations. Only by looking in detail at specific industrial relations contexts can this reality of the subject be conveyed. Yet at the same time it would be a mistake to ignore the power of modern technology for handling large samples: not least because this gives us a little more confidence when deciding whether or not results have any generalizability.

The optimum route, therefore, would seem to be one which seeks to take advantage of both approaches: gathering both quantitative and qualitative data to provide a broad context in which to examine the key issues of the enquiry in particular work contexts. It is this thinking which informs the present approach. The end result is in fact more quantitative and computer-dependent than we would have wished. This is partly because there was no satisfactory measure of IR climate that we could take off the shelf, and the process of generating and refining a measure of climate could only adequately be accomplished through large-scale testing, in order to pin down the important but nebulous concept of climate. However, the case-studies examined in chapter 6 represent an integral part of our analysis and indicate ways in which the influence of industrial relations climate can be tracked over time.

A word is necessary on the source of the data and its broader relevance and applicability. The quantitative and case-study material reported in later chapters is largely Canadian in origin. Given the various regulations and other specifics of different national contexts and their impact on the conduct of industrial relations, it is likely that many readers will judge the relevance of the study as pertaining primarily to that country. It will be our argument, however, that while the climate measure was developed and refined largely on the basis of Canadian data, it nevertheless could have wider applicability. The nature of Canadian industrial relations, the lengths taken to validate the measure and our efforts to create a general measure of IR climate which was equally applicable in car plants, hospitals, breweries, and hotels, gives us some confidence that the measure represents at least a good starting-point for studying industrial relations climates in countries outside Canada. Furthermore, in addition to the Canadian work, we have benefited from an early pilot-study undertaken in Britain (Dastmalchian *et al.* 1982), the extensive collection of climate data within an Australian national corporation (Zeffane *et al.* 1990), and from a series of discussions with managers in Britain and Australia concerning the nature of IR climate within their organizations.

PLAN OF THE BOOK

No period in history is static, but in terms of the context in which industrial relations takes place, the last ten years have been characterized by significant and widespread change – not since before World War II (and perhaps not even then) have two decades been characterized by such contrasting industrial relations milieux as the 1970s and 1980s. It was within this context of change that we were seeking to measure industrial relations climates in a diverse range of work organizations. Hence, it is appropriate to begin our study by reviewing some of the main aspects of that context and the sorts of changes taking place. This we do in chapter 2, at the same time considering in more detail the relative merits of the opposing arguments that industrial relations does/does not remain an important area for serious study. It will be no surprise to the reader (after all, we have a whole book ahead of us!) that the conclusion to this discussion supports a view of the continuing significance of industrial relations.

In chapter 3 we examine the concepts of organizational and industrial relations climate in more detail, and establish a model of how industrial relations climate relates both to the other major components of workplace industrial relations and to the various outcomes (agreements and disagreements, objective and subjective outcomes) of those relations. The testing of this model and the research questions outlined at the end of chapter 3 guide the empirical investigation discussed in subsequent chapters.

The methodology used in the study is discussed in chapter 4. This discussion developed into a longer chapter than we had originally envisaged, and is due to the tasks we seek to accomplish there: (i) summarizing the procedures adopted to establish a valid and reliable measure of industrial relations climate; (ii) an outline of the research design, sample and other measures used in the main study; and (iii) a description of our approach in the longitudinal study. We have been able to abbreviate this, however, since some stages of this lengthy journey have already been documented in journal articles, while other relevant, but not critical, information has been included in the appendix.

In chapters 5 and 6 we present the main findings of the study. Chapter 5 reports the testing of the overall model: how does climate relate both to the various organizational and industrial relations inputs and to a series of industrial relations outcomes? Case-studies are used more extensively in chapter 6, where a number of themes emerging from the general findings are examined in more detail, such as the importance of organizational flexibility and provisions for training on industrial relations climate and outcomes. In this chapter we benefit not only from the diversity of the organizations in the study, but also from the fact that in six of the organizations we were able to collect repeat information one-and-a-half to two years later than our first involvement with the organization. This gave us further valuable scope, not only for considering how our key variables operated over time, but also to track particular industrial relations issues through the workplace and evaluate the predictive capacity of our model. In the concluding chapter we seek to draw the study together, recapping on the main findings, and examining the new questions which the study poses.

2 Change and continuity in workplace industrial relations

Relations between employers and workers are never static, but are subject to both long- and shorter-term influences. Over long periods, changes in prevailing cultural beliefs and ideologies, towards authority, democracy, and the value of work, for example, will in turn affect the attitudinal context in which employer–employee and union–management relations take place. In the shorter term, those relations are influenced and constrained by a host of social, economic, and political factors, some acting in concert, others exerting contradictory pressures. Prominent among these influences would appear to be the condition of product, labour, and financial markets, the speed and direction of technological change, the extent and nature of state intervention in work relations, and the extent of trade union and employer organization. However, the potential list of such influences is a long one – even the weather can play a significant role in workplace relations.

The upshot is that workplace industrial relations contain a dynamic element in their character. Yet, to a significant degree, those same relations are also characterized by continuity. Though subject to various pressures, workplace relations endure over time. Bonds of shared attitudes and assumptions, mutual dependencies, and no doubt in many cases, bonds of reciprocity and shared loyalty, act to sustain those relations. Thus in many important respects, work relations in 1990 bear a close resemblance to those prevailing in 1980 or 1970; indeed, in terms of the way work is controlled and rewarded, and in the basic exchange relations between employer and employee, a number of comparisons can be drawn between the present and the work relations existing a century ago in 1890.

For many social scientists, continuity presents a problem. The notable exceptions here are those working within a structural functionalist tradition in which continuity and the maintenance of order is the explicit focus (see Parsons 1964). In general, however, academic researchers appear to pay more heed to change than continuity: change is widely perceived as more exciting, more newsworthy, more likely to be judged 'relevant' by policy makers, and probably more appealing to research-funding bodies. The danger in this of course is that, compared to continuity, change comes to be scrutinized disproportionately. Thus in the study of work organization, just as in other areas of social science, warning bells should ring when all the talk is of the new and excludes what remains from before.

It is this picture of change and continuity we wish to outline in the present chapter, addressing in particular one major aspect of change and one of continuity. First, we review the argument that a coincidence of various factors has acted (and continues to act) to reduce both the power of organized labour and the prominence of industrial relations within work organizations. In contrast, we explore the argument that patterns of organization and the nature of contemporary production processes (in relation to both goods and service production), in combination with the demands engendered by increasingly competitive and uncertain environments, guarantees the continued importance of securing and maintaining the active co-operation of labour. One outcome of this continued dependence is seen to be that, despite apparent swings of power in their favour, managers must continue to secure and sustain effective industrial relations.

By examining these two contrasting arguments, two outcomes are sought which will provide a general context for the remaining chapters. The first is a recognition of the ways in which the nature of work and industrial relations in most industrial societies has been changing over the recent past. Many of the changes so far evident appear intermediary or transitional in nature and presage further change in the near future. The present study of workplace climates reflects a number of these changes and can only be fully understood within that context. The second is a confirmation that studies such as this one have a continuing relevance in the broader study of work organization, and if anything this relevance is likely to grow rather than diminish in coming years. This is not seeking to make exaggerated claims for the present study or for industrial relations enquiry more generally. Rather it is a recognition of the heightening significance of social aspects of contemporary work organization, including industrial relations – albeit a different style of industrial relations to those which are seen to have typified the 1960s and 1970s.

CHANGES IN CONTEXT

As we have noted, workplace industrial relations do not occur in a vacuum but rather in the context of other events taking place both within the workplace (such as changes in technology) and in the wider organizational, market, and societal environments in which the workplace is situated. It is not necessary here to rehearse in full the internal and external changes which have been widespread in industrial countries in recent years. It is appropriate, however, to note briefly some of the most prominent of these factors which have impacted, directly or indirectly, on the nature of industrial relations.

The most global of these factors has been the intensifying of activity and competition in both industrial and service sectors during the 1970s and 1980s. The emergence of several newly industrializing countries (NICs), and the growth of multinational corporate activity, are both important here. The economic emergence of Japan and, more recently, of countries such as Taiwan, Korea, Singapore, and Brazil has heightened levels of international competition both in traditional industries (such as steel-making and vehicle production) and in more 'sunrise' industries, such as electronics. In part, this competitiveness reflects the installation of modern plant and equipment in locations most suited to current systems of transportation. Employers in NICs also benefit from generally lower labour costs, principally due to lower wage levels, lower non-wage labour costs, and longer hours of work. For example, average hours for industrial workers in South Korea were approximately 2,800 per year in the mid-1980s, and over 2,500 per year in China and Singapore; this compares with around 1,900 hours in the USA, and 1,800 in Britain at that time (Shimada and Hayami 1986; Blyton 1989a).

The diffusion of multinational activity, coupled with moves towards removing barriers to cross-national trade (such as the Canada–USA Free Trade Agreement, progress towards a Single European Market, and growing East–West trade following the decline of communist control in eastern Europe), is acting to increase levels of competition in many domestic markets. In terms of multinational activity, developments are particularly clear in vehicle production. Over the past ten years, most of the major Far Eastern producers have established assembly plants in other industrial countries; examples include Nissan in the UK, Honda and Hyundai in Canada, and Toyota in Australia, Canada and the UK (Crowther and Garrahan 1988; Rutherford 1990; Bamber 1989). The growth of joint ventures has also been marked in the vehicle industry, partly stemming from a desire to spread the high research and development costs attached to bringing new models to the market place; examples of joint ventures include the GM–Toyota plant at Freemont, California, GM–Suzuki at Ingersoll, Ontario, and the Honda–Rover relationship in the UK. Through such sole- and joint-venture activities, in conjunction with agreements on proportions of inputs sourced locally, foreign multi-nationals are increasingly able to circumvent quota regulations previously established to reduce the competition faced by domestic producers in their home markets. Moreover, this process shows no signs of slowing.

At the time of writing, there is much discussion of multinational vehicle manufacturers establishing assembly 'transplants' and joint venture activities in eastern Europe and the USSR, in order to take advantage of lower labour costs and understocked markets. The Japanese and Germans are again prominent in these moves; Suzuki Motors have signed a joint agreement with a bus company in Hungary, Daihatsu (a subsidiary of Toyota) is to build cars in Poland, and Mitsubishi is to build a car plant in eastern Germany (the *Independent*, 2 February 1990: 20). Similarly, Volkswagen and Daimler-Benz are preparing to produce cars in eastern Germany, while Opel have established a joint venture with Wartburg.

Several leading American, Japanese and German multinationals operate in the electronics sector, developing computer and microprocessor-based equipment both for producer and consumer markets. Technology based on microelectronics tends not only to be smaller, more reliable, and more flexible than previous technologies, but in some applications is also less expensive. These cost, adaptability, and portability factors have accelerated the diffusion of new techno-logies in both materials and information-handling settings. The linking of microelectronics to other technical advances in such fields as image processing and telecommunications has further extended the range of applications of various new technologies. Thus at a time when one way for individual employers to respond to increased competition is by technological modernization, the greater ease of diffusion of available technologies, coupled with their adaptability and their speed of obsolescence, ensures that only limited or tem-porary competitive advantage is generally obtainable from the tech-nology alone.

Besides the expansion of industrial and multinational activity and the spread of new technology, various other factors have also fuelled the growth in competition. For example, the world recession of 1980–82 resulted in the closure of a large number of manufacturing plants which have not since re-opened. Among those which did survive, many responded to slack markets by reducing capacity and/ or effecting major work-force reductions. The combined result has been that in various industrial sectors, older and less productive organizations perished and among the survivors, productivity improved through work-force reduction often coupled with plant relocation, technological change, and new work practices involving employees accepting operational changes which maintained production with lower manning levels. In such an environment, further sources of competitive gain become less easy to identify. One result of this has been a revival of managerial interest in the different social aspects of work organization. This has manifested itself in various ways, ranging from involvement schemes and profit-sharing to performance appraisal and flexible work practices, and has variously been designed to deliver lower labour costs, greater commitment, improved quality, and better responsiveness to change (McKinlay and Starkey 1991; Poole and Jenkins 1990; Blyton and Morris 1991; Oliver and Wilkinson 1988). This 'rediscovery' of the importance of people in work organizations is also reflected in the recent ascendancy of 'human resource management' both in managerial and educational circles (Strauss 1987; Storey 1989).

This growth in competition and its repercussions for work organizations has not been confined to the private sector. Following three decades of growth in public services in many western countries, the 1980s have witnessed a break from this pattern in such countries as the UK, the United States, and Canada. In these, the success of conservative parties in achieving power in the 1980s, and their advocacy of restrictions on public sector spending, the removal of public sector monopolies, and the promotion of privatization, have combined to create an emphasis on cost-cutting and competitiveness not dissimilar from (and in some cases more acute than) their private sector counterparts. Even where services have remained largely within the public sector, such as the Canadian and UK health services, increased attention to cost reduction has led to widespread changes in labour utilization, including greater use of part-time workers and the broadening of tasks performed by non-specialist staff (Ursell 1991).

In sum, contemporary industrial relations are taking place in environments where greater emphasis is being placed on competitiveness and productivity than hitherto, where sources of competitive advantage are becoming more difficult to locate and sustain, and where management has a heightened sense both of labour costs and labour potential. It is against this background that various changes in organizational activity have been widespread. Three areas are particularly noteworthy: changes in *organizational structure, production*, and *human resources*. Structural changes have included accelerated acquisition/disacquisition activity, upstream and downstream expansion/contraction, and the formation of joint ventures, franchising, and other collaborative arrangements. Through such changes, companies have been seeking to position themselves more effectively within existing markets, or to lay claim to new ones. Production changes include not only the use of more advanced technologies, but also the re-configuring of traditional machine layouts, not least to improve work-flow and move towards just-in-time principles of minimizing stocks and work-in-progress (Turnbull 1988; Hutchins 1988). The increased use of subcontracting to cover some aspects of production is also relevant here, as are the development of closer relations with main ('preferred') suppliers, and the extension of quality training and more widespread adoption of established quality assurance techniques such as statistical process control (SPC). Moreover, these changes are impacting upon the production of services as much as upon the production of goods. Important in this has been the expansion of information systems and technologies in such industries as banking and insurance, the growing use of new technology in health care, and the increase of private sector service organizations to handle subcontracted work such as cleaning and catering, formerly done in-house in the production industries (Child 1984a, 1984b; Appelbaum and Albin 1989; Coombs and Green 1989).

A variety of human resource responses to greater competition are also evident and will be prominent at several points in forthcoming chapters. One widespread development has been the moves to create more 'flexible' work-forces through, for example, reductions in job grades and demarcations, a growth in the use of part-time, temporary, and contract labour, the introduction of new working time arrangements, and changes in reward systems and pay bargaining to reinforce the link between pay and local performance (Atkinson 1984; Boyer 1988; Barkin 1987; Blyton and Morris 1991; Blyton 1991). However, while these issues have been much-studied in recent years, they have rarely been viewed explicitly in the context of broader moves towards 'organizational' flexibility, that is, organizations using such strategies as devolved responsibilities, local profit centres, flatter management structures, and even 'empty' organizations (where all work is contracted out), as ways of being more responsive to change.

This concept of organizational flexibility may help to integrate other aspects of discussion on flexibility. To date these have taken place on many levels, ranging from the global organization of production to the characteristics of national labour markets and the nature of work arrangements within individual workplaces (Piore and Sabel 1984; Boyer 1988; Meulders and Wilkin 1987; Atkinson 1984; Cross 1988; Hakim 1987). At the workplace level, much of the analysis has centred around work-force changes to effect greater functional and numerical flexibility. The notion of organizational flexibility broadens the workplace attention beyond changes in the work-force. In addition (and this is an issue we will develop in later chapters), the concept of organizational flexibility may act as a bridge between classical organizational studies such as Burns and Stalker (1961) on organic and mechanistic organizations, and the current interest in flexible firms. In the present study, flexibility in both organizational design and in human resource practices were found to be significant in organizations as diverse as hospitals, meat-packing companies, hotels, and breweries.

CHANGES IN INDUSTRIAL STRUCTURE

Plant closures in the early 1980s recession represents only part of longer-running and broader shifts occurring in the economic structures of mature industrial societies. In summarizing some of these major changes we can point to the following factors:

1 There has been a widespread decline in employment in older extractive and production industries, including coal, steel, textiles, and shipbuilding. In the steel industry, for example, the number employed in the UK by the biggest employer British Steel dropped from over 229,000 in 1977 to less than 52,000 by 1989; similarly, in the United States, employment in the steel industry fell from over 379,000 in the late 1970s to under 166,000 by the late 1980s (Buchan 1989; see also Whetton 1980 and Zammuto and Cameron 1985 for an organizational analysis of decline).

2 There has been a decline in traditional industrial areas and working-class communities, and the siting of new manufacturing and service organizations has tended to be on 'greenfield' sites often in rural and semi-rural areas, away from old industrial areas and the traditional heartlands of trade unionism. This decline of industrial conurbations was accelerated by the recession in the early 1980s, but is a feature of the last generation rather than the

last decade. In Britain between 1960 and 1978, for example, the level of manufacturing employment in rural areas (districts in which all settlements have fewer than 35,000 people) rose by 38 per cent, compared to a fall of 26.5 per cent in the country's six traditional industrial conurbations (Massey 1988: 61). Corresponding declines have occurred in other countries, such as parts of northern France and the north-eastern United States (Hudson and Sadler 1989; Adams and Mueller 1986; Hoerr 1988).

3 There has been a continued absolute and relative growth in service sector industry, particularly private sector services. In Organization for Economic Co-operation and Development (OECD) countries as a whole, service sector employment grew at a rate of over 2½ per cent per annum in the 1975–79 period; this fell to 1.5 per cent in the early 1980s, but had recovered its former growth rate by 1984. By the mid-1980s, approximately six employed people in every ten in the OECD countries worked in service activities, compared with around three in every ten in goods production, and under one in ten in agriculture. In a number of countries, including the United States, Canada, and Australia, the proportion of the total work-force employed in the service sector now approaches seven out of ten (Blyton 1989b: 36). In the UK, service sector employment rose from 60 per cent to 67 per cent of total employment between 1980 and 1986, compared with a fall from 28 per cent to 22 per cent engaged in manufacturing during that period (Sisson 1989: 27).

One consequence of these shifts in economic activity is that industrial relations are increasingly taking place in different arenas from those more typical of a generation ago. If large engineering factories were ever 'typical' contexts in which to study industrial relations (and they were often taken to be so by many researchers in the 1960s and 1970s), they are even less so today. Contemporary accounts and investigations of industrial relations need to take this structural change and diversification fully into account.

CHANGES IN WORK-FORCE COMPOSITION

One of the most significant developments in industrial relations over the past two decades has been the changing composition of the work-force engaged in those relations. We noted above the increased likelihood for workers to be employed in service activities rather than in manufacturing. Closely related to this growth in service employment has been the increase in female and part-time employment. In the OECD countries, the growth in part-time employment was particularly marked during the 1970s, and it continued to rise during the 1980s. Of the major industrial nations in the OECD, only Italy and Ireland fail to demonstrate a substantial growth in part-time working over this period. (In the case of Italy, this is at least partly due to social security provisions which are unfavourable to hiring part-timers rather than full-timers, and also partly due to the high level of moonlighting in Italy which both represents unrecorded part-time work and reduces the supply of labour seeking part-time work in the recorded sectors.) In the OECD as a whole, approximately one-sixth of the total work-force work part-time; in Scandinavian countries, this level is substantially higher (e.g. over 30 per cent in Norway), and in the UK it is projected to rise to over 27 per cent by 1995 (Sisson 1989: 47). As well as increases in part-time working, there are indications that the level of temporary working and working from home also increased during the 1980s, though the extent of this growth is disputed, and analysis is hampered both by a lack of earlier information and definitional problems about what constitutes temporary employment (Casey 1988 and Hakim 1988: 610).

Women hold an increasing proportion of jobs in industrial countries. Overall in the OECD countries, female participation rates (that is, the proportion of the female population of working age who are active in the labour market) increased from 50 per cent to 56 per cent between the mid-1970s and the mid-1980s; in contrast, the corresponding figures for males show a decline in this period, from 87 per cent to 84 per cent (Blyton 1989b). Most part-time jobs are held by women; in the large majority of industrial countries, at least seven out of every ten part-timers are female; in western Germany, Austria, Luxembourg, and the UK, women hold nine out of every ten part-time jobs. This continued growth in female, part-time, and service sector employment means that the frequent portrayal in the past of employment as typically involving male manual workers in manufacturing industry is increasingly less and less appropriate (though it is a perception which continues to be sustained in many books and articles on industrial relations).

Another group which has been more prominent in the past decade than during the previous three is the unemployed. Unemployment increased rapidly in most western countries during the early 1980s (exceptions being Austria, Japan, Norway, Sweden, and Switzerland) and by 1984 had reached a level at or near one-tenth of the labour force in eleven OECD countries (Hughes 1989: 70–71). Economic growth in the mid- and late 1980s tended to be less labour intensive than corresponding growth in the 1960s and 1970s, with the result that in several countries, unemployment has persisted at relatively high levels despite several years of economic expansion. In coming years, demographic changes are likely to ease continuing unemployment problems in many industrial countries; in the shorter term this reflects a reduction in the number of 16–19 year olds entering the labour force, combined with a relatively large proportion of the population reaching retirement age. In the medium and longer term, lower birth rates will bring about net decreases in the population of working age in many industrial countries by the year 2,000 (International Labour Organization 1986). Any expansion in working populations will be the result of further increases in female participation rates.

CHANGES IN TRADE UNIONISM

Union movements in different industrial countries have experienced mixed fortunes during the past decade. Where unemployment has remained low (e.g. in Scandinavia), or where falls in private sector unionism have been compensated for by union growth in the public sector (e.g. Australia, Canada), levels of union density increased during the first half of the 1980s. Elsewhere, however, it was precisely this period, characterized by rising unemployment and the decline of manufacturing employment, which saw a marked reduction in union membership levels. In Britain, union membership levels fell from 13.3 million in 1979 (a union density level of over 54 per cent) to 10.7 million by 1985 (and a union density level of 43 per cent) (Price 1989: 178). The United States, France, Netherlands, and Ireland similarly experienced marked falls in union membership during the first half of the 1980s. Further, even in many contexts where membership levels remained relatively buoyant in the 1980s, the influence of trade unions was apparently significantly reduced. In some situations this was reflected in 'no strike' agreements, 'flexibility' agreements, and 'concession' bargaining, all of which would have been almost unthinkable a decade earlier (Bassett 1986; Wickens 1987; Kochan *et al.* 1986). In others, the State has been active in restricting union power, either through legislation to restrict industrial action (as in the UK) or in confrontations with public sector unions including the replacement of union strikers with other staff (as in the case of air traffic controllers in the USA).

While the UK evidence is that managements have rarely used their enhanced power position to destroy the trade union presence in their organizations (as has been more apparent in the United States; see Kochan *et al.* 1986), various case-studies nevertheless attest to a diminution of union powers, with trade unions being forced more often into accepting management's *faites accomplis* over the devolution of bargaining away from national and towards local settlements, as well as over substantive issues such as pay settlements, working arrangements, redundancies, and facilities provided for union representatives (Terry 1986). Even where union membership levels have held up, such as in Canada (Meltz 1988), commentators have argued that the scope of union influence is under threat given a political climate encouraging individualism rather than collectivism (for example, see Dion and Hebert 1989). Indeed, increased government intervention to circumscribe union action has become more evident in Canada in recent years through, for example, the increased use of 'Back to Work Legislation' to end strikes (Sack and Lee 1989).

More generally the revival of consultation, Quality of Working Life, Joint Labour–Management committees and other involvement schemes on both sides of the Atlantic may indicate (following the argument by McCarthy 1966) trade unions insufficiently strong to protect bargaining relations and thus being forced to accept the reduced levels of influence implicit in consultative relations (Starkey and McKinlay 1989; Wood 1988; Marchington 1989).

This spread of involvement schemes appears to reflect both a widespread diminution of the trade union role as sole channel of interest representation (the emphasis in most schemes being on 'employee' rather than 'union representative' involvement) and a corresponding reduction in collective bargaining as the sole focus of collective relations. We return to this issue of involvement schemes below.

INDUSTRIAL RELATIONS – RIP?

Where is the foregoing discussion leading us? One impression could be that in some countries at least, industrial relations as traditionally understood is as good as dead, with union power withering on the bough, economic restructuring shifting employment away from former union strongholds, technology offering management the opportunity to reduce their reliance on large numbers of workers and worker-situated skills, various governments creating conditions increasingly hostile to the exercise of union power, and workers becoming increasingly compliant in the face of greater job insecurity than was generally typical two decades ago. It is clear that in the US trade unionism if not dead is at least unconscious in several industrial sectors and has remained virtually stillborn in others. The overall union density in the US of just over 17 per cent in 1987 is unevenly distributed: density is only 14 per cent in the private sector, much of which is concentrated in a small number of industries (e.g. transportation and automobiles) and occupations (e.g. machine operators) (Freeman 1989). The continuation of various trends noted above: the shift out of large-scale manufacturing in major conurbations to smaller operations away from the big cities, coupled with the further fragmentation of the work-force reflecting the growth of part-time, self-employed, temporary and subcontracted labour, create further problems for future union growth. Where union funds are already stretched due to lower income from a smaller membership, the recruitment difficulties involved in organizing smaller and more isolated groups are correspondingly heightened.

Yet, despite these factors, three arguments encourage a more sanguine view of the overall future of industrial relations and trade unionism. The first is simply that union movements have been in difficult circumstances before and have not only survived but have gone on to prosper. The UK is a good example here. Union membership in the UK was badly affected by the economic slumps in the 1920s and 1930s – a total membership level of over eight million in 1920 (45.2 per cent density) had been virtually halved to 4.4 million by 1933 (22.6 per cent density). However, economic revival stimulated a corresponding revival in trade union fortunes such that by 1945 membership levels in the UK were again approaching eight million and union density was almost 40 per cent (Bain 1970; also Rubery 1986). In a more recent discussion of union density, Bain (1986) notes that the recent decline in union members in the 1980s in the UK only takes total membership back to levels prevailing at the beginning of the 1970s and does not represent a wholesale reversal of the post-war growth in trade unionism. Supporting this argument, Kelly (1988) points out that the growth in unemployment accounted for much of the loss in union membership, rather than those in work giving up their union membership. For Kelly and others this is an encouraging sign that the basis of unionism remains intact and that as labour market conditions improve, so membership levels have the potential to recover.

To achieve a revival in density levels, trade unions face the challenge of organizing in sectors and occupations that in the past have not been conducive to unionization. Again, however, history is encouraging on trade unions' ability to adapt to changed circumstances. To cite Bain again, he notes that, having begun among skilled groups, unionism 'spread to groups of workers which were initially thought to be unorganizable – the semi-skilled and unskilled, public employees, white-collar employees and women'. On this evidence, argues Bain, 'it is reasonable to predict ... that the basic parameters of the unionisation equation will shift in the future in such a way as to enable unions to expand' (Bain 1986: 158).

Extending this first argument a little, it is evident that while perhaps at a low ebb in Britain and elsewhere, trade union power and organization has far from disappeared altogether. In the area of strike activity, most commentators in recent years have remarked mainly on reasons for the decline in strike levels in various countries. However, given the harshness of the political and economic environments facing trade unions in several countries, what is perhaps just as remarkable is the number of strikes which *did* occur. In the UK, for example, 1989–90 witnessed major disputes in engineering and docks, railways, London Underground, and the ambulance service, among others. Irrespective of their outcome, such strikes indicate the maintenance not only of unions' continuing ability to organize strikes, but also members' willingness to take strike action despite a general absence of conditions favourable to union success.

A second factor pointing to a significant future for industrial relations is that while the changes which have occurred in employment and industrial relations have attracted most attention and comment, in practice many of the changes being discussed are taking place in a minority of work contexts, leaving many or the majority of enterprises pursuing industrial relations in much the same way as before, albeit within a different political and economic context. Here we are back to our earlier argument: that too often in academic enquiry it is the changes rather than the continuities which are emphasized, with insufficient consideration being given to the magnitude of the latter compared to the former. In discussing the importance of new forms of participation and worker involvement, Sisson makes a similar point that while team briefings and quality circle arrangements have grown considerably in Britain in the 1980s (and the references to these in the management literature grown even more), it is still only a small percentage of manufacturing establishments which have introduced such activities (Sisson 1989: 33). The same may be argued in relation to recent departures in industrial relations such as 'concession bargaining' and 'no-strike' agreements. Likewise in the area of changing work arrangements, where a recent study by one of the leading researchers in this area (Cross 1988) found that, in a majority of organizations, the changes being implemented were relatively small.

All this is not to say that the changes which have occurred are not significant or potentially long-lasting. Also, it is important to recognize that many of the most important changes to occur – for example the revival of managerial prerogative – do not easily show up in investigations. Nevertheless, when referring to national (or international) economies and the enterprises operating therein, it is important to remember the *diversity* of activities that this incorporates, including the vast numbers of small and medium-sized organizations long-established in mature industries, many serving local markets, with their managers relatively unexposed either to national or international competition, or to new managerial thinking and practices connected with 'human resource strategies'. In these circumstances the tendency will be for industrial relations to continue more or less as they did before, particularly where those relations have been viewed as generally successful. One reason for this is that the traditional form of industrial relations, in which employees are represented by trade unions, can offer managers a number of benefits. Not the least of these is that unions enable managers to deal with one or a small number of representative bodies rather than with disparate groups of employees. Also, by abiding to, and working within established grievance procedures, unions in effect act as (to use the now time-honoured phrase) 'managers of discontent' (Watson 1988), legitimizing the procedures and suppressing unsustainable grievances which, if pursued, would lower the union's own credibility, *vis-à-vis* management.

The third argument for the view that trade unions and industrial relations will figure prominently in coming years is based on a heightened significance of the social or human factor within current and future work organizations. This argument comprises not one but several strands. The growth in capital intensity and any reduction in union power has not diminished the importance to management of securing effective industrial relations which deliver a work-force not only willing to work intensively, but also prepared to co-operate with changes, including the introduction of new technologies and new work arrangements. Though industrial relations may take a markedly different form in coming years (for example, a reduced emphasis on collective bargaining as the primary mechanism of industrial relations), those relations – and within them the role of trade unions – are unlikely to be less important than hitherto; if anything they will be more important. The following section looks at these issues in a little more detail.

THE CONTINUING IMPORTANCE OF INDUSTRIAL RELATIONS

A principal indicator of the continuing importance of workplace relations (a term which may be useful in denoting a broader meaning than the more traditional 'industrial relations') has been the various attempts to develop more integrative or 'collaborative' relations via different forms of communication and involvement schemes. 'Participation in decision making' in its various guises has a long history stretching back more than a century. The latest expressions of interest in worker involvement have led to the growth of both direct forms (that is, directly involving workers in quality circles and other production-oriented meetings) and indirect forms (based on committees with worker representatives). Evidence from several countries indicates a growth of both these types of involvement over the past decade. In the UK, for example, Collard and Dale conclude that there has been 'a very considerable growth' in the number of quality circles since the late 1970s (Collard and Dale 1989: 357). Likewise, most commentators agree that there has been a revival of joint consultation schemes in the UK during the 1970s and 1980s (Daniel and Millward 1983; Marchington 1989). A similar pattern is evident in North America, both in relation to work group meetings and quality of work life (QWL) programmes, as well as indirect mechanisms (for example, joint labour–management and joint productivity committees). These joint committees appear to have prospered, particularly in manufacturing. Cooke, for example, found that among 350 US manufacturing plants surveyed, 45 per cent had introduced joint committees and almost nine out of every ten of these had been introduced since 1980 (Cooke 1989: 300). (Cooke also concludes that these forms of involvement do deliver in terms of higher productivity and quality levels.) McNally, in a study that surveyed 201 organizations in western Canada found that in addition to mandatory committees, about 30 per cent of the firms voluntarily formed joint consultation committees in the 1980s (McNally 1989). These joint committees have been particularly prominent in the auto industry (Wood 1988). Activities such as General Motors' QWL Program and Ford's Employee Involvement Program (also introduced in Britain, see Starkey and McKinlay 1989) represent both a significant change in the traditional organization of workplace relations and also one response[1] to other changes taking place not only in the way that automobiles are produced but also the level of competition faced in that industry, particularly from Far Eastern manufacturers.

However, while there is evidence that the development of involvement schemes is widespread, there are several possible interpretations of what it signifies. As noted earlier, at one level these schemes (particularly those offering involvement but little real influence to workers) may simply reflect weakened union power and the unions' inability to translate a managerial need for co-operation into a widening of the collective bargaining relationship. A related view is that in searching for greater productivity, managers are using different forms of involvement as a human relations approach designed to lower resistance to change, gain the necessary co-operation and commitment, and generally to accomplish the required 'attitudinal structuring' for more efficient working.

This argument in fact takes us back to one of the fundamental dilemmas and challenges for managers under capitalism – how to realize effective control over a work-force and at the same time acquire the necessary consent and co-operation needed for capitalist production to be sustained at a profitable level. A recent variant of this argument holds that as competition grows and enterprises search for new market advantage, and also as technology makes smaller production runs and frequent tooling changes more economic, companies such as auto producers are beginning to augment their traditional standardized mass production approach with a mode of production which generates greater diversity and higher quality, but not at the cost of lower productivity. For this to occur, however, the work-force must be sufficiently willing to move away from highly routinized tasks with short cycle-times and adopt methods of working which demand greater competence over a wider range of tasks, and also a greater degree of adaptability to variations in the production process. This argument thus maintains that in contemporary large-scale operations, the logic of fordism (based on a high division of labour and tight supervision) is no longer sufficient in contexts which demand greater flexibility, broader job function, and self-regulation. In these environments the control aspects of fordism need to be supplemented by other managerial styles designed to deliver worker co-operation and commitment, partly through the use of different forms of 'involvement' (Sabel 1982).

It is important not to apply this argument unilaterally or in an exaggerated fashion: mass, standardized production has never been the norm for many (or most) work processes. Also, the extent to which many products are becoming less standardized (rather than a standardized product capable of accepting a range of minor modifications) is questionable. However, even if we accept the retention of standardized mass production operations, Wood is probably right in describing many of these contexts as having been 'work studied to perfection' leaving little room for further productivity gains without major organizational changes (Wood 1989: 22). One such change is to seek higher efficiencies not through closer supervision and control but through harnessing worker co-operation via different forms of participation scheme. The objectives behind such schemes are often diverse and diffuse; they include, for example, increased performance, lower costs, less resistance to change, altered worker attitudes, and 'getting management's message across'. Cooke points out that these attempts at collaborative relations are often also intended to increase performance 'through indirect efforts aimed at improving employee well-being and/or the *labour–management relations climate*' (Cooke 1989: 300, our emphasis). We return to this below, but whatever their explicit, implicit, or unintended outcomes, these different participation and involvement schemes indicate a continuing management need to secure effective workplace relations based on more than direct control.

New technology, a widening of task boundaries, and changes in quality measurement and inspection are some of the ways we have already noted in which work processes are changing on a significant scale. Another area of change is in the ways materials are processed – how they are ordered, utilized in the production process, and handled once the process is completed. Much recent discussion on these topics has centred around the notion of 'just-in-time' (JIT), whereby materials and components are purchased and arrive at the relevant point of production 'just in time' to be incorporated into the assembly, which in turn is completed just in time to supply an order (Hutchins 1988). This concept involves not only a marked reduction, if not elimination, of stock holding and banks of work-in-progress, but also complex intra- and inter-organizational information systems to allow the necessary materials-planning and -scheduling to take place.

The relevance of this for industrial relations is that by removing previous buffers in the system (stocks of materials and finished goods, work-in-progress, etc.), and by timing operations with little margin for error (the timing of transporting materials to work stations being organized if not on a split-second, at least on a split-minute basis), there is an increased reliance on the system running smoothly. Indeed a common metaphor in the JIT literature is one of materials and production 'flowing' uninterruptedly through the manufacturing system. Clearly, as well as suppliers failing to deliver on time, or the technology breaking down (including the information technology upon which the JIT system is so dependent), a key factor in this continuity is the maintenance of worker compliance in both the supplying and assembling organizations. As the significance of the co-ordination of activities increases, the overall management dependence on work-force co-operation appears to grow rather than diminish, when compared to previous production regimes. The effects of losing this co-operation have been clearly demonstrated in a number of industrial disputes; one example here is the 1988 Ford strike in the UK where the closure of Ford factories in the UK very rapidly led to closures throughout Ford's European operations, due largely to the company's reliance on daily deliveries of components (such as axles and engines from South Wales) rather than the holding of stocks at different plants (Wilkinson and Oliver 1990).

To sum up, various changes which are currently taking place (the diffusion of new technology; the demand for more flexible ways of working; the pressure to increase quality; the adoption of just-in-time techniques; and more generally management's desire to compete through cost reductions and improved performance and productivity levels) all rely for their success – at least in the medium- and longer-term – on securing active work-force co-operation and, by extension, by ensuring an effective system of workplace relations. Though certain indices (levels of unemployment and trade union membership) denote a weakening of labour power in a number of countries and industries since the late 1970s, current changes in production and work organization suggest that management's dependence on labour – especially that part of the labour force qualified in particular skills – has not markedly declined, but in certain contexts has probably increased.

One way in which workplace relations have been affected by these changes is through some managements attempting to secure the necessary co-operation and commitment via greater *individualized* relations with employees. This underpins practices such as direct communication with employees rather than via trade unions, individual merit and performance-related pay systems, employee share-ownership schemes, individual appraisal and career development systems – in sum, developments which place emphasis on the worker as an individual employee rather than as part of a collective (particularly a trade union collective). This approach is likely to continue and indeed grow in the future as managers look to controlling labour costs through a closer relationship between pay and perfor-mance, and seek to reinforce company identification by the extension of share ownership and similar schemes. However, where unions are present, the tendency is more likely to remain a dual approach by management: securing the necessary co-operation and agreement both through direct appeals to individuals and through more traditional formal and informal agreements within the industrial relations framework.

As part of creating the necessary context for achieving performance and productivity goals, we anticipate a continued significance being placed on establishing and maintaining an effective industrial relations climate. A low-trust and hostile industrial relations context is unlikely to represent a favourable base upon which either to embark on major changes in work arrangements or to achieve levels of working relationships necessary for the new arrangements to be productive (Fox 1974). Thus, despite the recent period representing a cold climate for many trade union movements, the coming years appear to contain conditions favourable to the retention and even the extension of industrial relations.

In the continuing study of those relations, one of the more intractable questions has been how to pin down and measure the general 'atmosphere' or 'climate' of workplace industrial relations. Though acknowledged as an important, and possibly a key, constituent of workplace relations, with a few exceptions it has generally evaded explicit and detailed study. Understanding and measuring climate involves to some degree a 'codification of the invisible' – that combination of feelings and attitudes which collectively comprise climate. It is to an examination of the climate concept that we now turn, drawing first on the literature of organization theory in order to clarify our understanding not only of the concept of industrial relations climate, but also of how the concept fits into and potentially mediates other aspects of industrial relations structure and process.

NOTE

[1] Other responses include a growth in joint ventures, a spate of concession bargaining in the 1980s, the widespread upgrading of plant and equipment, and the opening of new and non-union plants, for example in the southern and western states of the USA.

3 The climate concept

'There is nothing so practical as a good theory' is as true in the study of industrial relations as it is in any other field of enquiry. However, in a subject which has been bereft of adequate theory in many of its key areas, there is a valuable role for the development of intermediary or working models and frameworks to act as way-stations *en route* to more definitive theories. This is especially true in the present study where the objectives were to address deceptively simple questions such as: what comprises an industrial relations climate? why does climate vary from one organization to another and from one part of an organization to another? and how does climate influence the behaviour of industrial relations actors? In pursuing these questions, we are not many steps away from posing questions such as, why are industrial relations like they are? i.e. the central theoretical question in industrial relations (and in any other branch of enquiry into social or natural phenomena). In the present study we can hope to gain only a little ground on such elusive a prey. In our defence we would argue that we are attempting to proceed in a rigorous way: trying in fact to create a sound base for subsequent theorizing and empirical investigation. However, we will remain deficient in many aspects and a long way short of definitive answers; indeed, we remain open-minded as to whether we yet have the right set of definitive questions.

In this chapter we consider the climate concept and the way it has been applied in other areas of organizational research. We also examine the few instances in which notions of climate have been applied to industrial relations research. Though relatively isolated, these studies, together with an early enquiry by two of the present authors, were sufficiently encouraging to undertake a more thorough-going study of the climate concept and its applications to industrial relations. What follows from this discussion is an outline of our own model of climate and how climate is embedded in a broader set of relationships involving a series of organizational and wider inputs, industrial relations processes, and a number of different types of industrial relations outcomes.

This model is not presented as any sort of last-word or final statement. Indeed, readers of our earlier journal articles on this subject, particularly that which appeared in the *Journal of Industrial Relations*, (Blyton *et al.* 1987) will note that the model reproduced here has already undergone a number of amendments from our earlier position. What was needed was a model which summarized a diverse body of literature on the relationships which may exist between organizational and other variables, industrial relations context and climate, and various industrial relations outcomes, including both agreements/successful negotiations and individual and group expressions of conflict or dissatisfaction. Such a model would thus guide the collection of appropriate information, offer a way of categorizing that information, and represent a basis for initial data analysis.

Our intention was to create a working model of how climate fitted in to the industrial relations structure and process taking place at the establishment level, and then commence the task of devising a reliable measure of climate and applying this to as wide a range as possible of industrial relations contexts. While we were always aware of the need to take in the influences of head offices and centralizing aspects of industrial relations, our main attention was clearly directed to the workplace arenas where union representatives met management on a day to day basis to conduct industrial relations. In this, our overarching aim was to use climate as a vehicle for understanding in more detail the links between organization and other structures, industrial relations processes, and different industrial relations outcomes.

THE CLIMATE CONCEPT IN ORGANIZATIONAL LITERATURE

The concept of organizational climate has been widely researched over the past two decades. It has generally been viewed as a variable, or set of variables, that represents the norms, feelings and attitudes prevailing at a workplace (Payne 1971; Litwin and Stringer 1968). For many writers on organizational climate, the concept is seen to comprise the combined perceptions of organizational members describing the atmosphere in their organization. However, even at this general level, several problems are immediately apparent. First, the variety of ways in which the climate concept has been taken up has led to a 'lack of boundaries differentiating what climate is from what it is not' (Rousseau 1988: 140). One way of overcoming this is the way we have adopted: becoming more specific as to the organizational area to which the climate concept is applied (e.g. the climate of union–management relations).

Second, the practice of deriving organizational-level variables (such as 'organizational climate') by aggregating individual perceptions of climate is not uncontroversial. Indeed, for some writers the issue of aggregation lies at the heart of conceptual and methodological debates on the future direction of research on climate (see, for example, James *et al.* 1988; and Glick 1988). Roberts *et al.*, in their discussion of aggregation problems, argue that two types of data are used in organizational research to describe characteristics of groups and organizations: 'global data not divisible across individuals (such as organizational ownership) and aggregate data based on some composite of lower level scores'. They go on to argue that, 'Although both global and aggregate characteristics can be used to describe groups and organizations, the use of aggregate data and concepts makes it more likely that interpreters will be confused and information lost. A future disadvantage is that aggregate data are not directly linked to the level of aggregation about which inferences are made' (Roberts *et al.* 1978: 84–5).

Thus, aggregate concepts such as perceived organizational climate have, by definition, a degree of ambiguity attached to them. However, we believe that such ambiguity is more methodological than conceptual and agree with Glick that pursuing the debate on whether climate is an individual attribute (i.e. psychological climate) or an organization one (i.e. organizational climate), is not likely to be productive (Glick, 1985, 1988). There are clearly two well-established positions among researchers on this aspect of climate, and we subscribe to the position that perceived climate is an aggregate concept and an 'organizational' phenomenon.

A further point here is that in operationalizing the climate concept, care is needed to overcome the methodological difficulties associated with aggregate data. Roberts *et al.* (1978) suggest a way in which this can be achieved. Using an example from a climate study by Drexler (1977), they argue that a measure of within-organization variance provides an index tied to the organization rather than to the individual. A small within-organization variance (relative to between-organization variance) would suggest that climate is useful and representative of an organizational attribute. Glick (1985) has further stressed this point, and other more recent climate studies as well as our own have taken this into account (Ansari *et al.* 1982; James *et al.* 1984; Kozlowski and Hults 1987; James 1982; Dastmalchian *et al.* 1989). In other words, an acceptable measure of climate is only obtainable where there is a relatively high level of agreement between the individual respondents (Lincoln and Zeitz 1980; Angle and Perry 1986).

Third, as Roberts *et al.* (1978) have pointed out, even if the legitimacy of aggregation is established, the question remains of the appropriate constituency for the aggregation. Is climate a feature that characterizes a company, individual divisions, single establishments, departments within those establishments, or even perhaps sections within those departments? Few studies have focused on departmental or sub-unit climate. Among those that have are the conceptual work of Powell and Butterfield (1978) and the study of climate in R & D units by Abbey and Dickson (1983). One would expect that the shared characteristics of a unit within an organization contribute to the perceptions of particular climates shared by the unit members. But how much homogeneity of perception should be attributed to the similar context and structure of the unit, and how much is likely to be due to the larger organization? Also, how influential are the characteristics of the individuals forming the unit? Questions such as these are still open to investigation. Our own work has shown that for workplace industrial relations climate, membership of the same union is likely to affect the shared perception of climate more so than does departmental affiliation (Dastmalchian *et al.* 1989). But, does this mean that the appropriate level of analysis for studying industrial relations climate is that of union affiliation? We would hold that the answer to this very much depends on the focus of the research. If the theory and the underlying research questions relate to the organization as a whole, then somehow the measurement of climate should correspond to this, with the focus directed at the organizational level. However, there is no doubt that the question of level of analysis for aggregation has a direct bearing on the utility of the concept of climate, and is one that has further complicated the various debates on the concept.

One further problem area for the climate concept has been the question of its volatility. If climate is viewed as being subject to a great deal of turbulence (caused, for example, by individual day to day events occurring in the organization), then its measurement – and any subsequent characterizing of an organization as displaying a particular climate – is highly problematic. For most researchers in this area, however, climate has been viewed as sufficiently broad-based to have a degree of endurance over time, usually changing only relatively gradually rather than mirroring each and every frisson caused by individual events. A comparison here can be drawn with meteorology, and the distinction between climate and weather. The climate in Saskatoon in the winter is cold and that in Cardiff is mild and damp. This is not to say that individual weather patterns in February don't bring occasionally balmy days to the Canadian prairies, or very cold and dry spells to South Wales. But these individual fluctuations are not in themselves sufficient (unless repeated many times over a sustained period) to negate the general characterizing of the winter climates in the two locations.

Since first discussed in the late 1950s, the overall climate concept has been much scrutinized, and at least twelve reviews of the climate literature have been published (see, for example, Argyris 1958; Payne and Pugh 1976; James and Jones 1974; Joyce and Slocum 1979; Schneider and Reichers 1983; Ekvall 1987; Rousseau 1988). The recent growth of interest in organizational 'cultures' has added a further stimulus to this general area of research work though, as we noted in chapter 1, the linkage of climate and culture research has been less than fully exploited (see, for example Ashforth 1985; Rousseau 1988).

For us, the attitudinal climate in an organization is one contributing factor to the organizational culture which in turn represents a more general set of beliefs and way of working that (usually) develops over a relatively long period and is fairly resistant to short-term pressures. The two concepts of climate and culture share a number of similarities and in many ways can be regarded as indistinguishable. They are both essentially consensual in nature (for instance they both seek to portray a general characteristic applicable across an organization). In addition, both concepts are based on individual interpretations, both have a degree of stability over time (the culture concept more so than climate), and both are believed to shape behaviour. However, the two concepts also demonstrate important differences which signal the inappropriateness of considering climate and culture as identical concepts. First, while climate has been viewed as a shared perception, culture has been characterized more as a shared belief or assumption. Further, climate has tended to be employed as a descriptive concept, while much of the discussion on culture has been imbued with a prescriptive or normative slant. Moreover, while climate is seen to exist in all situations, it is possible to characterize an organization (or part thereof) as having no culture.

Also, organizational climate normally starts from the individual level and is aggregated upward to the organizational level whilst culture is normally attributed to the aggregate level and then moved downward to the level of the individual.[1]

Despite our attempts to highlight the differences between the two concepts, it is important to remind ourselves that in developing these, or any other concept in organizational analysis, we are bound by methodological constraints. In this sense, research on culture and climate has in many ways been faced with similar kinds of problems and issues. In fact, the kinds of debates that are currently going on in the climate literature (e.g. Glick 1988; James *et al.* 1988) could easily be taking place with regard to organizational culture. Pursuing the symbolic interactionist perspective, and relying on more qualitative methodologies in the culture literature may be one of the current differences in the research strategies between the two areas (e.g. Morey and Luthans 1985). However, whether such differences in research strategies (i.e. one is more qualitative and the other more quantitative), which have originated in the disciplinary roots of the two concepts, will result in sharpening and clarifying our understanding of the relationships between the two concepts or not, is a matter that requires more empirical and conceptual work.

Much of the work on organizational climate during the 1970s and 1980s has progressed along a variety of courses rather than a single one. There has also been a widespread lack of agreement emerging on the status of climate in overall models of organizations, or on how the climate variable should be operationalized and measured. Several writers on this subject, however, do agree that the concept of climate can be viewed as an intervening variable between organizational inputs and constraints on the one hand and individual behaviour on the other. This follows a broader view (argued, for example, by Brass 1981, and by Rousseau 1978, 1988, among others) that 'the impact of organizational and other characteristics on individual responses (e.g. structure's impact on attitudes, technology's effect on performance) is mediated by individual perceptions of the situation' (Rousseau 1988; 139). In similar vein, a number of writers on climate have explicitly or implicitly followed similar assumptions, employing climate as an intervening variable, linking contextual factors to individual and group behaviour (Litwin and Stringer 1968; Payne and Mansfield 1973; Payne and Pugh 1976; Joyce and Slocum 1979).

In addition and following our earlier discussion, one of the problems in the past has been the potential breadth of the climate concept, resulting in a lack of precision both in the concept itself and in the instruments used to measure it. One response to this has been to reduce the scope of the concept by viewing organizations as maintaining several different climates pertaining to different aspects of the organization. To this end, by the late 1970s and early 1980s, the climate concept was being applied to particular facets of organizations, giving rise to notions of a climate for service (Schneider *et al*. 1980), a safety climate (Zohar 1980), and retaliation against a 'whistle-blowing' climate (Micelli and Near 1985). In the same way, Nicholson (1979) was one of the first writers to highlight the possibility of using the climate concept in industrial relations, and in particular for its utility in providing a theoretical bridge between the structural aspects of organizations and industrial relations outcomes, including the manifestation of conflict. Both in this and in a small number of other studies, users of the climate concept underlined the variety of attitudinal elements relevant to an IR climate measure and the potential for linking climate to a variety of organizational and individual outcomes (Warr *et al*. 1978; Nicholson 1979; Kelly and Nicholson 1980; Dastmalchian *et al*. 1982; Katz *et al*. 1983; Angle and Perry 1986).

The investigation by Warr and his colleagues (1978) is a broad study of employee relations, part of which highlights the importance of industrial relations climate, though without examining it in any systematic way. One of the researchers in the Warr team, Nigel Nicholson, took the concept further in a later article (Nicholson 1979), using case-study material to argue that the concept of IR climate can be used to integrate organizational issues and IR outcomes, such as industrial conflict. He also raises the possibility that the idea of issues-centred vs. person-centred climates can be used to diagnose the quality of outcomes of IR in the steel plant under study. Kelly and Nicholson (1980) take this last argument further and sketch out a conceptual model that attempts to explain the incidence of strikes, with IR climate as an integral part of that model. Dastmalchian *et al*. (1982) subsequently utilized Nicholson's notion of IR climate in a small-scale mail questionnaire study of twenty-eight manufacturing plants in South Wales. Their findings suggested a relationship between IR climate and company effectiveness (measured in terms of adaptability and readiness to change). The findings also suggested that this relationship was moderated by the extent of unionization and the firm's economic performance.

Yet, while identifying the potential significance of an industrial relations climate variable, these studies only took the first tentative steps in the process of refining the concept or establishing how it could be satisfactorily measured in different types of work organization, or indeed how it could intervene between or mediate any relations between structures and outcomes. In addition, later studies conducted in the United States contained other shortcomings which limited their usefulness as the basis for an adequate climate measure. For example, Katz *et al.* (1983) examined the effects of the introduction of Quality of Work Life programmes on IR and economic performance in eighteen plants of a division of GM in the United States. As part of this, they made use of the results of a short (five-item) questionnaire administered by GM to its managers and supervisors over three years: this represented their measure of IR climate (high scores represented more co-operation). The relatively low standard deviation in the results (mean = 2.9; s.d. = 0.5) reflects a problem of using information collected by management (that is, the tendency for the supervisors and other managers to report an exaggeratedly positive climate). In addition, the climate data was available for less than half of the observations (65 out of 176) over the three-year period of the study. Nevertheless, this climate measure was found to relate positively to a number of measures indicating less IR conflict, as well as to labour efficiency and product quality.

In a later study, Angle and Perry (1986) studied dual commitment and union-management relationships in twenty-two municipal bus companies in western US. For climate they used twenty-three statements from the Michigan Organizational Assessment Package (MOAP) (Institute of Social Research 1975), which they then collapsed into one climate measure. This study, however, leaves many important questions unanswered. For example, despite the reporting of Alpha coefficients for management (n=67) and union (n=53) respondents, there is no evidence about the validity of the measure and the 'modifications' that are reported to have been made to the MOAP battery of items: did the measure adopted from elsewhere and the modifications undertaken make sense in the context of this study? Is the climate measure uni-dimensional (this is almost taken for granted by the researchers)? Is there evidence that the perceptions of the managers and union officers towards climate in their respective plants share some common variance (i.e. is there any level of agreement between the two groups for each plant?)? From our review of the climate literature, this last issue has been identified as important: it is not possible to speak of the existence of climate without demonstrating a certain degree of agreement on it (James, 1982; Glick, 1985; Joyce and Slocum, 1984).[2]

It was clear that to improve our understanding and measurement of the climate variable, it would be necessary to adopt a more systematic approach to the concept's construction. This would initially involve reviewing the industrial relations and organizational behaviour/theory literatures to establish both the possible components of a model of climate, and the major factors impacting upon that climate. Empirical study could then be used to test and refine the climate concept, and to assign weights to the factors influencing climate.

THE MODEL

The dearth of industrial relations theory and theory testing becomes evident as soon as we consider what is the nature and role of factors influencing the overall industrial relations process and subsequent outcomes. Take the example of industrial relations systems theory. In his early work, Dunlop (1958) identified the importance of such contextual variables as technology, labour and product markets, budgetary constraints (including the funds available to the industrial relations system), and the distribution of power in society. Groups of actors, bound by a set of beliefs defining and legitimizing their roles, were seen to act within these contextual constraints to produce substantive and procedural rules. Even in this simple model, little attempt is made to suggest relative weights for the different input or contextual variables: indeed the main objective was to lay out the model, not to consider how it may be operationalized.

Subsequently this model has been elaborated with the addition of many more input factors, for example by Craig (1983) and Anderson *et al.* (1989). Craig's input variables, though representing an impressive list, range all the way from the legal system to the weather, which brings us back to the immense difficulties involved in the adequate testing of such multi-variable and interactive models. Assigning appropriate weights to these input factors is a major empirical study in its own right. Indeed, achieving an accurate picture of how industrial relations is affected by such variables as the nature of labour markets, the political context, social value systems, and so on, requires both a large-scale international study and ideally one that is longitudinal in design to gauge the impact of inputs on outputs in real time.

It is not only others who are guilty of presenting models which have worthwhile taxonomic properties but are little use as operational models. When we first began discussing the present work we generated a long list of inputs to the industrial relations system which included value systems, political, economic, and legal contexts, and changing

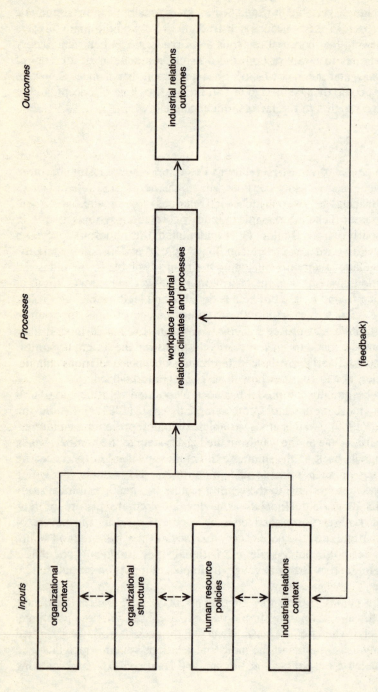

Figure 3.1 A model for studying workplace industrial relations climate (WIRC)

Inputs

organizational context

organizational structure

human resource policies

industrial relations context

Processes

workplace industrial relations climates and processes

Outcomes

industrial relations outcomes

(feedback)

demographic patterns (Blyton *et al.* 1987: 213). It is important not to lose sight of such overall schemes; however, as our primary interests became more narrowly focused on how climates operate within individual work organizations, it was necessary to create a more middle-range model which could be treated fairly rigorously within a sample of organizations.

This required a more organizational focus to the model, which in turn necessitated an expansion and modification of the organizational factors, and the omitting of many of the broader environmental factors (though we return to these in our later discussion). Whilst never overlooking the ways in which head offices and other central bodies exert influence on plant-level industrial relations, a focus at establishment level allowed us to examine the level at which most day to day industrial relations take place between managers and worker representatives, and how these relations help to establish, and are themselves influenced by, the climate of attitudes surrounding the union–management relationship.

INPUTS

On the basis of existing organization theory and industrial relations literatures, four categories of organization-level inputs can be identified as having a potential impact both on workplace relations climate and industrial relations outcomes: organizational context, organizational structure, human resource or personnel practices, and IR context (see figure 3.1). As is evident from the discussion below, in relation to a number of the factors in our model, we remained open as to the expected direction of association with the climate variable. In these cases, and on the basis of extant evidence, the case for *a priori* propositions could be equally well made for either a positive or negative relationship with the climate variable.

Among the context variables, *size* of organization has frequently been shown to be associated with aspects of industrial relations such as level of unionization. Holding other factors constant, there is also some evidence that size is related to strike propensity (Brett and Goldberg 1979). Further, organizational size has been shown to relate to climates characterized by 'matters relating to work itself', and to administrative efficiency (Payne and Mansfield 1973; Mansfield and Payne 1977). This, Payne and Mansfield have argued, is due to the increased complexity resulting from greater size and the greater financial resources of larger organizations (1973). Payne and Pugh, in reviewing the evidence, concluded that 'size has related more pervasively to different climate variables than any other structural variable' (Payne and Pugh 1976: 1,157).

In terms of the relevance of other organizational characteristics, given arguments such as, on the one hand, the tendency that industrial relations practices will 'mature' over time (leading among other things to the more complete institutionalization of conflict; see Ross and Hartman 1960), or (in contrast) the tendency that industrial relations practices will tend to ossify around out-dated procedures, it might also be expected that the *age* of an organization could have a bearing on climate. A number of studies have also identified associations between the types of *technology* employed (and the control systems typically attached to them) and the nature of union–management relations (Woodward 1965; Eisele 1974; Rousseau 1978). A Norwegian study by Peterson (1975) identified a relationship between technology and climate; small batch and process technologies were positively associated with the perceptions of white collar staff on such issues as intrinsic motivation, commitment, and organic style of management. This supports the contention of Woodward (1965) and Blauner (1964) in highlighting the effects of technology on work and the behaviour of employees. That is, in both small batch and process technologies, the organization is likely to be characterized as beng more organic, more adaptive, with fewer procedures, and less formalization and standardization. In addition, more craft oriented, and less mass production oriented, technologies are less likely to contribute to worker alienation.

The nature of *ownership*, including whether the enterprise is domestically or foreign-owned, has also been shown (in British studies at least) to affect the industrial relations process adopted (Enderwick, 1985), and the degree to which longer term industrial relations strategies are formulated (Marginson *et al.* 1988).

In addition to the nature of ownership, the organizational climate literature has shown that the extent of an organization's *dependence on owners* (i.e. on a parent organization) has certain influences on the climate development within the focal organization. Dependence on owners has generally been characterized by a situation where the focal organization is relatively small, is a plant or a subsidiary of a larger group, and has limited influence on the central policy-making body of the parent organization (Pugh and Hickson 1976). In these situations, research has shown that there appears to be a tendency on the part of the management of the dependent organization to create climates characterized by psychological closeness between managers and employees and a general atmosphere of friendliness (Payne and Mansfield 1973; Dastmalchian 1986).

Further, in a separate study, one of the present authors has examined the link between organizational climate and degree of organizational *dependency on labour markets*. Through developing an index of the organization's dependency on labour, based on the conceptual work of Emerson (1962) and Jacobs (1974), representing both scarcity of labour in the markets and the importance of the scarce labour to the firm, this study showed strong relationships between labour dependency and climates characterized by psychological closeness of management and employees, reward orientation, sociability, and management concern for employee involvement. That is, when organizations face high dependency on external labour markets, the managements attempt to deal with this through creating a more attractive working climate as a means of retaining the existing personnel (Dastmalchian 1986). For example, firms may put increased efforts into the internal labour market, resulting in, for example, better opportunities for training and promotion. Hence from this we might infer that different levels of labour market dependency will tend to give rise to different industrial relations climates. Finally, in this organizational context group of factors, it is likely that the degree of turbulence or organizational *change* will potentially exert an influence on climate, either through the heightened levels of insecurity and uncertainty which can be generated in periods of major organizational change or, more positively, through the opportunities for new working arrangements which reorganization can engender.

A second group of organizational factors in the present model are those relating to organizational structure. Aspects of organizational structure and context have been shown to have significant impact on the perception of organizational climate (Payne and Mansfield 1973; Payne and Pugh 1976). Research on organizational structure and climate has shown that, for example, more bureaucratic structures are likely to relate to climates characterized by rules orientation, conventionality, and generally more concerned with getting the work done. A less bureaucratic organization is likely to demonstrate a climate of psychological closeness between managers and employees (see Pugh and Payne 1977 for a comprehensive discussion of research in this area).

There is also some evidence that the structure of an organization, especially the degree of *centralization* and *formalization* of decision making, influences the nature of grievance handling, the resolution of labour disputes, attitudes and practices towards unionization, and the incidence of strikes (Brett and Goldberg 1979; Thompson 1967; Barbash 1975; Brett 1980; Turner *et al.* 1977).[3] The general direction seems to be that the more centralized (and/or bureaucratized) the

organizational structure, the more unfavourable the industrial relations climate and practices are likely to be. For example, Ng and
Dastmalchian, in a study of grievance outcomes, have shown that
decision-making centralization relates to the settlement of grievances
at higher levels in the organization (regional offices, headquarters),
rather than at the work unit level, causing more delays and unneces-
sary tension and frustration (Ng and Dastmalchian 1989). Elsewhere,
based on their analysis of six case-studies from their grievance
outcomes data, Dastmalchian and Ng have shown that the above
situation also contributes to the existence of less co-operative climates
between unions and managements (Dastmalchian and Ng 1990). In
contrast, we might anticipate that positive industrial relations
climates will be more associated with structures which are more
decentralized and *participative*.[4] To take one example from many,
Katz *et al.* found some support for a link between the presence of
participation through quality of work life programmes, and positive
industrial relations outcomes (Katz *et al.* 1983).

The industrial relations context itself can also be expected to exert
a significant influence on the attitude climate.[5] The extent and
pattern of unionization (union density, proportion of male/female
members, number and composition of unions, recent bargaining
history, bargaining structure, level of union involvement/attachment,
etc.) can be expected not only to exert influence but in turn can be
influenced by the climate of workplace relations and the pattern of
industrial relations outcomes. This interrelationship can be seen in
relation to specific strikes, for example. It is fairly common for the
cause of a strike to be all or partly understandable in terms of the
unsatisfactory resolution of a previous dispute, which left the attitudes
to union–management relations hostile; see, for example, the discussion of a strike at Ford by Hyman (1972). Likewise, fragmented
bargaining systems and high levels of unionization are among the
factors which have been positively associated with propensity to
strike (Clegg 1979).

The broader employee or human resource context is a fourth area
of input likely to impact upon the nature of the WIRC. The
composition of the labour force (male/female, part-time/full-time,
blue-collar/white-collar ratios, etc.), together with such factors as the
extent to which an internal labour market exists (particularly opportunities for promotion), the provision for training and education
within the organization, and the degree to which personnel practices are
undergoing changes (e.g. efforts to increase labour flexibility) will all in
turn potentially influence the nature of the industrial relations climate.

To summarize, what the first part of this model predicts is that there are a series of organizationally-based variables which will tend to impact upon the nature of the workplace industrial relations climate variable.

Dimensions of industrial relations climate

Following the analysis of organizational climate, industrial relations climate (IRC) concerns the attitudes and beliefs held by management and employees (and their representatives) towards industrial relations. Also, based on the literature on industrial relations climate (e.g. Nicholson 1979) we anticipated that any climate construct would not be unidimensional. One of the key writings on attitudes in industrial relations which has influenced our own thinking is that of Fox (1974), who identified *trust* and *distrust* as containing important explanatory power in the analysis of industrial relations, and in the broader study of contemporary society: 'The reciprocation of distrust [between management and work-force] ... has had massive consequences not only for the work organization ... but also for society at large in shaping the nature of intergroup conflict' (Fox 1974: 14). For Fox, increasing division of labour has led to low-discretion jobs which have militated against the creation of personal obligations and trust in the workplace, but have engendered feelings of suspicion. As well as trust, we anticipated based on our previous experience (Dastmalchian *et al.* 1982; Osborne and Blyton 1985) that related feelings such as co-operation, mutual regard, and hostility would also be important components in the climate measure. However, with relatively little to guide us in this area, it was important to develop the climate measure empirically through information collected from parties directly involved in industrial relations. This process we describe in the next chapter (see also Dastmalchian *et al.* 1986).

OUTCOMES

Following the model through, the question is posed as to how different workplace climates impact upon the practice and outcomes of labour relations within organizations. The theoretical argument here is that the characteristics of organizational structure and context will affect the IR outcomes and that these relationships will be mediated by the perception by industrial relations actors of the IRC. Put another way, if the notion is correct that climate intervenes in relations between a series of inputs and industrial relations outcomes, we would expect that any associations between inputs and outcomes will be stronger when the climate variable is taken into account.

In the introduction and chapter 2 we argued for a broader definition of industrial relations than has often been the case in the past. Similarly, this fuller appreciation of industrial relations requires the adoption of a broader view of what constitutes the outputs of an industrial relations system (IRS). For Dunlop (1958) and many of his followers, outputs of the system were seen to be bodies or 'webs' of rules – substantive rules governing the employment relationship, and procedural rules elaborating the procedures to be adopted for resolving questions arising from the interpretation of substantive agreements. A later writer within the systems tradition, Craig, described substantive rule-making as 'the allocation of rewards to employees for their services and the determination of conditions under which they work'. This led Craig to identify two types of output from the IRS: those outputs concerned with the organization of both work and trade unions, and those outputs more specifically focused on the wage-effort bargain, job rights, and other worker-oriented benefits (Craig 1983).

However, by not treating *conflict* explicitly as a possible outcome of industrial relations, models such as Craig's would seem to over-state the functional and positive nature of industrial relations outcomes. By recognizing various aspects of conflict as outcomes in their own right (rather than temporary hindrances to the achievement of other outcomes), this serves to highlight the potential for IR outcomes to de-stabilize or worsen a situation as well as maintain its order. Thus, in the present model, the measure of industrial relations outcomes comprises two categories: the first emphasizing consensual outcomes (such as successful agreements, effective grievance handling, and perceived positive industrial relations negotiations); the second identifying potentially conflictual outcomes, such as employee absence and turnover together with strikes and other industrial action.

In addition to recognizing conflict as a possible outcome, the present outcomes measure contains not only objective aspects but also subjective ones (e.g. perception of negotiations). Subjective outcomes of industrial relations can have as important a bearing on future relations as objective outcomes. We have already noted how in Hyman's (1972) account of a dispute at Ford, the strike under study was in important part a result of the perceived mishandling of an earlier dispute. Gouldner's account of the background to a wildcat

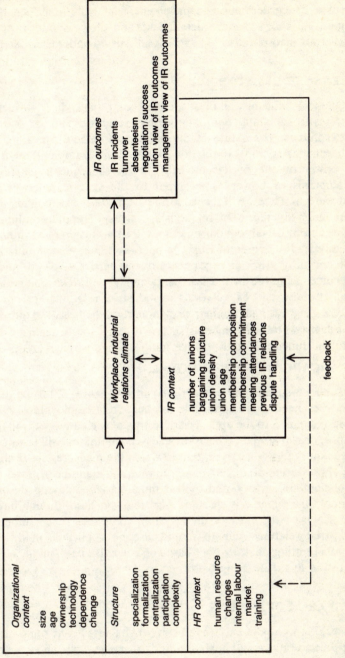

Inputs

Organizational context

size
age
ownership
technology
dependence
change

Structure

specialization
formalization
centralization
participation
complexity

HR context

human resource
changes
internal labour
market
training

Processes

Workplace industrial
relations climate

IR context

number of unions
bargaining structure
union density
union age
membership composition
membership commitment
meeting attendances
previous IR relations
dispute handling

feedback

Outcomes

IR outcomes

IR incidents
turnover
absenteeism
negotiation/success
union view of IR outcomes
management view of IR outcomes

Figure 3.2 The industrial relations climate model and summary of relevant factors

strike in a gypsum mine similarly points to the importance of attitudes created by earlier union–management relations (Gouldner 1954). Figure 3.2 shows a more detailed version of the model proposed earlier, by incorporating the variables discussed under each category.

FEEDBACK RELATIONS

Gouldner's account well illustrates the point that industrial relations systems are not static, but that outcomes resulting from one period in turn influence the nature of the inputs and climate prevailing in a subsequent period(s). In relation to inputs, for example, the exercise of power by the parties at Time 1 will subsequently affect the perceptions of power as an input to the system. Likewise, the outcomes at Time 1 will thence form part of the bargaining history of that union–management relationship, again potentially influencing expectations of subsequent outcomes. The atmosphere of industrial relations – the degree of trust, co-operation, etc. – will similarly be influenced by previous experiences of the parties involved, and the outcomes achieved in the last bargaining round. The point here is that attitudes and expectations in industrial relations are not formulated in a vacuum, but in important part on the basis of experiences and previous interactions.

APPLICABILITY OF THE MODEL

For models such as the one outlined above (figure 3.2) to be of real use, they need to be applicable in almost any employment setting. Thus one guide to the appropriate testing of such a model is that the sample drawn up should be as diverse as possible; this will ensure that the enquiry examines the extent to which the measures are usable in widely differing contexts (union/non-union; manufacturing/service; public/private sector), and that as much variance among the input variables as possible is created. Also relevant here, though beyond the scope of the present investigation, is that a robust model of industrial relations climate should also be applicable in different national settings, at least ones based on collective bargaining. We will return to this issue again below.

RESEARCH QUESTIONS

In seeking to model patterns of social behaviour, constructs such as the present one should have descriptive, explanatory, and predictive capabilities if they are to contribute towards more general theory-building. In terms of a model of industrial relations climate, we are thus interested in being able to describe systematically in what ways climate and outcomes differ from one situation to another, examine the reasons why these differences should occur, and be able to predict what the likely effects on climate and outcomes are, should a change take place in the input variables.

Disaggregating these objectives provides us with a number of general and specific research questions. In terms of the first part of the model a key question will be:

- Do some aspects of structure relate more strongly to climate than others? In particular, what are the configurations of input variables which tend to be associated with more co-operative/consensual/positive industrial relations climates, and what are the configurations which tend to be associated with more conflictual/negative climates? Are similar configurations identifiable across markedly different types of work organization (e.g. manufacturing and service organizations)?
- Within these overall configurations of input variables, what is the strength and direction of specific factors (which other studies would suggest might be particularly important)? Do the organizations with positive industrial relations climates have a noticeably stronger commitment to participative management, for example? Are they the more flexibly designed organizations? Does the presence of strong unionism tend to be associated with a more co-operative or more hostile industrial relations climate?

Testing the importance for climate of the different elements which comprise organizational structure, together with organizational, human resource, and industrial relations contexts is not as simple as might first appear. In practice these contextual and structural variables exist not in isolation but in various constellations in different organizations. Different elements, in particular constellations, could conceivably exert contrasting effects on climate, thus potentially neutralizing (and masking) one another's effect. For example, a high level of formalization in an organization may tend to have a negative influence on the nature of WIRC. However, if the formalization is operated partly through a high level of (formal) employee involvement in decision-making processes, this could impact positively on climate. Conversely, where formalization is accompanied by a high level of centralization of decision-making power, the result may be disproportionately to heighten the negative impact on WIRC.

Given the growth of attention paid to the concept of flexibility in organizations in recent years, we were also interested in the constellation of factors (and that constellation's individual components) representing more- and less-flexibly designed organizations and, in particular, whether more flexible organizations manifested different climates and industrial relations outcomes, compared to more rigid ones.

Moving through the model and to the question of whether the climate variable acts as an intervening variable between inputs and outputs, this gives rise to such research questions as:

● Does the climate variable strengthen our understanding of the relation between industrial relations/organizational inputs and industrial relations outcomes? That is, are the patterns of association stronger if we take a mediating role of climate into account – does the placing of the climate variable between input and output information improve the explanatory power of the model?

Also relevant to this question of whether the model is an appropriate description of relationships in the real world is:

● Does the model appear to work in the directions suggested? For example, is it more appropriate to conceptualize climate as an intervening variable in the model rather than as a subjective part of the outcome variables?

CONCLUSIONS

The central argument of this chapter has been that the concept of workplace industrial relations climate represents a potentially valuable path towards greater understanding of the determinants of industrial relations outcomes. Climate has provided a durable concept in organizational research. Over three decades there has been much discussion and elaboration but while researchers may have criticized particular approaches to measuring climate, there has been little evidence of attempts to refute or replace the concept. The few studies which have utilized climate within an industrial relations setting encourage a belief in the value of taking the development of the concept further. Up to now, however, only limited progress has been made in identifying what the major constituents of industrial relations climate are, and in understanding how climate fits into the broader picture of factors which influence the character of industrial relations outcomes. It is to these questions that we now turn, drawing on a series of studies which have sought first to formulate a valid and reliable measure of climate in a wide range of manufacturing and service organizations, in order to understand a little more clearly how climate is influenced by different patterns of organizational and industrial relations variables, and how in turn these variables, together with climate, impact upon a range of industrial relations outcomes.

NOTES

1 Furthermore, the relations between climate and culture are likely to be asymmetrical. The influence of climate on culture is easier to conceive of (that is, the individual perception-based concept influencing the group-based one), than vice versa.

To illustrate this last point (and more generally the difference between the two concepts), we can make use of the meteorological metaphor of climate discussed earlier, and of an anthropological metaphor of culture. In any geographical region, climate and culture could coexist. Climate, viewed in this way, is likely to have a profound and continuing effect on culture; for example different climates would contribute to the development of different habits, customs and beliefs – and, more importantly, to the means by which those assumptions are expressed and transmitted. The impact of culture on a region's climate however, has traditionally been more problematic to identify (though of course current events in different cultures are altering this, such as through massive deforestation and the destruction of the ozone layer, which are both impacting on climate).

It should be noted that our aim has been to stress the interrelated nature of the two concepts, and to highlight some of their more obvious similarities and differences. We admit that depending on the position that one takes, and the paradigm and metaphors that one subscribes to, additional explanations as to the relationships between organizational cultures and climate can be developed. For example, Payne referring to Tagiuri and Litwin's (1968) work, stressed that

far from obvious is the differentiation [of climate] from other common terms referring to what surrounds the individual such as *environment, ecology, milieu, culture, atmosphere, situation, setting, behaviour setting, conditions* ... What the term provides ... is a synthetic, molar concept of the environment: a kind of middle range concept instead of a middle-range theory.

(Payne 1971: 143–4)

Payne and Pugh, using a geographical analogy to explain the basis of the relationships between organizational context/structure and climate, pointed out that:

the organizational context and structure variables are the hills and rivers or physical features of the geographical area. Climate dimensions such as progressiveness and development, risk taking, warmth, support, and control correspond to temperature, rainfall, and wind velocity which have been generated by the interactions of physical features with the sun's energy. Social systems' equivalent energy sources are people who also create and are part of the climate. Although both physical and social climates may affect their respective structures, the context and structure of a social system are more stable than its people, whose energies may not always be spent in predictable cycles.

(Payne and Pugh 1976: 1127)

In other words, if one agrees with the above view, one is likely to conclude that organizational culture (assuming it is defined as a part of the organizational context) does affect climate.

Further, if one accepts the concept of organizational culture as a 'root metaphor' for understanding and analyzing organizations (Smircich 1983), in that a 'cultural model' of organization replaces open-system models (Pondy and Mitroff 1979), one is bound to see the internal features of the organization (including climate) as being embedded within the whole cultural milieu. The research questions will then become those relating to a discovery and an understanding of how the organizational life is possible, rather than prediction, generalizability, and causality.

2 Of a more serious nature is a criticism of the way in which climate scores have been assigned to each of the 1,057 individual respondents in the study. Angle and Perry report that they obtained between four and eleven responses on climate for each of the twenty-two plants (reflecting the fact that the climate questionnaires were given only to union representatives and management personnel); they do not specify the characteristics of these management and union respondents (age, level, involvement in IR matters, etc.):

> To derive scores for labour–management relationship climate for each organization, [they] first aggregated the scores within each organization for (1) labour leaders and (2) managers ... then assigned the mean of these two scores as an organization's score on labour–management relations climate. All rank-and-file members received one of twenty-two climate scores that were based on the consensus of the labour leaders and the managers from their own organizations.
>
> (Angle and Perry 1986: 39)

We think that this approach of assigning the climate scores to individuals is in a number of ways irregular. First, it violates the essence of the notion of climate in the sense that climate by definition has to be the perception and the cognitive interpretation of the 'individual' in question, not a score taken from the perception of others and then regarded as an individual property. Second, the use of the word 'consensus' is misleading here, as no attempt has been made to assess this. Third, the climate score derived in this way can only be used as an organizational property if evidence is provided that convinces the reader of some degree of shared perception between the respondents in each organization. None of these have been demonstrated in the article. Given these circumstances it may have been more appropriate to *drop* the term climate from the measure and the title of the article, and be more specific as to the nature of their measurement (means of union and management perceptions of their relationship, perhaps?).

3 The general pattern of relationships discussed here are notwithstanding the theoretical debates in the organization theory literature on the interrelationships among these structural dimensions. A quick review of, for instance, Child's suggestions on 'strategies of control' would imply that these dimensions (e.g. centralization, formalization, specialization) interact, and viewing them purely as separate facets of structure could be misleading (Child 1972, 1984; see also Zeffane 1989 for a thorough review of the issue).

4 One reason for distinguishing between centralization/decentralization and participation is to emphasize the conceptual differences between the two. The former is simply a hierarchical *level* at which decisions take place, and the latter is a reflection of the *processes* that take place in an attempt to involve lower level employees in the decision making (see Hage 1980; Carter and Cullen 1984; Dastmalchian and Javidan 1987 for additional discussion on this issue).

5 Here we have deliberately concentrated on 'context' (factors that are by and large given, such as membership, bargaining structure, etc.) rather than 'process' variables. Our emphasis on IR context variables implies that this category is seen from our standpoint as exerting an influence over climate. Process factors (such as the process of dispute handling) have to a large extent been left out of the discussion due to the restrictions of our proposed model. This, however, does not imply that IR processes are not important for understanding climate variations. We have discussed the importance of the process factors in our earlier work (Blyton *et al.* 1987).

4 The research design

In this chapter we outline the methodology adopted and procedures employed in the different stages of the research process. We begin with a brief overview of an early and small-scale study of British firms in 1981–82 which whetted our appetites for undertaking a more thorough study of workplace industrial relations climate. The development of the concept and measure of workplace industrial relations climate were the next steps in the sequence of events for this project. Below we describe the pilot-study that helped to determine the climate measure. Following this, a case-study involving two very different organizations was conducted in an effort to validate the measures. This is described, followed by the main study involving fifty-one Canadian organizations. Finally, a longitudinal study of seven organizations from our study is outlined.

The methodological concerns of the main study will necessarily be the prime focus of this chapter. However, it is important also to include the earlier programme of work in order to emphasize the developmental phases that this project has gone through. In many ways the present study has been a research journey which at times has left the researchers feeling more like explorers than package tourists. Moreover this journey was often being undertaken on different sides of the Atlantic. Not only the physical location of the researchers involved in the project, but also the geographical spread of the research sites, availability of research funds, and the length of time it took to complete various parts of the study have caused difficulties and delays from time to time, which we will address in this chapter.

BACKGROUND TO THE MAIN STUDY

The British study

In 1981–82 a study of twenty-eight manufacturing firms in South Wales examined possible relationships between the climate of industrial relations and organizational performance (Dastmalchian *et al.* 1982). The idea was based on Nicholson's case-study of a steelworks in Britain in which he demonstrated the potential utility of the industrial relations climate concept (Nicholson 1979). Our own study showed that even a fairly crude measure of industrial relations climate could be shown to have a direct impact on various behavioural indicators of effectiveness, such as the adaptability of the work-force to change. Even though there were no clear associations between climate and economic performance, this study identified the potential value of developing the idea of industrial relations climate further by more systematic theory and measurement.

Subsequent Canadian work

Our interest in the topic continued despite the disruption caused by one of the researchers (Ali Dastmalchian) moving to Canada. In 1983 we teamed up with another interested academic from Canada (Ray Adamson) and through grants obtained from the British Council and Canada's Social Sciences and Humanities Research Council we managed to keep the project's momentum going. We concentrated on two related aspects of the project in 1984–85. One was the development of the conceptual argument, as described in the previous chapter (Dastmalchian and Adamson 1984; Blyton *et al.* 1987). The other was to develop a more satisfactory measure of industrial relations climate (Dastmalchian *et al.* 1985, 1986).

As an initial stage in formulating a measure of climate, previous literature on union–management relationships was used as a basis for devising fifty-five attitude statements (Martin 1976; Martin and Biasatti 1979; Warr *et al.* 1978; Derber *et al.* 1958; Nicholson 1979; Dastmalchian *et al.* 1982). These were in relation to ten *a priori* climate scales: co-operation, apathy, hostility, aggression, support for unionism, joint participation, trust, fairness, goal identification, and power balance. After consideration of the face validity, wording and clarity of the questions (using seven independent raters, three of whom were union representatives and four who were personnel managers of local firms), this initial list of statements was reduced to forty.

These forty questions formed the initial questionnaire which was then sent to a group of industrial relations managers (150), union representatives (150), and labour arbitrators (40). The managers were identified by personnel associations in three Canadian provinces as having industrial relations responsibilities. The union representatives were identified by first approaching fourteen unions in Saskatchewan, and then by randomly selecting 136 union offices from the telephone directories of four additional provinces. The arbitrators were approached using public listings in Ontario. Out of the total of 340 potential respondents, seventy could not be reached by mail (mainly due to change of address), and twelve questionnaires could not be used due to extensive missing information. Of the 258 remaining, 161 responded by returning usable questionnaires (a response rate of 62 per cent). These comprised ninety-one managers, fifty-five union representatives, and fifteen arbitrators. The respondents were asked to rate the relevance of each of the forty statements to the practice of industrial relations in general, using a five-point scale. (For more details see Dastmalchian *et al.* 1986).

The central object of this pilot-study was to determine the relevance of the items devised for capturing certain dimensions of the climate of industrial relations. The respondents were not asked to relate the questions to their specific work situations but rather to think in more general terms and rate the meaningfulness of the statements to typical industrial relations situations. In this sense the rating of the *relevance* of the items was the most important outcome of this exercise, rather than the scalability of the overall dimensions. The analysis of the frequencies of the responses showed that fourteen items had the highest relevance ratings, while six were deemed to be of little value for understanding the climate of industral relations. These ratings are shown in table 4.1 (page 55).

As can be seen from table 4.1, items such as 'keeping their word', 'fairness of employment conditions', 'sincerity in solving problems', 'negotiating in good faith', and 'the existence of informal consultation' are rated among the highest. On the other hand, items such as 'aggressiveness' and 'hostility' between the parties, 'lack of communication between union and management', 'using threats' and 'quibbling over issues', as well as 'apathy' on the part of the membership were rated lower in terms of their relevance to industrial relations. The attribution of a lower relevance to the statements that were more reflective of conflictual situations between industrial relations actors was in some ways surprising. In fact this was an issue that confronted us again at a later stage, and is described in more detail below.

In terms of the characteristics of the respondents, over 80 per cent of the employees in the food packing firm belonged to operative, clerical, or support categories, and had been with the company for over ten years. In the health care organization, on the other hand, a majority (about 60 per cent) were from the professional category who had been with the organization for an average of five years. Among other contrasting features of the two organizations were: 74 per cent of employees in the health care organization were female as compared to 13 per cent in the food packing plant; the food packing organization was more heavily unionized and concentrated mostly in one major union, compared with the health care organization where level of unionization was lower and spread across six different bargaining units.

The procedure for validating the measure consisted of: (i) factor analysis to test the dimensionality of the climate scales; (ii) one-way analysis of variance to test the differences between the two organizations; (iii) internal consistency reliability of the scales; and (iv) an examination of the levels of agreement on climate scales within each organization (i.e. within organization reliability tests; see Glick 1985).

The twenty-six-item questionnaire measured the six a priori dimensions of climate we had identified in the earlier pilot-study. The respondents were asked to indicate their agreement with each item on a five-point scale, ranging from 'strongly agree' (scoring 5) to 'strongly disagree' (scoring 1). The distribution of the questionnaire was undertaken by the personnel departments (a covering letter by the authors accompanied each questionnaire). The responses were returned to the authors directly using pre-paid envelopes.

The questionnaire data for the two organizations were factor analyzed using principal component analysis with varimax rotation. This yielded five factors accounting for 59.7 per cent of the variance. For twenty-four of the twenty-six items the loadings on factors were between 0.43 and 0.71. For the remaining two items (referring to the role of the shop steward, and the use of aggressiveness in negotiations) the loadings were comparatively weaker (0.35 and 0.37) but (following Harris 1967) were considered sufficiently high to include in the factors. The five factors that resulted from this analysis were named: harmony, openness, hostility, apathy, and promptness. Comparing these factors, or climate scales, with the a priori scales in our earlier pilot-study, the 'hostility' and 'apathy' scales remained unchanged.

The four original scales, or dimensions, representing co-operation, mutual regard, trust/fairness, and joint participation, on the other

Table 4.4 Factor analysis of the IR climate data from the validation study (N=728)

IR climate items	Factor 1: harmony	Factor 2: openness	Factor 3: hostility	Factor 4: apathy	Factor 5: promptness
1 Union and management work together to make this organization a better place in which to work	56	36	-18	-22	09
2 Union and management have respect for each other's goals	59	31	-19	-14	12
3 The parties in this organization keep their word	65	19	-31	-19	18
4 In this organization, joint management–union committees achieve definite results	49	32	-09	-23	14
5 There is a great deal of concern for the other party's point of view in the union–management relationship	48	36	-24	-24	12
6 In this organization negotiations take place in an atmosphere of good faith	61	40	-26	-08	15
7 Employees have a positive view on joint union–management committees in this organization	48	28	-17	-30	16
8 The collective agreement is regarded as fair by employees in this organization	60	07	-27	-27	18
9 Employees generally view the conditions of their employment here as fair	50	16	-22	-04	-08
10 A sense of fairness is associated with union–management dealings in this place	53	32	-28	-21	29
11 Generally, employees here do not have much interest in the quality of the union–management relationship	-02	-20	21	61	-07
12 People in this organization are not committed to the unions	-20	-05	06	71	-04
13 In this organization unions have the strong support of their members	28	31	03	-57	18

Item					
14 Employees here rarely express interest in the outcome of negotiations	-05	-04	35	*50*	-09
15 Shop stewards are treated with respect here	30	35	-20	*-37*	24
16 Union and management in this organization tend to dislike each other	-32	-38	51	27	-06
17 The union–management relations in this organization can best be characterized as hostile	-27	-30	60	31	-13
18 Management often opposes the changes advocated by unions here	-30	-20	48	14	-14
19 The parties regularly quarrel over minor issues	32	-24	65	18	-15
20 The best way to get anything accomplished here is for the parties to resort to aggressiveness	-26	-20	35	02	-09
21 Joint union–management committees are a common means of implementing important changes in conditions	19	45	-20	-22	-20
22 The parties exchange information freely in this organization	26	57	-25	-11	08
23 There is not much communication between management and unions in this organization	-17	-44	25	20	-09
24 Management often seeks input from the union before initiating changes	29	43	-18	-08	10
25 Grievances are normally settled promptly in this organization	26	21	-18	-18	*71*
26 Management and unions take a long time to resolve their differences in this organization	-34	-20	41	19	-46
Eigenvalues	11.7	1.6	1.2	1.1	1.0
Percentage of variance	41.6	47.8	52.3	56.2	59.7

Source: Dastmalchian *et al.* (1986: 26)
Note: Decimal points omitted for factor loadings.

hand, were altered and the items reflecting them were re-grouped under three closely related scales of 'harmony', 'openness', and 'promptness'. These scales all reflect positive interaction between unions and managements; however, by reducing the overall number of scales the extent of overlap between the scales has been reduced. Table 4.4 shows the result of the factor analysis.

Table 4.5 shows the means, standard deviations of each scale, together with their reliability estimates, the differences in means between the two organizations, as well as the agreement coefficients representing the extent of shared perception on each scale (Shrout and Fleiss 1979). The first conclusion from the results reported in table 4.5 is that in terms of four of the climate scales, the two organizations demonstrate substantial differences, with the health care organization showing a more co-operative and generally more positive industrial relations climate. The other general observation from the table is that there appears to be a considerably greater homogeneity in perceptions in the food packing plant compared with the health care organization. Given the objective characteristics of the union membership as well as some organizational attributes noted earlier, such closeness in the nature of perceptions of employees in the food packing firm was anticipated. The within-unit agreement coefficients of the two organizations based on union vs. non-union, bargaining units, and departments were also analyzed (Dastmalchian *et al.* 1989: 27–8). This showed that the level of agreement on climate was highest when the union vs. non-union employees were compared, and weakest when different departments were compared.

Thus the case-study served a number of purposes that were necessary prior to embarking on the main study. It indicated to us that the items selected for measuring workplace industrial relations climate were on the whole relevant and able to capture aspects of the union–management relationship climate that we had considered theoretically and practically meaningful. It also increased our confidence in the predictive and diagnostic utility of the climate measures and in the conceptual model guiding the research.

THE MAIN STUDY

Throughout the earlier stages of this project, it was clear that in order to be able to claim a degree of generalizability for the climate measure, and also test the viability of the model as a whole, a relatively large-scale study involving organizations of different scale and located in different industrial sectors, was required. Our validation

Table 4.5 Descriptive statistics, reliability, and agreement estimates of IR climate scales from the validation study

| IR climate scales | Number of items | Health care organization (N=327) | | Food Packing organization (N=402) | | Differences between A and B (F ratio) | Within-organization agreement coefficient ICC (1, K)[a] |
		Mean (SD)	Coefficient α	Mean (SD)	Coefficient α		
1 Harmony	10	32.30 (5.72)	0.846	27.12 (8.74)	0.920	81.08**	0.987
2 Openness	4	6.10 (2.41)	0.649	5.54 (3.26)	0.745	6.40*	0.843
3 Hostility	5	13.35 (3.37)	0.768	15.89 (4.50)	0.808	60.86**	0.983
4 Apathy	5	2.37 (3.17)	0.663	2.27 (4.39)	0.803	1.63	0.389
5 Promptness	2	-0.01 (1.75)	0.682	-0.667 (2.13)	0.744	19.87**	0.949
Total	26					Median:	0.949

* $P \leq 0.01$
** $P \leq 0.001$.

[a] Refers to inter-class correlation, which is used as a measure of within-organization agreement (for further details see Shrout and Fleiss 1979; also Glick 1985). It is computed by the formula *Between Group Mean Squared minus Within Group Mean Squared, divided by Between Group Mean Squared*

Source: Dastmalchian et al. (1989: 27)

study, described above, had a major influence in the choice of our research approach and methodology. Consistent with the approach used in that study, a predominantly cross-sectional method was adopted in which the required information would be collected from a variety of sources in each organization using three different means of data collection (in addition a smaller longitudinal element was included; this is described below.)

The sources of information included: top management (either the chief executive officers or vice presidents); other senior management (at least one key functional head and the manager in charge of human resources); all local union and employee association representatives; a randomly selected group of employees, both unionized and non-unionized; written documents (e.g. company policy, union contract) and personnel records (e.g. pertaining to absenteeism, turnover, grievances, etc.). The data were collected by means of (i) structured interviews with some informants, (ii) semi-structured and open-ended interviews with others, (iii) distributing a climate questionnaire to a group of employees in each organization, and (iv) consulting written confirmatory documents and personnel records. A summary of the data sources and methods of data collection is provided in appendix 2.

Sampling procedure

The data for the main study were obtained from a total of fifty-one organizations in Canada between July 1987 and March 1988. The conceptual framework guiding the study, as described earlier, did not require us to concentrate on specific industries or types of organizations. In fact, our belief was that given the ubiquity of industrial relations climate in all workplaces, the issues should be tested in a sample of organizations that was as varied as possible in terms of size, industry, nature of operation, industrial relations structure, and so on.

In the event, this broad view of the nature of the desired sample caused a certain amount of difficulty and introduced additional uncertainty into the process, given the resources that we had available at the time. In selecting the list of potential organizations to approach our first primary constraint was the source of information. Most industry listings, for example, do not provide information about unionization. Additionally, in Canada such information, however incomplete, is provided provincially rather than nationally. Another related problem was the choice of location of the target organization (anyone who has looked at a map of Canada will readily appreciate the vastness of the country and the real problems it creates for any study of this sort that intends to be 'national'!). Our decision, then, was to approach organizations in regions that were relatively close to the locations of the two Canadian members of our research team: western Canada and southern Ontario.

The prime source of information about the organizations were the listings provided by the Departments of Labour in Saskatchewan, Alberta, and Manitoba in western Canada, and the Kitchner/Waterloo area in Ontario. Based on this, 190 organizations were approached (150 in the prairie provinces and 40 in the Waterloo area). These organizations were broadly selected to include those that, according to our information, had at least one recognized bargaining unit or an internal employee association. Upon identification of the organizations, a letter with the outline of the study was sent to both management and union/employee association(s). This was followed by telephone calls to management and union representatives in order to enlist their participation. Of 190 organizations, fifty-one agreed to participate. This agreement had to be reached with *both* the management and the union/association, since the willingness of both parties to participate in the study was deemed to be crucial. There were an additional forty-three organizations in which one party was willing to participate but they had to withdraw due to a lack of co-operation from the other party. The remaining ninety-six organizations were either unwilling to take part in the study (thirty-six organizations) or had to decline due to ongoing or upcoming negotiations (forty organizations), or those who either had no longer a union representing their work-force (nine organizations) or could not be located and did not reply to our request (eleven organizations).

An additional (and to some extent inevitable) problem that we were faced with later on in the study was the refusal of some organizations to allow the distribution of the climate questionnaire to employees. This was despite their earlier agreement to full participation, and understandably was beyond our control. As will be discussed later, in some cases the reversal in their decisions was due to internal matters (e.g. disagreement of management and union over certain items that should or should not be in the questionnaire). In one case, the president of a retail/wholesale organization left the company before the study was complete, and the new manager declined to participate in the survey distribution part of the project. In a number of other situations, the local union representatives who were in agreement with the study procedure received directions from their provincial offices not to take part in any attitude-type surveys (particularly if the managements had endorsed them!). As a result the number of organizations for which both interview and question-naire data were available was reduced to a maximum of thirty-five organizations.

Characteristics of the sample

Our main sample (which according to sampling definitions is a 'convenient' sample) consists of fifty-one organizations drawn from twenty-two different industry groups. Twenty-eight of the organiza-tions belonged to the manufacturing sector while twenty-three were in service industries. In all, thirteen different industries were included in the manufacturing group: six organizations from brewing, three each from chemical/petrochemical, telecommunication equipment, and textiles, two each from upholstered furniture and basic metal, and one organization in each of food processing, automotive parts, pulp and paper, beverages, printing, agricultural, and transportation equipment. In the service sector, our sample consisted of enterprises from nine industries: eleven from health care, two each from hospitality (hotels, restaurants), recreation/sports, education, and retail/wholesale, and one library, correction (prison) service, elec-tricity provider, and an agricultural servicing business.

Tables 4.6 and 4.7 show size classification (number of employees), age, status, and the service/manufacturing breakdown of the sample. As can be seen, a majority of the establishments in the sample employ between 100 and 500 employees, with an overall mean of 725 (and standard deviation of 1,448). The smallest organization in the sample was a hospital/clinic with nineteen full-time equivalent employees, while the largest was a petrochemical firm with 7,000 employees.

The age of the companies in the sample ranged from thirteen years (an electronics firm) to over 200 years (a brewery), with a mean of 63.6 years and a standard deviation of 40.6. In terms of the status of the organizations, by far the majority of the sample were principle operating units (58.8 per cent), with a remainder of the establish-ments being either subsidiaries of a larger organization (13.7 per cent), head branches with legal identity (9.8 per cent), or branches (17.6 per cent). About 36 per cent of the organizations in the sample (eighteen of them) were owned 75 per cent or more by various levels of government (municipal, provincial, and federal), and 30 per cent of the sample had public share offering.

Table 4.6 Size, age, and service/manufacturing classification of the sample by industry type (N=51)

Industry	<100	100–199	200–499	>500	Average age (Years)	Totals
I Manufacturing						
1 Brewing	2	4	–	–	145	6
2 Agricultural equipment	–	–	1	–	16	1
3 Transportation equipment	–	1	–	–	18	1
4 Basic Metals	–	2	–	–	68	2
5 Chemical, petrochemical and refinery	–	–	2	3	63	5
6 Telecommunication or microelectronics	–	1	2	–	22	3
7 Textile	–	1	2	–	48	3
8 Printing/publishing	1	–	–	–	76	1
9 Carbonated beverages	–	–	1	–	52	1
10 Pulp and paper	–	–	1	–	21	1
11 Automotive parts	–	–	1	–	23	1
12 Upholstered furniture	–	–	2	–	64	2
13 Food processing/packaging	–	–	–	1	95	1
Manufacturing Total						28
II Service						
14 Library	1	–	–	–	74	1
15 Hotel/restaurant	1	1	–	–	34	2
16 Recreation/sports	1	1	–	–	80	2
17 Education	–	–	2	–	93	2
18 Retail/wholesale	–	1	1	–	45	2
19 Correction/prison	–	–	–	1	45	1
20 Health care	4	2	–	3	59	11
21 Electricity services	–	–	1	1	26	1
22 Agricultural business services	–	–	–	1	63	1
Service Total						23
Totals	10	14	15	12	–	51

Table 4.7 Status of the organizations in sample by industry type

Industry	Organizational status				Totals
	Principal unit	Subsidiary	Head branch	Branch	
I Manufacturing					
1 Brewing			3	3	6
2 Agricultural equipment		1			1
3 Transportation equipment	1				1
4 Basic metals	1	1			2
5 Chemical, petrochemical and refinery	1	4			5
6 Telecommunication or microelectronics	2			1	3
7 Textile	1	1	1		3
8 Printing/publishing	1				1
9 Carbonated beverages	1				1
10 Pulp and paper				1	1
11 Automotive parts	1				1
12 Upholstered furniture	1		1		2
13 Food processing/packaging				1	1
II Service					
14 Library	1				1
15 Hospitality	1			1	2
16 Recreation/sports	2				2
17 Education	2				2
18 Retail/wholesale	1			1	2
19 Correction/prison		1			1
20 Health care	11				11
21 Electricity services	1				1
22 Agricultural business services	1				1
Totals:	30	8	5	8	51

Characteristics of questionnaire sample

As explained earlier, the data collection design included the distribution of the climate questionnaire among a varied sample of employees in each of the organizations studied. After the completion of the interviews, the agreement of both management and union representatives was sought regarding the distribution of the questionnaire and the procedure to do so. The procedure for the distribution of the questionnaire was usually finalized with the personnel/human resource managers. Our minimum requirement in terms of the number of people surveyed was about 10 per cent of the employees, varying in terms of their hierarchical levels, departmental affiliation, and union versus non-union membership. Typically, depending on the agreement reached regarding the number of people to be surveyed, names of people from a list of all employees provided by the personnel department were selected (e.g. every third, fifth, or seventh name on the list was chosen). A questionnaire, a covering letter from us explaining the purposes of the project and assuring the confidentiality as well as the voluntary nature of the survey, and a self-addressed envelope were then sent to each potential respondent. The respondent was asked to complete the questionnaire and mail it directly to the researchers. On each questionnaire a number of control questions were also asked. These included: age, education, union membership, length of service, departmental affiliation, and position/level of the respondents.

Of some three thousand questionnaires that were sent to employees from thirty-five organizations, 1,686 usable responses were received. Table 4.8 shows the overall characteristics of the respondents in terms of their age, sex, education, length of service, position, and union/association membership. This information shows that a majority of the respondents were in their late 20s or early 30s, have finished high school, college, or university, and have been with the organization for an average of ten years. There appears to be an equal number of respondents in skilled and unskilled categories, and, for the known cases, the proportions of male and female employees are similar. Also, by far the largest proportion of the respondents are unionized.

Table 4.9 shows the characteristics of the respondents to the climate questionnaire for each of the thirty-five organizations under study. This information shows that the respondents on average represent 16 per cent of the total employment in the thirty-five establishments (and 22 per cent of full-time employees); and the average number of respondents from each organization is forty-eight

Table 4.8 Age, sex, length of service, education, position, and union
membership of the respondents to the climate questionnaire (N=1686)

	Score	Frequency	%
Age			
17–25	–	132	14.2
26–35	–	356	38.2
36–45	–	242	25.9
46–55	–	136	15.7
56–71	–	66	6.0
Unknown	–	754	–
		1,686	100.0
Sex			
Female	–	470	49.0
Male	–	489	51.0
Unknown	–	727	–
		1,686	100.0
Service (years)			
Up to 1 year	–	162	10.4
2–5 years	–	443	28.5
6–10 years	–	395	25.4
11–20 years	–	406	26.1
20 years +	–	151	9.7
Unknown	–	129	–
		1,686	100.0
Education			
Not finished high school	0	84	8.7
High school completed	1	249	25.9
Some post secondary	2	114	11.9
Technical training/college	3	248	25.8
University graduate	4	266	27.7
Unknown	–	725	–
		1,686	100.0
Position			
Unskilled	0	413	28.5
Semi-skilled	1	285	19.6
Skilled	2	432	29.8
Supervisory	3	208	14.3
Dept. heads/management	4	99	6.8
Senior management	5	14	1.0
Unknown	–	235	–
		1,686	100.0
Union/association membership			
Not member	0	321	20.6
Member	1	1,241	79.4
Unknown	–	124	–
		1,686	100.0

Table 4.9 Characteristics of the questionnaire sample by organization*

Organization	Average age of respondents	Average position**	Average tenure	Average education**	Number of respondents (A)	Size (number of employees (B)	A/B
1	37.58	2.81	9.42	2.93	43	500	0.09
2	34.80	2.50	10.99	3.14	36	342	0.11
3	47.38	2.13	10.61	2.67	9	22	0.41
4	42.73	2.33	11.41	2.52	23	354	0.06
5	35.98	2.00	8.42	3.07	56	657	0.09
6	38.48	2.82	10.95	2.89	28	318	0.09
7	38.42	2.92	9.50	2.75	12	144	0.08
8	47.00	2.64	15.91	2.45	11	34	0.32
9	39.56	2.38	11.28	2.89	9	19	0.47
10	37.27	1.12	9.75	1.27	48	240	0.20
11	32.44	1.31	3.57	1.15	41	201	0.20
12	35.97	0.91	9.69	1.42	93	350	0.27
13	37.00	1.06	10.40	0.97	37	192	0.19
14	32.36	0.95	4.35	0.98	50	392	0.13
15	24.29	1.14	4.21	1.86	7	160	0.04
16	34.57	1.14	6.21	2.71	7	97	0.07
17	32.63	1.55	4.39	2.50	20	100	0.20
18	33.00	1.19	5.83	3.30	21	105	0.20
19	30.25	2.50	9.75	1.88	9	110	0.08
20	37.44	1.88	8.59	2.94	16	151	0.11
21	38.24	1.51	8.71	2.00	45	183	0.25
23	39.20	1.36	9.73	2.93	74	6416	0.01[a]
26	29.06	2.00	4.91	2.76	17	200	0.09
27	35.63	1.89	11.44	2.22	9	90	0.10
28	28.85	1.56	2.56	2.11	36	300	0.12
30	37.91	2.55	9.77	2.91	11	60	0.18
31	35.65	2.59	6.97	2.65	17	145	0.12
32	44.71	1.29	16.71	1.43	7	97	0.07
33	37.53	2.13	10.27	3.85	47	900	0.05
34	44.63	2.96	17.00	2.73	52	2600	0.02[b]
36	30.17	1.85	3.01	3.20	41	130	0.32
48	–	1.40	5.53	–	275	1620	0.17
49	–	.49	13.17	–	402	2375	0.17
50	–	2.12	5.20	–	32	70	0.46
51	43.53	3.11	12.36	2.67	45	1500	0.03[c]
Mean	36.70	1.89	8.93	2.43	48.2	604.92	0.16[d]

* Total of thirty-five organizations with 1686 respondents
** For the scoring procedure for these variables, see table 4.8

a Since the survey was distributed to union members only (N=1050), the actual rate is about 7%
b The unit under study had 600 employees, thus the actual rate is closer to 9%
c This represents 100% of the management in organization 51
d Given the 35% non full-time employees, this figure would change to 22% for full-time employees

employees. The actual response rate, however, is over 56 per cent (i.e. the number returned as a proportion of the total number of questionnaires distributed). Moreover, it shows that in terms of the position, tenure and the educational level of the respondents, there is sufficient variation across the establishments under study which has to be taken into consideration in further analysis of the climate data.

Measurements

Consistent with our working conceptual model, as described in chapter 3, six categories of variables were measured in this study:

1 organizational context and environment;
2 organizational structure;
3 human resources practices and policies;
4 industrial relations context and issues;
5 workplace industrial relations climates; and
6 outcomes of union–management relationships.

In the next section, the operational definitions and measurements employed as well as the statistics relating to the measures will be outlined. The interview schedule and the climate questionnaire are presented in appendix 1.

1 Organizational context and environment

The aspects of organizational context and environment included in the study were: size, age, technology, dependencies on owners and on labour markets, and the extent of organizational change.

Size

Size of organization was measured in terms of the number of full-time equivalent employees. A logarithm of the number of employees was computed to represent size. (The mean of this log scale was 2.41 with a standard deviation of 0.58.)

Age

Age refers to the number of years the organization had been in existence with its present identity and in its present form (Mean=63.6, SD=40.6).

Technology

Two different measures of technology were used. One was based on Woodward's classification of small batch (scoring 1), large batch (scoring 2), and process technologies (scoring 3) (Woodward 1965). In addition, given the number of service organizations in our sample, a score of 4 was given to denote this category. In total, about 12 per cent of the sample had small batch technology, an equal number fell in the process category, 33 per cent had large batch or mass production technology, and 43 per cent belonged to service. The mean score for this variable was 2.86 (SD=1.11).

The second measure of technology used was based on Thompson's (1967) classification of intensive (scoring 3), long-linked (scoring 2), and mediating (scoring 1) technologies. This measure was selected for its ability to reflect task interdependencies among various units or departments in the organization, without being tied to production versus service technologies. In all, 47 per cent of the sample belonged to the intensive technology group in which more intensive and reciprocal interdependency is required. Among the remainder, 43 per cent had long-linked technologies in which line units in each organization had more sequential interdependencies with others, while 10 per cent of the organizations had mediating technologies indicating a relatively low level of interdependence among departments. The mean score for this variable was 2.37 (SD=0.66).

Owner dependency

This variable is defined as the extent to which an organization, as a unit of analysis, is dependent on its owners. It is based on the notion of 'dependence on parent organization' as used by the Aston research team (Pugh and Hickson 1976). The adapted measure used here has been successfully employed before (e.g. Dastmalchian 1984; Dastmalchian and Javidan 1987). It consists of six items, measuring: (i) the status of the unit in terms of whether the organization is a principal unit, a subsidiary, a head branch with legal identity, or a branch (on a four-point scale); (ii) the extent of ownership by individuals or a family, measured on a four-point scale (where less than 10 per cent scores 1, and more than 75 per cent scores 4); (iii) the extent of ownership by government (on a four-point scale, as above); (iv) the extent of ownership by one or two organizations (on a four-point scale, as above); (v) whether the shares are quoted in a stock market (a score of 1 for an affirmative response); and (vi) the number of structural levels in the parent organization. Owner dependence was computed by adding the scores on these six items. The average inter-correlation among the six items was 0.38, and Alpha for five items (excluding the one binary variable) was 0.73. The mean score for the total measure was 11.70 (SD=4.84).

Labour market dependence

This variable refers to the extent to which the organization is dependent on the external labour market for staffing its current positions regarding different categories of employees (i.e. managerial, professional, manual, and clerical). The measure used consists of five items referring to: (i) the extent to which the organization is generally unable to fill vacancies within a reasonable time; (ii) the extent to which training is needed due to lack of availability of qualified personnel; (iii) the extent to which the organization has current unfilled positions; (iv) and (v) the availability of the required employees at local and industrial levels. All the items were measured on four-point scales. For the first three items, the scale ranged from 'never' (scoring 1) to 'almost always' (scoring 4). For items four and five, the scales ranged from 'very available' (scoring 1) to 'virtually non-existent' (scoring 4). These questions were repeated for the four categories of managerial, professional/technical, clerical, and manual employees. For each category a dependency index was computed by adding the scores on the five questions. A total measure of labour market dependency was then computed by taking the average of dependency scores of the four categories. This total labour market dependency score had a mean of 7.63 and a standard deviation of 1.99. The reliability estimate (Cronbach 1951), showing the internal consistency reliability of the items forming labour market dependency was Alpha = 0.894.

Major changes

In order to reflect the extent to which the organization has recently been undergoing major changes, a general question to this effect was asked in the senior management interviews. After analyzing the contents of their responses, a measure was constructed to show the extent of change for our comparative analysis. Ten items were identified from the descriptive responses. These were: reorganization; relocation; incorporation changes; ownership changes; automation and/or computerization; product/service diversification; expansion;

renovating building, equipment or facilities; downsizing; and divestment. A score of 1 was given for positive responses to each of the above. A total measure was computed by adding the scores on the ten items (mean=3.34, SD=1.60).

2 Organizational structure

Aspects of organizational structure were measured in order to reflect the framework within which tasks are performed and to have a set of 'organizational' variables that depict the nature of interactions likely to take place among organizational members. These include aspects of decision making (three aspects: centralization, decision sharing, and distance were measured), formalization of roles and jobs, specialization of various functions, and organizational complexity.

Centralization

This refers to the hierarchical level at which actions on a list of decisions can be initiated. This was measured by asking senior managers to describe the most junior level at which decisions pertaining to sixteen areas were normally made. The hierarchical levels were measured on a seven-point scale, ranging from 'above the organization' (scoring 7), through various management and supervisory levels, to 'operative level' (scoring 1). This is a modified version of the centralization measure used by the Aston group (Pugh *et al.* 1968; Pugh and Hickson 1976), and in particular by the more recent versions of the instrument (e.g. Wheeler *et al.* 1980; Dastmalchian 1984; Dastmalchian and Javidan 1987). The sixteen decision areas concerned: introduction of new products/services; elimination of products/services; changes or modifications to products/services; introduction of new policies; departmental budget allocation; hiring; promotion; dismissal; number of employees required (manning levels); salaries of non-unionized staff; training needs; purchasing capital items; purchasing other items; organization of departments and personnel; closing deals with customers; and pricing.

The total measure of centralization was computed by adding the scores of all sixteen items. This had a mean of 58.9 and a standard deviation of 13.84. The average intercorrelation among the items was 0.40, the corrected item-total correlation was 0.56, and the estimate of internal consistency reliability was 0.89 (Cronbach's Alpha). In addition, a sub-scale measuring the centralization of decisions relating directly to the human resource function was computed by adding the scores on six relevant items (i.e. hiring, promotion, dismissal, manning levels, salaries, and training). This was termed *HR Centralization* (mean=20.98, SD=5.19, Alpha=0.83).

Decision sharing and distance

Two aspects of 'participation' were measured by ascertaining: (i) the number of different hierarchical levels involved in the process of making decisions (sharing); and (ii) the distance between the highest and the lowest hierarchical levels involved in decisions (distance). For these measures the centralization scale with its sixteen decision items was used. This measure was based on Hage's (1980) notion of participation, and more recent discussion regarding the utility of including these aspects in any centralization/decentralization measurements (Carter and Cullen 1984). For decision sharing, the mean score was 40.64 (SD=12.66, and for distance 28.18 (SD=12.08). The internal consistency reliability estimates for these sales were 0.89 and 0.86 respectively (Cronbach's Alpha).

Similar to the other measures of structure, sub-scales of sharing and distance pertaining to the human resources function were computed, by adding the scores on the six decision-making items relating to human resources (see 'Centralization' page 75, for details). These were termed *HR Sharing* (mean=14.34, SD=4.70, Alpha=0.81) and *HR Distance* (mean=9.57, SD=4.97, Alpha=0.80).

Formalization

This refers to the extent to which written documents are used to define and prescribe the role of people in the organization. It is based on Pugh *et al.*'s (1968) formalization of role definition, and the actual items are modifications of Aston's abbreviated measures (Inkson *et al.* 1970), which has been used in previous research (e.g. Dastmalchian 1984, 1986). This measure consists of eleven items (Inkson's original measure had twelve items) operationalizing the existence of: job descriptions for different levels of management and employees (four items); an organizational chart and its distribution (two items); existence and distribution of information booklets (two items); written policies (one item); and written procedures and operating instructions (two items). The only item that had to be deleted from the original scale was that referring to the existence of written research reports or plans (no organization had a score for this item).

With the exception of two items dealing with the distribution of documents (the distribution of chart and booklets, measured on 0 to 4 scales), all the items had binary scales (score of 0 for the absence and 1 for the presence of a document). In computing the reliability of the measure, the two items with ordinal scales were converted to binary ones. The mean item analysis value (Brogden 1949; Levy and Pugh 1969) of the formalization items was 0.67. A total measure of formalization was then computed by adding the scores on the eleven items (mean=10.68, SD=3.89).

Specialization

Specialization refers to the extent to which full-time employees are employed to deal exclusively with various specialized activities in the organization. Twenty-one activities were identified to represent a wide range of specializations across different functional areas. Thirteen were taken from Inkson *et al.*'s (1970) earlier study. In addition, given our own interests, eight items were added to the list to identify various specialities within a typical personnel department (i.e. recruitment, benefits, salary, training, industrial relations, health and safety, organization development, and other employment matters). A score of 1 was given to an activity for which the organization had a specialist, and 0 for those for which it did not. The overall score for specialization was computed by summing the scores on the twenty-one items. The mean item analysis value, as an estimate of the scale's reliability was a very satisfactory 0.88 (Brogden 1949). The mean score for the scale was 10.02 (SD=5.48). In addition, a sub-scale of *HR Specialization* was computed by considering the eight items pertaining to the human resources unit (mean=2.64, SD=2.62, and reliability estimate of 0.85).

3 Human resource practices and policies

Four aspects of the organization's human resource practices, policies, and issues were measured: the existence of an internal labour market (ILM); provision for employee training and education; human resource changes; and organizational changes.

Internal labour market

This refers to the existence of a promotion ladder within the organization. As discussed in chapter 3, we have made a distinction between ILM (or firm-specific ILM) and training, even though the existing literature tends to view both as being part of the same concept. In order to gauge ILM, a measure based on the categories provided by Pfeffer and Cohen (1984) was developed. This consisted of eight questions referring to: level of required experience; chances of promotion with minimum experience; percentage of vacancies filled from within and from outside; percentage of employees promoted in the last five years; chances of moving from unskilled to semi-skilled jobs, and from semi-skilled to skilled positions; and the existence of a ladder for promotion. All the eight questions were measured on a four-point scale (with 4 representing the highest, and 1 the lowest, value), and were repeated for four categories of employees (managerial, professional, clerical, and manual). An average of the four categories formed the overall ILM score (mean=20.07, SD=4.28). The reliability estimate for all the thirty-two items was 0.86, and the average intercorrelation among the four sub-categories forming the overall scale was 0.71.

Training and education

This variable refers to the provision for training and education, both on- and off-the-job, made in each organization. The measure consists of four items: (i) provision for training prior to new employees taking up their duties; (ii) provision for in-house training programmes; (iii) formal on-the-job training; and (iv) support for training outside the organization. These were measured on a four-point scale, ranging from 'no training' (scoring 1), training for few (2 points), and many positions (scoring 3), to training for all positions (scoring 4). These four questions were asked for managerial, professional, clerical, and manual employees separately. An average of the training scores was taken across the four employment categories to arrive at an overall training and education score, which had a mean of 11.95 (SD=3.05) with the reliability estimate of Alpha=0.92.

Human resources change

This variable refers to the overall changes that have taken place in the recent past in the staff requirements of the organization. Seven items were devised to measure this variable: significant changes in job descriptions; requirements for new skills (within existing skill areas); requirements for whole new skill areas; changes due to new and different equipment; creation of whole new jobs; higher job qualifications; and increased legal and technical requirement for jobs. A score of 1 was given when an item applied, and 0 for no changes. A total score was computed by summing the scores for the seven items. The mean score for this variable was 4.65 with a standard deviation of 1.73. Mean item analysis value, as an estimate of the scales's reliability was 0.60.

Organizational change

This is similar to the extent of change measured as part of the context variables. However, it concentrates on the key changes identified by the human resource managers that had direct bearing on the nature of staffing and human resource practices in the organization. Three categories were included in this measure: undertaking an expansion programme involving new facilities; becoming more specialized as to the type of products/services offered; and offering a new range of products/services. Again these items were measured on a binary scale, and a total measure was computed by adding the scores on the three items. The mean was 1.74 (SD=1.01), and the mean item analysis value was 0.58.

4 Industrial relations context and issues

The variables under this category were included in order to take into account some of the more objective features of the industrial relations setting of each organization. Clearly, one would expect the current perceived climate of the union–management relationship to be influenced by such variables as the size of the union membership, the bargaining structure, and so on. The following variables were selected to represent some key aspects of the industrial relations context.

Number of unions/associations

A majority of the organizations in the sample had one union representing their employees (twenty-seven organizations). Twelve organizations had two bargaining units, two had five unions, and single organizations had three, six, and twenty-five unions. Six organizations did not have a union representing their employees, but in four cases some alternative mechanism (employee committees, consultation groups, etc.) were formed to act in a collective fashion in employment relations matters. The mean number of bargaining units was 2.10 (SD=3.66).

Number of union members

The mean size of union/association membership was 351 with a standard deviation of 576. Forty-six per cent of the organizations had a membership size of up to 100 employees, with another 44 per cent indicating their union membership to be between 100 and 900. About 10 per cent of the available responses indicated unionization levels of between 1,500 and 2,250 employees. The rate of unionization was also computed using a four-point scale (1 for under 10 per cent, 2 for 11 to 40 per cent, 3 for 41 to 70 per cent, and 4 for over 70 per cent). The mean for the sample was 3.06 (SD=1.07), indicating union density of over 70 per cent.

Proportion of males and females

These refer to the proportion of the union/association members who were male or female. The means and the standard deviations of these two variables were quite similar. For proportion of male employees, the mean was 50.58 (SD=36.60), with about 8 per cent of the organizations having no male membership, and up to 25 per cent having 10 per cent or less. For females the mean was 51.46 (SD=36.86), with under one-third of the sample having less than 10 per cent female membership.

Level of bargaining

A total of 71 per cent of the sample operated local bargaining structures. Bargaining at the industry or province levels was much less common among the organizations studied. About 31 per cent of the sample had provincial bargaining structures while only 17 per cent indicated the existence of some form of industry-wide bargaining. In the case of the six brewing organizations, as well as a school system, local bargaining was in conjunction with either industry-wide, or province-wide structures.

Length of union presence

The mean length of union/association presence in the organization was 17.5 years, with a standard deviation of 12.34. A total of 24 per cent of the organizations had had unions for eight years or less, and up to 80 per cent of the sample for twenty-five years or less. The range was from 1 to 47 years.

Information also was obtained on main methods of grievance handling, and on the outcome of the last collective negotiations. For grievances, 76 per cent of the sample indicated 'formal' methods (scoring 1), and 24 per cent had 'informal' methods (scoring 2). The mean score was 1.23 (SD=0.43). For outcome of last negotiations, the favourability of the outcomes from the union's standpoint was measured using a four-point scale (ranging from 1 indicating 'poor' to 4 denoting 'very favourable' outcomes). The mean score was 2.26, with SD of 0.80.

5 Workplace industrial relations climate

Our measure of workplace industrial relations climate refers to the perceived work atmosphere surrounding the union–management relationships. Initially the twenty-six items (grouped in terms of five climate scales) that resulted from our validation study were to form the measure of industrial relations climate (Dastmalchian *et al.* 1989). However, in discussions with the five organizations that were interviewed in the first stage of the study it became apparent that eight questions were being criticized and were not considered suitable for inclusion in the questionnaire. The interesting issue here was that all the eight items were in some ways dealing with negative or conflict-related matters, as can be seen from the following list:

1 People in this organization are not committed to the unions.
2 Employees here rarely express interest in the outcomes of negotiations.
3 Union and management in this organization tend to dislike each other.
4 The union–management relationship in this organization can best be described as hostile.
5 The parties regularly quibble over minor issues.
6 The best way to get anything accomplished here is for the parties to resort to aggressiveness.
7 There is not much communication between management and unions in this organization.
8 Management and unions take a long time to resolve their differences in this organization.

The first two items were a part of the 'apathy' scale. The next four items were included in the 'hostility' scale, and the last two statements were related to lack of openness and promptness. In their

Table 4.10 Factor analysis of the workplace industrial relations climate items (with varimax rotation N=1686)

	Factor 1 (fairness)	Factor 2 (U/M consultation)	Factor 3 (mutual regard)	Factor 4 (member support)	Factor 5 (union legitimacy)
1 The collective agreement is regarded as fair by employees in this organization (Q10)		0.611			
2 A sense of fairness is associated with management dealings in this place (Q19)		0.592	0.452		
3 In this organization, negotiations take place in an atmosphere of good faith (Q8)	0.519				
4 The parties in this organization keep their word (Q3)	0.503		0.440		
5 Employees generally view the conditions of their employment here as fair (Q14)	0.496				
6 Grievances are normally settled promptly in this organization (Q13)	0.436				
7 Unions and management in this organization make sincere efforts to solve common problems (Q24)		0.551			
8 Management often seeks input from unions before initiating changes (Q23)		0.532			
9 Management and unions cooperate to settle disputes in this organization (Q17)	0.474	0.496			
10 The parties exchange information freely in this organization (Q16)		0.453			
11 There is a great deal of concern for the other party's point of view in the union–management relationship (Q6)		0.429	0.403		

	Q12–Q22 item	F1	F2	F3	F4	F5
12	Joint union–management committees are a common means of implementing important changes in conditions (Q12)		0.421			
13	Unions and management work together to make this organization a better place to work (Q1)		0.404	0.601		
14	Unions and management have respect for each other's goals (Q2)			0.596		
15	In this organization, joint union–management committees achieve definite results (Q5)			0.439		
16	Generally, employees do not have much interest in the quality of the union–management relationship (Q11)				−0.529	
17	In this organization, unions have the strong support of their members (Q15)				0.495	
18	Unions make a positive contribution to this organization (Q4)				0.408	
19	Shop stewards in this organization generally play a helpful role (Q21)					0.401
20	People are encouraged to get involved in union activities here (Q22)				0.490	0.476
	% Variance	37.6	44.6	49.1	53.3	57.3
	Eigenvalue	9.030	1.665	1.077	1.029	0.939

place, six statements from our original forty-item questionnaire were selected. As a result of these alterations, the total number of items on the climate instrument was reduced to twenty-four. These items were devised to measure the employees' perception of the climate of industrial relations in the organization (i.e. workplace industrial relations climate). The respondents were asked to indicate the extent of their agreement with each item using a five-point scale, ranging from 'strongly agree' (scoring 5) to 'strongly disagree' (scoring 1).

These twenty-four items were then factor analyzed, using principal component analysis with varimax rotation. This produced five factors accounting for over 57 per cent of variance. Table 4.10 shows the result of the factor analysis.

Even though there are some minimal degrees of overlap between loadings on the first three factors, and one observed overlap between factors four and five, the outcome is quite interesting and consistent with the earlier version of the survey used in our validation case study. Factor 1 refers to fairness and harmony in dealings between union and management and their active co-operation to solve common problems. Items under factor 2 are concerned with union–management consultation, joint participation, openness, and respect – the main ingredients of building a co-operative relationship. Factor 3 includes aspects of union–management relationships focusing on mutual regard and having respect for one another's goals. Factor 4 deals with membership support for unions, whereas factor 5 reflects the general legitimacy of the union within the organization. Three items (questions 7, 9, 18 and 20) had weak loadings (less than 0.40) under factor 1. Due to this they were excluded from our final scales. Therefore the final version of our workplace industrial relations climate has twenty items grouped under five scales.

Table 4.11 shows the means, standard deviations, ranges, reliability estimates (Cronbach's Alpha), and corrected item-total correlations, as well as within-organization agreement coefficients (Shrout and Fleiss 1979; Glick 1985).

As shown in table 4.11 the internal consistent reliability (Alpha) coefficients, and the corrected item-total correlations are quite strong (over 0.90) for the first three scales (fairness, consultation, and mutual regard) and comparatively weaker, but acceptable (0.78 and 0.75), for the remaining two scales (membership support and union legitimacy). As for the within-organization agreement coefficients, table 4.11 shows that for four of the scales the agreement within each organization is quite high, and for one of the scales (i.e. member support) is comparatively weaker. However, as the average of the

Table 4.11 Means, standard deviations, reliability estimates, and within-organization agreement coefficients for workplace industrial relations climate scales

Climate scales	Number of items	Mean (SD)	Range	Cronbach's α	Mean corrected item-total correlation	Within-organization agreement coefficient (ICC)*
1 Fairness	6	19.66 (2.40)	13.73–24.25	0.926	0.788	0.904
2 Union-management consultation	6	18.71 (2.33)	10.80–22.26	0.931	0.801	0.875
3 Mutual regard	3	9.51 (1.43)	5.73–11.76	0.947	0.894	0.943
4 Membership support for unions	3	3.67 (1.13)	0.26– 5.88	0.782	0.525	0.489
5 Union legitimacy	2	6.72	3.60– 7.88	0.747	0.596	0.734
		(0.74)			Average	0.789

* See footnote, table 4.5

agreement coefficients of 0.79 is well above what has been reported in the literature on organizational climate (Glick 1985; Dastmalchian 1986) we deemed this to be acceptable. That is, there appears to be an acceptable level of agreement on the climate scales within each of the thirty-four organizations to justify considering an average score for each organization as reflecting an 'organizational' or a 'workplace' phenomenon.

6 Industrial relations outputs

In order to measure a set of variables that pertain to the outcome of union–management and employee–management relationships, three different sets of items were employed: those relating to employees; those relating to union–management interactions; and those relating to unions and their membership.

Employees

For the first category, two measures were selected: turnover, and absenteeism. Turnover was measured in terms of the percentage of employees that had left the organization voluntarily in the past year. Absenteeism measured the recorded absences for employees according to the personnel files. In both cases, confirmatory records were obtained (or observed) where possible. These variables were measured for the four categories on managerial, professional, manual, and clerical employees separately, using a four-point scale ranging from less than 1 per cent (scoring 1) to more than 10 per cent (scoring 4). Overall measures were computed by averaging the rates for the four categories. In addition, four to six months after the completion of the interviews, contacts were made with the human resource managers to obtain an update on turnover and absenteeism figures (as will be mentioned later, this update also included information on industrial relations events and the overall industrial relations rating). If the update information was different to the ones previously obtained, the new information was included (in fact, in the case of eight organizations the new information was sufficiently different that it had to replace the original data). The mean score for turnover was 2.0 (SD=0.99), with the lowest mean belonging to the managerial employees (mean=1.6) and the highest to the manual category (mean=2.18). The mean absenteeism score was 1.9 (SD=0.78), with the managerial category as the lowest (mean=1.33) and the manual group as the highest (mean=2.12).

Union–management interaction

For the second category of industrial relations outcome variables, referring to the interactive dimension of union management relations, the following information was obtained: general success in negotiations (from the union's standpoint), major industrial relations events or incidents, and the descriptions of the overall industrial relations situation from both the management (overall industrial relations situation), and the union/association (industrial relations scene) representatives.

The procedure for obtaining the information on the interactive category was to ask open-ended questions to the respondents (human resource managers and union/association representatives). For example, for 'overall industrial relations situation' and 'industrial relations scene', the question 'how would you describe the industrial relations situation in this organization?' was asked. The descriptive information was then content analyzed and, for the purpose of the comparative analyses, was given quantitative scores.

For the union's success in negotiation a four-point scale ranging from 'unsuccessful' (scoring 1) to 'very successful' (scoring 4) was used. Of the valid responses (ten organizations), 24 per cent indicated unsuccessful negotiations, whilst only 4 per cent (two organizations) described the pattern of negotiations as very successful. The mean score for this variable was 2.12 (SD=0.83).

The variable 'industrial relations events' was included to measure the existence of major conflictual outcomes in the year in which the study took place. This information was also updated four to six months after the interviews. This variable was measured on a five-point scale, ranging from 'no major events' (scoring 1), 'minor events', 'major outstanding grievances', and 'walk-outs', to 'strike actions' (scoring 5). An almost equal number of organizations indicated either 'no events' (29 per cent) or 'strike actions' (27 per cent), with the remaining organizations falling almost entirely into 'some minor events' (18 per cent) and 'outstanding grievances' (25 per cent). Only one organization reported a walk-out.

Overall industrial relations situation, described by the managers, and industrial relations scene representing the union's view on the industrial relations situation of the organization, were quantified using four-point scales. These ranged from 'poor' (scoring 1), through 'fair' and 'good' (scoring 2 and 3 respectively) to 'excellent' (scoring 4). Overall industrial relations had a mean score of 2.69 (SD=0.92), and industrial relations scene had a mean of 2.17 (SD=0.82). About

45 per cent of the views expressed by the managers were either poor or fair, whereas the equivalent figure for the union/association representatives was 62 per cent. Only one union representative described the industrial relations situation as excellent, while in eleven of the organizations the managers rated the industrial relations as such.

Unions and union membership

The third category was concerned with aspects of industrial relations outputs that pertained primarily to union membership. These were: attendance at the union/association meetings, overall commitment of the membership to the union/association, and the extent to which the membership wanted industrial relations changes to take place.

During the interviews with the union representatives, two questions regarding the level of membership commitment to the union and the rate of attendance at union meetings were asked. The descriptive responses for commitment, and the figures for attendance levels, were then converted into three-point scales, ranging from 'low' for the former, and less than 10 per cent for the latter (scoring 1), to 'high' and over 50 per cent (scoring 3). Mean attendance score was 1.85 (SD=0.69), with over 30 per cent of the respondents indicating less than 10 per cent attendance. For commitment, the mean score was 1.92 (SD=0.76), again with almost one-third of the valid responses indicating low commitment.

Desire of the union membership for industrial relations changes, was quantified with positive (scoring 1) and negative (scoring 0) categories. Nine organizations (about 22 per cent) indicated no desire for change, while 32 organizations (78 per cent of valid responses) expressed strong desire for change in industrial relations-related practices and policies in the organization (mean=0.78, SD=0.42).

THE LONGITUDINAL STUDY

In May 1989, eighteen months after the start of the main study, we contacted twenty of the organizations in our original sample in order to gain access for repeating the study. A letter was sent to the top management in each organization asking them to participate in the second stage of the study. This participation involved agreeing to personal interviews and the distribution of the climate questionnaire in as similar a fashion as in the 1987 study. In choosing the organizations, the criteria were: their location (i.e. western Canada), and their expressed willingness during the first stage to participate in the second stage. Of the twenty organizations contacted, we received fourteen favourable responses. We then contacted the human resource managers and the union representatives to discuss the details and to obtain their support. During this process, seven organizations and their unions agreed to the second round of data collections. The reasons for this reduction in the number of participating organizations included: the timing of our proposed data collection; delays in clearing the matter with headquarters; and obtaining permission from central union organizations.

The data collection took place between July and November 1989. The methods of data collection and the variables were identical to our main study (as described earlier in this chapter). The only difference was that the interviewees tended to elaborate on the nature of changes over the intervening two years, and provided us with their descriptive accounts of the changes. Therefore, in addition to the data from the structured interviews and the questionnaire, this stage of the study allowed us to obtain a considerable amount of descriptive information about the dynamics and the nature of changes in their organizations, environments, and union–management relationships.

In total, we conducted twenty-one interviews for the seven organizations, lasting between one and three hours each (three to four interviewees per organization) with senior managers, human resource managers, and union representatives. A summary of the descriptive statistics for the key variables measured (i.e. context and environment, organizational structure, industrial relations context and outcomes, and human resource practices) is shown in table 4.12.

Regarding the climate questionnaire, one organization decided to withdraw from the survey part of the study, due to internal reasons. For the remaining six organizations, a total of 580 questionnaires were distributed, of which 245 usable ones were received by the end of November 1989. This represents a response rate of 42 per cent. This also represents 15 per cent of the total employment in these six organizations. The characteristics of the respondents were fairly similar to those of the 1987 survey in terms of their length of service and age. The proportion of female respondents is less (41 per cent as opposed to 49 per cent, see table 4.8 for the 1987 survey), so is the percentage of unionized respondents (62 per cent as compared to 79 per cent in 1987). Also, there appears to be relatively more skilled employees and supervisory personnel in our 1989 data (37 per cent rather than 22 per cent in our earlier data). Table 4.13 shows the size and industry classification of these six organizations, as well as the characteristics of the respondents.

Table 4.12 Descriptive statistics of selected variables for the longitudinal study (N=7)

Variable	Mean	SD	Minimum	Maximum	N
Organizational context					
Log. size	2.53	0.75	1.80	3.73	7
Owner dependency	8.14	4.60	4.00	16.00	7
Labour market dependency	8.07	1.37	6.25	10.00	7
Organization change	1.00	1.29	0.00	3.00	7
Organizational structure					
Formalization	13.71	3.20	7.00	17.00	7
Specialization		5.35	4.00	19.00	7
Distance	31.57	9.95	18.00	43.00	7
Sharing	46.17	9.11	34.00	55.00	6
Centralization	59.14	9.97	45.00	71.00	7
Complexity	13.29	4.68	9.00	21.00	7
Flexibility	85.50	17.56	61.00	101.00	6
Bureaucracy	86.14	15.05	61.00	106.00	7
Industrial relations context and outcomes					
Number of unions	5.71	8.77	1	25.00	7
Number of members	567.70	842.51	12	1800	7
% female	40.86	38.37	0	95	7
Age of union	21.43	17.39	3	49	7
Local bargaining	1(100%)	0.00	1	1	7
Negotiation success	2.57	0.79	2	4	7
Outcome of last negotiations	2.71	0.76	2	4	7
IR scene	2.14	0.69	1	3	7
Method of grievances	1.33	0.52	1	2	6
Attendance at union meetings	2.14	0.69	1	3	7
Commitment to union	1.71	0.76	1	3	7
Turnover	2.00	1.00	1	4	7
Absenteeism	2.00	0.58	1	3	7
Human resource practices					
Training	10.64	2.58	7.00	14.25	7
ILM	19.71	3.81	14.50	23.75	7
HR changes	3.14	2.12	1.00	7.00	7

Table 4.13 Characteristics of the seven organizations in the longitudinal study

Organization*	Size (number of employees)	Industry	Data from climate questionnaire						
			Number of respondents	Response rate	Represen- tation	Average age	Average position	Average tenure	Average education
17	63	Recreation/ sports	9	36%	14%	37.13	1.56	5.94	2.8
18	159	Library	45	46%	28%	35.88	1.84	8.20	3.4
20	121	Brewery	24	25%	20%	36.92	2.38	8.89	3.0
21	153	Brewery	26	21%	17%	36.73	1.50	11.04	2.0
[23	5351	Education	–	–	–	–	–	–	–]
30	169	Printing/ publishing	10	40%	6%	42.00	1.78	12.90	2.0
34	2824	Agricultural business services	131	61%	5%	38.40	2.50	14.32	2.09
Total			245	Overall: 42%	15%	37.84	1.92	10.23	2.6

* Organization numbers correspond to those in table 4.9

Table 4.14 Means, standard deviations, reliability estimates, and agreement coefficients for workplace industrial relations climate scales for six organizations (N=245) in the second data set (1989)

Climate scales	Mean (SD)	Range	Cronbach's α	Within-organization agreement coefficient (ICC)*
1 Fairness	19.05 (2.40)	15.35–22.22	0.915	0.901
2 Union–management consultation	17.69 (1.78)	14.50–19.44	0.868	0.778
3 Mutual regard	8.81 (1.35)	6.31–10.10	0.835	0.869
4 Membership support for unions	3.32 (0.97)	2.11– 4.24	0.606	0.861
5 Union legitimacy	6.45 (0.67)	5.78– 7.56	0.658	0.867

* See footnote in table 4.5 for an explanation of this coefficient

Table 4.14 shows the means, standard deviations, and the reliability estimates of the workplace industrial relations climate scales for the 1989 data. The internal consistency reliability estimates of the climate scales are acceptable, even though they are slightly weaker than expected for support for unions and for union legitimacy scales. The within-organization agreement coefficients are considerably higher on average than the 1987 data (average of 0.86 as compared to 0.79 for the 1987 data).

Even though there is no quantitative analysis reported on this second data in this volume (except to compare the actual scores between the 1987 and 1989 data), it is hoped that the above information on the data collection procedures and measures will serve as an indication of acceptability of our small scale longitudinal data. Chapter 6 will be devoted to analyzing and understanding the qualitative and the quantitative information on changes that have taken place in these six cases, and their relationships with our proposed model.

5 The overall findings

In this chapter we examine the overall pattern of relationships in the model using both quantitative and qualitative data collected from our sample organizations. As we discussed in chapter 4, because full sets of data on industrial relations climate were forthcoming from thirty-four of the fifty-one organizations in the sample, our analysis in this chapter is focused on these thirty-four enterprises. In addition, having discussed the correlation matrices and descriptive statistics of the main variables in chapter 4 (see also the appendices) we are able in this chapter to turn our attention to the presentation and interpretation of the overall relationships between the various input variables, climate, and industrial relations outcomes.

The main technique used for investigating the soundness of the model was path analysis (Duncan 1966; Nie *et al.* 1975). Path analysis has a number of advantages over other techniques in that it enables us to identify and examine both direct and indirect effects of a set of variables, and it provides a convenient way in which intervening variables (in our case aspects of climate) can be included in the model. Using ordinary least squares regression, it tests the causal relationships among a set of variables (Billings and Wroten 1978). Here a two-step approach has been adopted: the first step examines the determinants of industrial relations climate; the second step looks at the factors, including climate, that determine the outcome of the institution's industrial relations activities. Given our objectives in devising and testing the model (see chapter 3) the key questions guiding our analysis were as follows:

1 Which input factors (i.e. context, structure, and human resource practices) are more important for understanding workplace industrial relations climate?

2 Which factors (i.e. input and climate) are more important for predicting the nature of industrial relations outcomes?
3 Do the data provide support for the model? That is, by considering both input (structural and contextual) variables *and* workplace industrial relations climate, do we achieve a better understanding and an explanation of the outcomes of the organization's industrial relations activities?

In order to pursue these questions and determine the usefulness of the model, it was necessary first to simplify the range of variables actually measured and consider them in an aggregated form. Realizing the difficulties associated with aggregating variables (see, for example, Roberts *et al.* 1978), every attempt was made both to minimize the conceptual and methodological difficulties of this exercise and at the same time to make sure that the resulting simplifications were as meaningful as possible. The following section describes this process and identifies the main aggregated variables used in our subsequent analysis.

KEY VARIABLES IN THE OVERALL MODEL

Six categories of variables were considered for testing the model: organizational context; organizational structure; human resource practices; industrial relations context; workplace industrial relations climate; and industrial relations outcomes.

Organizational context

Aspects of organizational context that were originally measured include size, labour market dependence, dependence on owners, age, technology (i.e. technological interdependence), and the extent of major recent organizational changes. Based on the theoretical arguments developed in chapter 3, size, age, and labour market dependence would have particular relevance for our model. In addition, in our sub-sample of thirty-four organizations, there appears to be more variation in terms of these three aspects compared with the rest. Therefore in discussing the results more emphasis is placed on them.

Nevertheless, in an attempt to examine the overall configuration of the contextual variables, the six variables were subject to factor analysis. The varimax rotated solution produced two factors accounting for over 50 per cent of the variance. Table 5.1 shows the result of the factor analysis. The first factor consisted of: technology (negative loading), dependence on owners, age and labour market dependence (negative loading). This represents the context of organizations which resemble a typical manufacturing or operating plant, with production technologies similar to that of an assembly line (relatively low interdependence among key units), low skill requirements for labour (and thus less dependence on labour markets), owned by a larger group, and relatively older. On the other hand, low scores on this factor represent the context in which there is high interdependence among the functions, less dependence on owning groups (i.e. is not a branch or a subsidiary of a larger group), is likely to be a relatively new plant, and have higher skill requirements, and thus is likely to be more dependent on its labour markets. Therefore, a high score on this factor is likely to represent a configuration of organizational context that we term 'branch plant orientation'.

Table 5.1 Factor analysis of organizational context (with varimax rotation)

		Factor 1: Branch plant orientation	Factor 2: instability
1	Owner dependence	0.876	0.119
2	Technology[1]	−0.711	0.078
3	Labour market dependence	−0.209	−0.078
4	Organizational age	0.201	−0.185
5	Major changes	0.167	0.854
6	Size (log)	−0.006	−0.152
	% of Variance	30.2%	50.2%
	Eigenvalue	1.81	1.26

[1] Thompson's interdependence scale

The second factor corresponded to the situation in which an organization has gone through, or is currently undertaking, changes in ownership, and/or technology, product/market orientation, and so on. This factor also had a negative loading on size which shows that firms in our sub-sample that undergo major changes are also likely to be relatively smaller in size. We termed this characteristic of organizational context 'instability'.

Organizations that were high on 'branch plant orientation' included three breweries, a textile company, a tyre manufacturing plant, a division of a meat packing group, and a furniture manufacturing plant. All of these belonged to larger groups, have been in existence for over fifteen years, are by and large production units, are predominantly blue-collar firms with relatively less specialization and level of skill requirements, and are less dependent on labour markets for the required personnel. Those establishments that scored high on the 'instability' dimension were: a manufacturer of automotive parts, a manufacturer of agricultural equipment, a brewery plant, and a large sports/recreation facility. All of these units had gone, or were in the process of going, through some major changes regarding their ownership structure, production technology and automation, nature of products and services, and/or their markets.

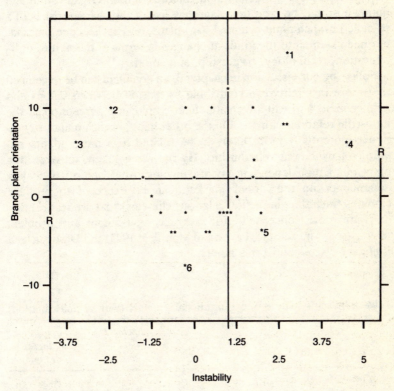

Key:
1 Brewery
2 Meat packing plant
3 Agricultural business corporation
4 Transportation equipment manufacturer
5 Library
6 Large hospital

Figure 5.1 Plot of organizational context dimensions

These two characteristics of organizational context are not mutually exclusive and, looking at figure 5.1, it is evident that approximately half of the organizations demonstrate either high or low scores on both branch plant orientation and instability. For example, organization 1 in figure 5.1 is a brewery plant which exhibits the features of a typical operating plant of a larger corporation. At the same time due to the introduction of a whole new production line (canned beer) as well as new plant and machinery, coupled with major changes in the structure of the ownership and other external factors (such as changes in the regulatory environment of the brewing industry), this organization exhibits a fairly unstable and volatile context. Organization 3, a major hospital, on the other hand has few of the characteristics of a so-called branch plant oriented workplace, and at the same time has not been subject to the kinds of changes in terms of the nature of its operation, technology, ownership, and so on.

Following our discussion in chapter 3, an argument can be developed that more instability can contribute to tension between unions and management and will adversely affect employees' perception of the industrial relations climate. On the other hand, branch plant orientation is potentially more likely to be related to a more adverserial union–management relationship. By the same token, an operating plant with a high dependence on the owning group, and relatively low dependence on the labour market, can be expected to produce climates (including industrial relations climates) that are less conflictual and more concerned with task accomplishment and problem solving (see, for example, Payne and Mansfield 1973, and Dastmalchian 1986, for discussion of this point).

Table 5.2 Factor analysis of organizational structure (with varimax rotation)

		Factor 1: flexible design	Factor 2: bureaucratic design
1	Sharing	0.897	0.132
2	Distance	0.867	−0.014
3	Specialization	0.503	0.223
4	Complexity	0.177	0.809
5	Formalization	0.222	0.737
6	Centralization	−0.380	0.473
% of variance		36.7%	58.8%
Eigenvalue		2.26	1.32

Organizational structure

Dimensions of organizational structure were also factor analyzed to establish the existence of underlying patterns among them, which could be used as a basis for their aggregation in testing the overall model. Using varimax rotation, two factors were revealed accounting for over 58 per cent of the variance. These are shown in table 5.2.

The first design factor consisted of decision sharing, distance, and specialization, which we termed 'flexible design'. The second factor had positive loadings on structural complexity, formalization, and centralization of decision making. This we will refer to as 'bureaucratic design'. It should be noted that despite our choice of terms used to describe these factors, the flexible and bureaucratic designs are not necessarily the opposite extremes of a continuum. In other words, it is conceivable to have a bureaucratic design as defined here (i.e. highly complex and formalized) which demonstrates a certain level of flexibility, e.g. in terms of participation in decision making (decision sharing and distance). The organization with the highest flexibility in its structural design was a medium-sized electronics firm, and among those with the lowest degree of structural flexibility were a textile manufacturing firm and a brewery. Organizations in our sub-sample which had the highest level of bureaucracy were two relatively large hospitals and a division of a federal government department. The same electronics firm referred to above also had the lowest score on bureaucracy. However, the least flexible firms (a textile company and a brewery) were not the most bureaucratic organizations in our sample. Similarly, the most bureaucratic institutions did not demonstrate the lowest flexibility. Thus, the two dimensions of organizational design reflect different aspects of the structure of the organization, rather than merely a continuum along which the overall design can be located.

Human resource practices

The three aspects of human resource practices under study (the development of an internal labour market, the extent of training and human resource changes) have been chosen to reflect certain policies and practices of human resource management. Even though two of these variables (ILM and training) have tended in the past to be considered as part of the same concept (Doeringer and Piore 1971; Althauser and Kalleberg 1981), we have argued elsewhere that these policies may in fact go in different directions and be used to pursue different human resource strategies (Dastmalchian and Blyton 1989). Conceptually, therefore, aggregating these variables does not make much sense. In addition, the data indicated poor grounds for aggregation (when an exploratory factor analysis was performed on the constituent items forming these variables, three distinct factors corresponding to the above three variables were found). Thus with no conceptual or methodological reasoning for aggregation, the variables are treated separately in our overall analysis.

Industrial relations context

Aspects of industrial relations that formed our measure of the context within which the union–management relationships take place include: number of unions, number of members (expressed in terms of union density), percentage of female union members, age of the union(s), bargaining structure (local, industry, or province-wide), method of handling grievances, outcome of last year's negotiations, membership commitment, and attendance at union meetings. Factor analysis of these items produced four factors accounting for over 73 per cent of the variance. Table 5.3 shows the results of this analysis.

Table 5.3 Factor analysis of industrial relations context (with varimax rotation)

	Factor 1: facilitative relations	Factor 2: membership commitment	Factor 3: single union dominance	Factor 4: union age
1 Last year's outcome	0.855			
2 % of female members	0.714			
3 Method of grievance handling	0.689			
4 Bargaining level (local, industry)	−0.630		0.417	−0.405
5 Attendance		0.938		
6 Commitment		0.664		0.526
7 Number of unions			−0.781	
8 Union density			0.726	
9 Union age				0.807
% variance	28.4%	47.2%	62.2%	73.7%
Eigenvalue	2.55	1.69	1.34	1.03

The first factor consists of favourable outcomes from the previous round of negotiations (as seen from the union's standpoint), percentage of female membership, informality of handling disputes, and industry or province-wide bargaining structure. This factor we have labelled 'facilitative relations'. The second represents membership commitment while the third factor characterizes single-union dominance. Commitment represents a situation where membership attendance of the union meetings, and the union representatives' perception of general levels of commitment to the union are both high. Single-union dominance refers to high union density combined with few unions. The extreme point on this factor would be that of one union representing all the employees in an organization. The fourth factor has the single item of age of union.

As discussed in previous chapters, our argument is that these characteristics of the industrial relations context influence the interaction between unions and management. For example, organizations with more facilitative contexts (e.g. a number of hospitals in our subsample scored highly on this dimension) are more likely to exhibit more harmonious climates and more positive outcomes. Firms with high single-union dominance on the other hand are likely to be those in which the relationship between the dominant union and the management could take an extreme form (i.e. either very co-operative or conflictual). A furniture manufacturing plant and a tyre manufacturer are two of the companies with high scores on single-union dominance. Both have had major disputes and strike actions in the recent past. On the other hand, an electronics firm with a high union dominance score has demonstrated a fairly co-operative relationship with its dominant union. Figure 5.2 shows the plot of the scores for facilitative relations and single union dominance. As can be seen from figure 5.2, it appears that most of the service organizations (i.e. hospitals, a school board, and a hotel) fall into the higher facilitative contexts, with some (e.g. several medium-sized hospitals) showing low domination by a single union, and others (e.g. a school board) demonstrating higher single-union dominance. Most of the organizations in our sample scoring low facilitative relations are in the manufacturing sector, with firms such as a textile company and a furniture manufacturer showing higher single-union dominance, and others (e.g. a high-technology firm and a division of a federal government department) exhibiting low dominance by a single union. Membership commitment and age of union do not appear to have any association with other context dimensions. In the overall analysis which follows, we will concentrate more on facilitative relations and single-union dominance as aspects of industrial relations context.

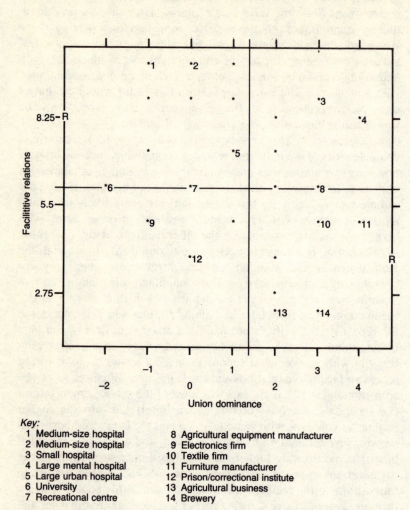

Figure 5.2   IR context: plot of facilitative relations and union dominance

Key:
1 Medium-size hospital
2 Medium-size hospital
3 Small hospital
4 Large mental hospital
5 Large urban hospital
6 University
7 Recreational centre
8 Agricultural equipment manufacturer
9 Electronics firm
10 Textile firm
11 Furniture manufacturer
12 Prison/correctional institute
13 Agricultural business
14 Brewery

Workplace industrial relations climate

As described in chapter 4, the measure of climate in this study consists of five aspects of: extent of union–management consultation, fairness, mutual regard, membership support, and union legitimacy. For the purpose of the overall analysis in this chapter, these five aspects of climate were factor analyzed. A one-factor solution consisted of all the climate aspects (with positive loadings), and accounted for over 72 per cent of their variance. Given the initial aims of model testing, the five climate dimensions were then summed to create a single climate measure. This aggregated measure of workplace industrial relations climate characterized on the one hand climates that are more co-operative (more fairness, consultation, and mutual regard) and at the same time more supportive of unions (more membership support and more legitimacy given by the organization to the role of the union). On the other hand, it could also characterize the climate of lack of co-operation coupled with lack of support for unions. While useful to us at this stage, it is important to note that this aggregation also acts to subsume patterns of relationships *among* these climate dimensions that are themselves revealing and could form a basis for creating taxonomies of union–management relationships.

The organizations with the highest overall climate score were: two small hospitals, two breweries, and a government department. Those with lowest scores on climate were: a recreational facility, a brewery, a meat packing plant, and a transportation equipment factory.

Industrial relations outputs

As described in the previous chapter, six variables formed our industrial relations outputs measure. These were: managers and unions' views of the industrial relations situation in their organization, industrial relations events (from minor disputes to strikes), success in negotiations (from the union's viewpoint), employee turnover, and absenteeism. In an attempt to form a composite scale or scales for outputs, these variables were factor analyzed. Varimax rotation of the factors produced two factors accounting for 67 per cent of the variance. These are shown in table 5.4. The first factor had positive loadings on both managers' and unions' views of the industrial relations situation and a negative loading on industrial relations events. This factor we termed 'IR situation'. The second factor has positive loadings on turnover and absenteeism, and a negative loading on union's perceived negotiation success. This aspect of outputs we termed 'employee responses'. These two factors, however, had a strong negative correlation (–0.71); this led us to subtract the score on employee response from industrial relations situation to arrive at a single composite indicator of industrial relations outcomes. A high score on industrial relations outcomes, therefore, represents positive views on the IR situation by the key actors, lack of a major industrial action, low employee turnover and absenteeism, and high perceived negotiation success of the unions. A recreational institution in our sub-sample had the highest score on outcomes and a meat packing plant demonstrated the lowest score.

Table 5.4 Factor analysis of IR outcomes (with varimax rotation)

		Factor 1: IR situation	Factor 2: employee responses
1	IR events	−0.814	0.041
2	IR situation (management's view)	0.682	−0.263
3	Success in negotiation	0.442	−0.718
4	IR situation (union's view)	0.794	−0.276
5	Turnover	−0.078	0.836
6	Absenteeism	−0.191	0.796
	% of variance	49.4%	66.6%
	Eigenvalue	2.96	1.02

TESTING THE MODEL

Step 1: interrelations between the 'input' variables

The first task in examining the overall model was to analyze the correlations among the input variables selected, in order to detect any pattern of relationships that need to be taken into account in our subsequent analyses. The correlation matrix for the variables is shown in table 5.5.

Based on the correlations in table 5.5 it is apparent that larger operating units in our sample are more flexible, pay less attention to training, but at the same time are more inclined to have an internal labour market, operate in less facilitative industrial relations contexts, and are ones characterized by less single-union dominance, with older unions; they are also likely to have less favourable industrial relations outcomes.

Branch plant organizations (as an aspect of their organizational context) are those that have considerably less facilitative industrial relations contexts, tend to be dominated by a single union, and exhibit marginally less favourable industrial relations outputs. Organizations in our sample which are operating in more volatile and changeable contexts, on the other hand, are more likely to be those in which unions are relatively new to the scene and have less favourable workplace industrial relations climates.

Table 5.5 Correlation matrix of the aggregate variables in the overall model

	1	2	3	4	5	6	7	8	9	10	11	12	13	14
1 Size (log)	1.0000 (34)													
2 Branch plant orientation	-0.0336 (32)	1.0000 (32)												
3 Instability	-0.4692a (34)	0.2371* (32)	1.0000 (34)											
4 Flexibility (design)	0.2449* (34)	-0.2043 (32)	-0.1329 (32)	1.0000 (32)										
5 Bureaucracy (design)	0.0222 (32)	-0.1840 (30)	0.0258 (30)	-0.0524 (30)	1.0000 (30)									
6 Training	-0.2682* (30)	-0.2157 (28)	0.0085 (33)	-0.0585 (31)	0.1218 (29)	1.0000 (33)								
7 ILM	0.2495* (33)	0.6669 (31)	-0.0418 (32)	0.1837 (30)	-0.1442 (28)	-0.0720 (31)	1.0000 (32)							
8 HR changes	0.2702 (32)	-0.0222 (30)	-0.0413 (34)	0.1415 (32)	-0.2173 (30)	-0.0453 (33)	0.1291 (32)	1.0000 (34)						
9 Facilitative relations	-0.3333+ (30)	-0.7257a (28)	0.0611 (30)	-0.0009 (28)	0.2870* (27)	0.3953* (29)	-0.2081 (28)	-0.2154 (30)	1.0000 (30)					
10 Members' commitment	0.0022 (32)	0.0361 (30)	-0.1001 (32)	0.1528 (30)	0.3279+ (28)	0.0607 (31)	-0.0509 (30)	-0.2936+ (32)	-0.0139 (29)	1.0000 (32)				
11 Single-union dominance	-0.2241* (32)	0.4968a (31)	0.1008 (33)	-0.3760+ (31)	-0.1666 (29)	-0.0592 (32)	-0.0102 (31)	-0.0284 (33)	-0.3524* (30)	-0.1111 (32)	1.0000 (33)			
12 Union age	0.2420* (33)	-0.1715 (33)	-0.4974a (33)	-0.1482 (31)	-0.1506 (29)	-0.0079 (32)	0.1884 (31)	-0.0934 (33)	-0.0999 (30)	0.0762 (32)	0.0562 (33)	1.0000 (33)		
13 Workplace IR climate	-0.0402 (34)	-0.0803 (32)	-0.2236* (34)	0.1538 (32)	0.1781 (30)	0.1349 (33)	0.0104 (32)	-0.0537 (34)	0.3907+ (30)	0.0796 (32)	-0.1330 (33)	-0.0547 (34)	1.0000 (34)	
14 IR outputs	-0.4546a (30)	-0.2867* (29)	0.0744 (30)	0.0830 (28)	0.0017 (26)	0.5506a (29)	-0.0593 (28)	0.2251 (30)	0.5365a (27)	-0.1183 (29)	-0.0853 (30)	-0.1804 (30)	0.5426a (30)	1.0000 (30)

* P ≤ .10 + P ≤ .05 a P ≤ .01

Structural flexibility, apart from being related to the large size, tends also to be higher in organizations where there is considerably less evidence of single-union domination. Increased bureaucracy or rigidity in structure tends to be associated with more facilitative industrial relations contexts and higher membership commitment to unions.

In terms of human resource practices, provision for training in general relates to industrial relations contexts characterized by more facilitative relations, and is also associated with more positive industrial relations outcomes. The existence of an internal labour market and significant changes in human resource practices and policies have no noticeable relationships with other variables, except with size.

Industrial relations context characterized by facilitative relations seems to be associated with a number of other variables, some of which we have already mentioned. To summarize, a more facilitative industrial relations context relates to: small company size, lower branch plant orientation, higher bureaucratic elements of organizational structure, a greater emphasis on training, and a more favourable workplace relations climate; it also has a relatively strong association with industrial relations outcomes. Single-union dominance, as another aspect of industrial relations context, was found to be related to lower levels of structural flexibility and greater branch plant orientation. ·

In terms of climate, the correlational results indicate that organizational contexts characterized by more stability, and more facilitative industrial relations contexts tend to be associated with more favourable workplace relations climates. As regards the outputs of union–management relations, the correlational analysis indicates that industrial relations outcomes are related to small size of the unit, lower branch plant orientation, greater provision for training, a more facilitative industrial relations context, and more favourable climates.

Step 2: input variables and climate

To examine the combined influence of input factors on climate, and the extent to which consideration of both input factors and climate contribute to explaining IR outcomes, a series of multiple regressions were computed (as pointed out earlier, for each set, climate is first considered as a dependent variable and the input variables as independent; then outcome variables are viewed as the ultimate dependent variable with the remaining variables, including climate, as independent factors).

To address the three questions posed at the head of this chapter, first a series of step-wise regressions were computed with the above specifications. This enabled us to assess the extent to which each of the independent variables contribute to the explanation of each of our dependent variables (i.e. climate and outcomes). Tables 5.6 and 5.7 present these results. The difference between the two tables is that the former includes the branch plant orientation as organizational context, and the latter includes instability.

Table 5.6 Step-wise regressions of climate and outcomes on independent variables in the model (i branch plant orientation)

	Variable	β in	Final β	F (sig.)	R^2
I Dependent: workplace IR climate					
Step 1	Flexible design[a]	0.439**	0.481**	5.04(.030)	0.194
Step 2	IR context[b] (facilitative relations)	0.436**	0.518*	6.19(.008)	0.383
Step 3	Organizational context (branch plant orientation)	0.099	0.124	3.99(.020)	0.387
Step 4	Training	−0.040	−0.040	2.85(.050)	0.388
II Dependent: industrial relations outcomes					
Step 1	Training	0.579***	0.498***	10.62(.003)	0.336
Step 2	IR climate	0.530***	0.416**	15.96(.000)	0.614
Step 3	IR context (workability)	0.190	0.336	11.39(.000)	0.643
Step 4	Organizational context (branch plant)	0.148	0.164	8.41(.000)	0.652
Step 5	Structural flexibility	0.076	0.076	6.47(.001)	0.656

[a] Bureaucratic design did not produce significant regression results (F=NS)
[b] Other IR context variables did not produce significant regression results (F=NS)
*   t < 0.10
**   t < 0.05
*** t < 0.01

The results reported in tables 5.6 and 5.7 are encouraging and show that the step-wise regressions involving all the key variables of our model are significant. As shown in table 5.6 the flexibility of structure and industrial relations context of facilitative relations are the most significant factors explaining workplace relations climate. When the organizational context aspect of instability was introduced into the analysis (table 5.7) the same pattern of results persisted. These results indicate that aspects of organizational structure pertaining to increased participation (by increasing opportunities for decision-sharing and employee involvement in the decision processes) and increased specialization (including the specialization of human

Table 5.7 Step-wise regressions of climate and outcomes on independent variables in the model (ii instability)

	Variable	β in	Final β	F (sig.)	R^2
I Dependent: workplace IR climate					
Step 1	Flexible design[a]	0.416**	0.411**	4.59(0.040)	0.172
Step 2	IR context[b] (facilitative relations)	0.403**	0.432**	5.29(0.010)	0.335
Step 3	Organizational context (instability)	−0.160	−0.155	3.75(0.020)	0.360
Step 4	Training	−0.080	−0.080	2.73(0.050)	0.366
II Dependent: IR outcomes					
Step 1	IR climate	0.573***	0.564***	10.75(0.003)	0.328
Step 2	Training	0.530***	0.467***	16.34(0.000)	0.609
Step 3	Organizational context (instability)	0.181	0.168	11.84(0.000)	0.639
Step 4	IR context (facilitative relations)	0.156	0.166	9.15(0.000)	0.658
Step 5	Flexible design	0.038	0.038	6.97(0.000)	0.660

[a] Bureaucratic design did not produce significant regression results (F=NS)
[b] Other IR contents variables did not produce significant regression results (F=NS)
*   t < 0.10
**   t < 0.05
*** t < 0.01

resource and industrial relations functions) are most important in creating a climate in which consultation, mutual regard, fairness, and a general atmosphere of union support and legitimacy are achieved. This is a key finding in the study, for in the past organizational structure has rarely been considered a relevant and significant variable in studying and understanding the behavioural dimensions of industrial relations. It strengthens our belief in the proposed model in the sense that creating appropriate organizational design and structure is not a phenomenon that is only beneficial for the achievement of organizational technical objectives. Rather, these findings indicate that organizational design has wider-reaching implications for a whole host of organizationally relevant areas of concern, including the creation of more productive union–management relationships and perceived climates.

The second important variable for understanding workplace relations climate was the industrial relations context of 'facilitative' relations. To recap, this is a composite scale created from variables that include: percentage of female employees, informal methods of handling conflict, industry or provincial bargaining structures, and the favourability of outcome of the last round of negotiations. The range of this composite variable gives rise to some difficulty both in attaching a suitable label and in interpretation. Nevertheless, it does represent a context within which the present union–management relationships take place, and in this sense it has implications both for unions and management.

Tables 5.6 and 5.7 also show the results of step-wise regressions of input variables and climate on the outcomes of industrial relations. In both cases, climate and provision for training (as an aspect of the organization's human resource practices) are the most significant variables for explaining the outcomes, with the industrial relations context of facilitative relations as the third variable entering the equation. Thus, these results suggest that the creation of more positive workplace relations climates, and increasing the organization's training orientation in general, can have significant impacts on reducing the conflictual outcomes of the organization's industrial relations (e.g. absences, turnover, industrial actions) and increasing the chances of more harmonious outcomes of union–management relationships (e.g union and management's views of their relationships, success of negotiations).

In an attempt to examine these results more closely, particularly as far as aspects of organizational context (size, labour market conditions, and age of organization) are concerned, a separate set of step-wise regressions were computed using each one of the context variables as one of the independent variables. The results of these regressions are shown in the appendix at the end of this chapter (page 116). In summary, a strong similarity with the main findings is evidenced: structural flexibility and industrial relations context are the most important factors for explaining climate; also, climate and training are most significant for determining the outcomes of industrial relations. The only exception was the strong negative impact of organizational size on outcomes. This indicates that, controlling for other variables in the equation, smaller organizations tend to have more positive industrial relations outcomes than larger ones.

Step 3: the overall model tested

The next question to address is how well the data supports the model. To test this, we first compare the relationships as suggested in the model but omit workplace industrial relations climate as an intervening variable. Following this, the exercise is repeated but this time including climate as an intervening variable. In other words, the question becomes whether the input variables *on their own* explain more of the outcomes' variance, compared with the situation where

Table 5.8 A comparison of the explanatory power of the model

Dependent variable: IR outcomes

	Organizational context[a]	Organizational design[b]	IR context[c]	Training	IR climate	F (sig.)	R^2
Analysis I							
Equation 1	0.202	0.276*	0.551**	0.482***	–	5.49(0.004)	0.549
Equation 2	0.164	0.076	0.336	0.498***	0.416**	6.47(0.001)	0.656

	Organizational context[d]	Organizational design	IR context	Training	IR climate	F (sig.)	R^2
Analysis II							
Equation 1	0.089	0.245	0.384**	0.427**	–	4.71(0.008)	0.498
Equation 2	0.168	0.038	0.166	0.467***	0.504***	6.97(0.000)	0.660

[a] Branch plant orientation
[b] Flexible design/structure
[c] Facilitative relations
[d] Instability

$N = 30$
* $t \leqslant 0.10$
** $t \leqslant 0.05$
*** $t \leqslant 0.01$

climate is included in the model. This comparison is shown in table 5.8, where the results of the two regressions, both using industrial relations outcomes as the dependent variable, are compared. In addition, analysis (I) includes the organizational context aspect of branch plant orientation, while analysis (II) includes instability. In the first equation of each analysis in table 5.8, climate is excluded from the list of independent variables, while in the second one it is included. The results of both analyses in table 5.8 show that the inclusion of climate increases the explanatory power of the equations substantially (from 0.549 to 0.656 in analysis I, and from 0.498 to 0.660 in analysis II). Therefore, this clearly indicates that by including workplace relations climate in the model we are able to increase the percentage of explained variance of IR outcomes by 20 per cent and 33 per cent.

Step 4: further tests on the model

The next task is to examine the relationships suggested in our model using path analysis. In doing so the standardized regression coefficients shown earlier are illustrated in the form of diagrams following the path analysis conventions. In addition, the latent coefficient ($E = \sqrt{(1-R^2)}$) has been shown for each stage of the path model. The square of this coefficient shows the proportion of the variance in the dependent variable explained by factors other than the independent variables at each stage (Nie *et al.* 1975). The two overall path models are shown in figure 5.3. These differ only with respect to the organizational context variable: the first diagram includes branch plant orientation, and the second instability.

The path models explain about 65 per cent of the variation in industrial relations outcomes, and between 36 per cent to 38 per cent of the variance of climate. Given the evidence regarding other studies using organizations as units of analysis and having comparable sample sizes (e.g. Swamidass and Newell 1987), the results of path analysis are significant and indeed encouraging. Not only that, the pattern of direct and indirect associations summarized in figure 5.3 reinforce our earlier discussion about the value of considering workplace industrial relations climate in any model that attempts to explain the outcomes of union–management relationships. One important conclusion from this analysis is that the indirect paths of variables such as context (both IR and organizational) and organizational structure to outcomes are much stronger than their respective direct paths. That is, organizational context and structural variables

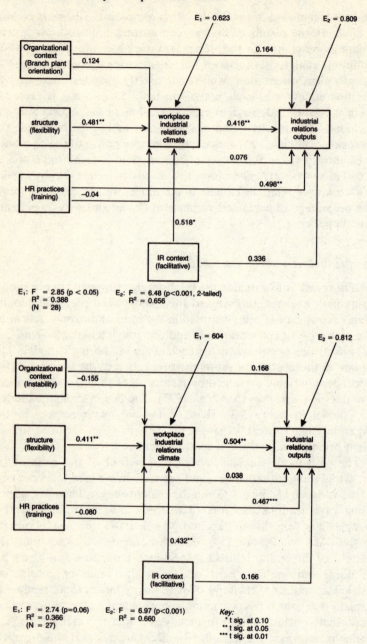

Figure 5.3 Tests of the overall model (path analyses involving branch plant orientation and instability as organizational contexts)

impact more strongly on outcomes through their effects on perceived climate than by any direct effects on those outcomes. Similarly, it can be argued that the contexts within which the interactions between union and management take place have their greatest influence on results through their potential impacts on employees' perceptions of the climate, rather than directly in the form of industrial actions, turnover, and the like.

In order to examine and interpret some of the above rather complex relationships further, we find it necessary at this point to reintroduce some of the key variables (particularly those relating to context), in a disaggregated form, to the model. Our intention is to do this selectively in an attempt to clarify and make better sense of the model's utility. For example, figure 5.4 shows the path analyses of the variables in the model with the organizational context being represented by size, labour market dependence, and age, rather than by a composite variable. The results are similar to the ones reported in figure 5.3. However, the effects of variables such as size and labour market dependence are more clearly represented. For example, whilst size has a direct negative effect on industrial relations outcomes, its path through climate shows a positive impact. This implies that in larger organizations in our sample, where there is higher chance of conflictual outcomes, attempts to create more co-operative or positive climates will have a significant impact on achieving more desirable industrial relations outcomes.

In addition, labour market dependency and organizational age both have negative, but weak, effects on climate and on outcomes. However, considering their indirect effects on outcomes through climate, it is conceivable that increases in labour market dependence and in age have a relatively weak but positive impact on outcomes.

Similarly, based on the results in figures 5.3 and 5.4, it is evident in this sample that a more positive IR context has a much stronger impact on the outcomes of industrial relations when one considers its effects through the creation of a more favourable workplace relations climate, rather than directly to outcomes. In other words, a facilitative background, a positive history, and policies and practices that encourage problem solving and informal handling of disputes, do affect people's perceptions of the quality of union–management relationships. It is through the creation and development of such perceptions that the results or outcomes of industrial relations are more positive.

Training, as an element of the organization's human resource practices, does not appear to have any impact on climate. Controlling

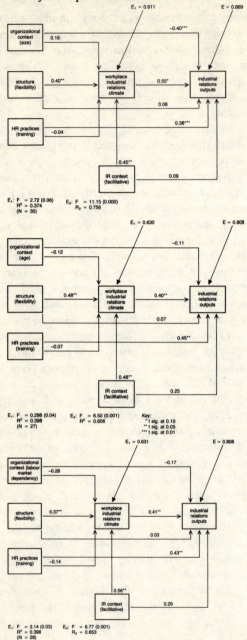

Figure 5.4   Tests of the overall model (path analyses including the size, age and labour market dependency as organizational contexts)

for the effects of other variables in the model (and in particular industrial relations context, which has a correlation of 0.40 with training), training shows a strong direct effect on the outcomes of industrial relations. In fact, further analysis revealed that training has a much stronger relationship with employee turnover and absenteeism than with other elements in the outcomes measure. It is possible that the potential impact of training on climate is suppressed by the influence that context has on both. On the other hand, when we looked at the characteristics of the organizations in our sample that had high levels of training, a further explanation was suggested. Two of the organizations with the highest scores on training are a hotel and a branch of a brewery. Both of these had been undergoing major technological and product/service changes at the time of the study. The hotel was in the process of complete renovation and the introduction of a new range of services. At the same time it appeared that a change of ownership was being contemplated. The increase in staff training was probably seen by employees and their union as an attempt by the organization to increase its control over the process, and did not help the tense feelings and mistrust associated with the major changes taking place. The brewery had just introduced a new production line, coupled with a downsizing (redundancy) programme which was a part of the new and automated technology. In this kind of situation, training was again seen as a prime effort by management to select out more suitable employees for the new production technology, rather than in any way relating to improvement of their long-term skills and abilities. A number of other units with relatively high scores on training also demonstrated similar situations (e.g. a tyre manufacturer, another brewery), which could have contributed to the lack of relationship between training and climate.

APPENDIX: ADDITIONAL STEP-WISE REGRESSION

Table 5.9 Additional step-wise regression (N=25)

Dependent variable: workplace IR climate

	Variable	β in	Final β	F(sig.)	R^2
Step 1	Flexible design	0.416/**	0.372**	4.59(0.040)	0.173
Step 2	Branch plant orientation	0.403**	0.555**	5.29(0.010)	0.335
Step 3	Labour market dependency	−0.240	−0.274	4.08(0.020)	0.379
Step 4	Training	−0.146	−0.146	3.14(0.030)	0.398

Dependent variable: IR outcomes

	Variable	β in	Final β	F(sig.)	R^2
Step 1	Climate	0.573***	0.415**	10.75(0.003)	0.328
Step 2	Training	0.530***	0.438***	16.34(0.000)	0.609
Step 3	Branch plant orientation	0.177	0.282	11.49(0.000)	0.633
Step 4	Labour market dependency	−0.171	−0.171	8.93(0.000)	0.653
Step 5	Flexible design	−0.065	−0.065	6.92(0.000)	0.657

Dependent variable: workplace IR climate

	Variable	β in	Final β	F(sig.)	R^2
Step 1	Flexible design	0.439**	0.483**	5.04(0.030)	0.194
Step 2	Branch plant orientation	0.436**	0.482**	6.19(0.008)	0.382
Step 3	Age of organization	−0.106	−0.124	4.11(0.020)	0.393
Step 4	Training	−0.077	−0.077	2.98(0.040)	0.398

Dependent variable: IR outcomes

	Variable	β in	Final β	F(sig.)	R^2
Step 1	Training	0.579***	0.454***	10.62(0.003)	0.336
Step 2	Climate	0.536***	0.404**	15.46(0.000)	0.615
Step 3	Branch plant orientation	−0.190	0.247	11.39(0.000)	0.643
Step 4	Age of organization	−0.102	−0.114	8.44(0.000)	0.652
Step 5	Flexible design	0.077	0.077	6.50(0.001)	0.657

Dependent variable: workplace IR climate

	Variable	β in	Final β	F(sig.)	R^2
Step 1	Flexible design	0.416**	0.405**	4.59(0.040)	0.172
Step 2	Branch plant orientation	0.403**	0.452**	5.29(0.010)	0.335
Step 3	Size	0.172	0.160	3.78(0.020)	0.362
Step 4	Training	−0.049	−0.049	2.72(0.060)	0.364

Dependent variable: IR outcomes

	Variable	β in	Final β	F(sig.)	R^2
Step 1	Climate	0.573***	0.545***	10.75(0.003)	0.328
Step 2	Training	0.530***	0.384***	16.34(0.000)	0.609
Step 3	Size	−0.395***	−0.386***	19.70(0.000)	0.748
Step 4	Branch plant orientation	0.081	0.099	14.04(0.000)	0.752
Step 5	Flexible design	0.073	0.073	11.15(0.000)	0.756

* $t \leqslant 0.10$
** $t \leqslant 0.05$
*** $t \leqslant 0.01$

6 The case-study analysis

In the last chapter the central focus was on identifying whether the climate measure could be used across very different types of work organization, and whether its inclusion secured a better understanding of the relationships between various inputs and industrial relations outcome variables. Despite the limitations of some of the available information, we are reasonably satisfied that the value of measuring climate, and the validity of viewing it as an intervening variable, have been established.

However, it was never the intention to be content with reporting only the kind of aggregate data (regressions, correlations, and so on) which supported or failed to support parts of the model. As discussed earlier, the broader aim was to mix a quantitative and a more qualitative approach in order to examine the importance of climate within individual work contexts and, if possible, over time. We were always aware of the problems (and insights) this could bring: what may be identifiable in terms of statistical significance among an organizational sample of thirty-four, and a questionnaire response from over eighteen hundred employees, may be much harder to unearth within the particularities and peculiarities of an individual work organization. Yet to have lasting value it is at this more local level that climate must be shown to be both relevant and measurable.

As will become clear when the cases are discussed, this analysis yields both supporting evidence for the general argument set out in chapter 5, and also instances where the relationships appear if not directly to contradict the model, at least to indicate the greater complexity of organizational reality than the general results have so far allowed for. Hopefully, what emerges at the end of this process is, first, a clearer picture of what some of the general relationships recorded in chapter 5 may actually *mean* in practice. It is one thing to discuss the impact of structural flexibility on industrial relations outcomes in the abstract (or at least from behind the screen of aggregated data from diverse organizations). It is quite another to trace that relationship through a particular organization and to know the case well enough to understand the wider context of the factors being considered. Second, these cases clearly attest to the dangers of over-simplification in the modelling of organizational dynamics. The list of factors which could influence climate are legion, even before account is taken of the manifold ways in which different combinations of these factors could themselves create distinct influences on both climate and outcomes.

In chapter 3 we discussed the compromises that were made to operationalize our model, for example making cuts to a much longer list of input factors as outlined in an earlier journal article (Blyton *et al*. 1987) in order to move closer to a testable model. However, in tracking the nature of workplace industrial relations within particular organizations, the door to this larger list of possible influencing factors is re-opened. That the findings outlined in chapter 5 retain at least some support is in fact reassuring, in that it suggests our process of operationalizing the factors made some sense in reality. However it is also evident from the cases that we are a long way from the last word on industrial relations climate, and in particular on the many potential influences upon that climate.

This chapter is divided into two main sections. The bulk of the chapter is devoted to reporting six case-studies in which we were able to repeat the 1987 study in 1989 and so draw out the changes that had occurred since 1987 and the respective movements of the climate, inputs, and outcome variables. While not fully longitudinal in approach (which would require constant contact with the organizations over the intervening time period), nevertheless this ability to repeat the study yielded considerable insight into the associations between variables over time. The chapter's second objective is to elaborate some of the cross-sectional findings discussed in the previous chapter by considering three cases from the 1987 data set for which we have considerably more information. These cases are summarized within this chapter; however, for those wanting further information on the three cases (auto parts, textile and furniture manufacturers), more detailed descriptions are given in appendix 2.

THE LONGITUDINAL CASE-STUDIES

We described in chapter 4 how we obtained our sample of cases for the longitudinal study. To recap briefly, our financial constraints required an approach only to twenty of the thirty-four organizations; the remainder were too geographically remote, and thus too expensive, for the research budget. Of these twenty, full data were gathered from six; a seventh organization participated in the follow-up study but provided insufficient data to allow a full comparison of the climate measures, hence it has been omitted from the present discussion. In this chapter we therefore focus on six organizations: two breweries, a city library, a printing company, a large social and recreational centre, and a major agricultural products handler. These six vary not only in their manufacturing/service orientation but also in their size, age, structure and industrial relations history. As we turn to examine the cases in more detail, it is also evident that these organizations vary too in the degree to which they conform to the major patterns of relationship between inputs, climate, and outcomes identified earlier.

Western Recreational Association

Western Recreational Association (WRA) is located in a medium-sized city in western Canada. It is a part of a group of fifty-four non-profit establishments located in major Canadian cities, providing sports, recreational, and skills training facilities to the communities. WRA was founded in 1910, initially as a centre to help immigrant women through the provision of accommodation and training in various skills, including household and craft skills, as well as to provide religious training. Changes in the needs of the communities and consequently in the goals of WRA took place in the 1950s. This resulted in a shift by the organization as a whole to a more focused direction of activities and a separation of facilities and programmes for personal development, and sports.

As a result of this, WRA went through a relatively slow process of change and expansion in the 1960s, and the 1970s. This was achieved mostly by fund-raising to expand and renovate existing facilities and by developing independent programmes for sports and recreation. The overall lack of facilities meant that it shared the rare sports facilities of the city with other organizations (e.g. university, schools, municipal organizations). It was not until the 1980s that adequate financial resources were available for a major project involving the building of a brand new sports complex, and the moving of the offices and the operation to a new location.

WRA moved to its new location in 1985; this has been the single most important event in the history of WRA. Within two years,

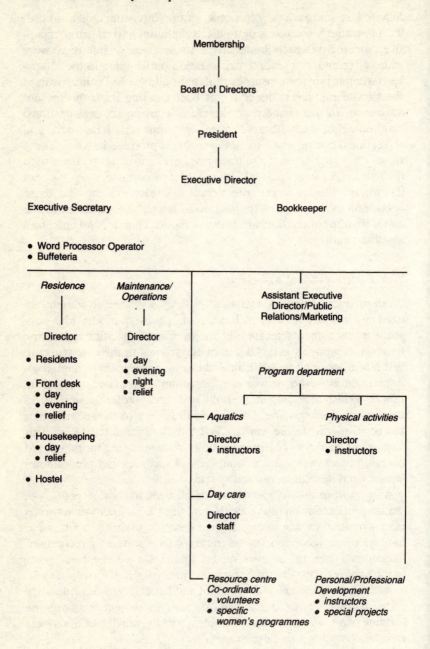

Figure 6.1   WRA organizational chart (1987)

WRA introduced a new range of programmes for the public. In 1987 WRA offered sixteen different recreational/sports programmes; maintained its residential services; ran fourteen different developmental (non-physical) courses (e.g. crafts, oil-painting, stress management); and introduced an expanded resource centre 'help line' for the public. The new and well-equipped gymnasium and swimming pool attracted more users and placed additional demands on the internal resources of WRA.

The growth period and the situation in 1987

The result of the move into the new facilities and the increase in the range and the quantity of services offered by WRA was being felt in 1987. The operating cost was almost doubled to 1.2 million dollars, and the number of full-time core staff had increased from twelve to twenty-one. The overall number of people employed by WRA (including part-time staff and instructors) was increased to 100 people. Figure 6.1 shows the organizational chart of WRA for 1987.

As seen from the chart, seven positions reported directly to the executive director of WRA. The co-ordinators and the directors of the programme departments (aquatics, physical activities, and professional development) reported to the assistant executive director. Overall, there appeared to be a fair degree of autonomy given to the departmental managers for operational decisions. Given the uncertainties attached to the implementation of the newer programmes, there also seemed to be a considerable degree of consultation and information-sharing among the staff and between the staff and the departmental managers/co-ordinators. Matters such as a scheduling of programmes, alterations and modifications to the programme plans, training, hiring, promotion, and minor purchases, were all handled by more junior managers in consultation with other more senior people. For decisions that were regarded as strategic (e.g. the introduction of new, or elimination of old programmes, budget allocation, and major purchases), the board retained its authority. This partly reflected a desire by the board to keep a closer eye on major decisions during this growth period.

The diversity of WRA's activities and the professional orientation of the line jobs (i.e. programme department) had resulted in a high level of functional specialization relative to its size. This in conjunction with relatively high levels of sharing and consultation in the processes of making operational decisions had caused the organization to be fairly flexible in terms of its structure (it had the third-highest flexibility score in the sample of thirty-four organizations, and the second-highest among the six cases discussed in this chapter).

Due to the nature of the services provided (i.e. service to the public) there was a relatively high degree of formalization of procedures and roles. In matters such as public health, safety and security in gymnasia, swimming pools, and so on, as well as in the day care, there existed a well-developed set of written procedures to follow. People received various written instructions for modifications and changes to the performance of their duties. Therefore, there was a significant degree of formalization of role definition at WRA (particularly in relation to its small size). Despite this, the extent of the structural bureaucracy at WRA was not particularly high in comparison to other organizations in the sample.

In terms of the human resource practices that were examined, WRA did not have an extensive internal labour market mechanism (WRA exhibited the lowest overall score for the existence of ILM among the six cases reported on in this chapter). Movement and mobility of personnel within the organization was very limited. There appeared to be a widespread lack of opportunity for promotion from within, and the few middle- and senior-level positions that had become available were filled by external candidates. On the other hand, WRA was clearly a training-oriented establishment. It had the highest score on provision for training for its employees. The organization not only provided extensive in-house training and development programmes on a regular basis, but had also encouraged and supported outside training and education activities by its employees.

WRA's manual and clerical staff were represented by the Service Employees International Union. In total there were twelve union members among the twenty-one core staff. The impression given both by management and the union representative in relation to the quality of the relationship between them was fairly positive. Member commitment to the union was not regarded as strong, however, probably reflecting the small size of the union local (union branch) and possibly the nature of the work organization. No major issues had been raised in the latest round of negotiations. The main items included wages and shift differentials for the maintenance staff, and the union representative indicated that all had been settled satisfactorily. The average score for the climate of workplace industrial relations was higher than average (60.5 as compared to the sample mean of 58) indicating the generally co-operative atmosphere surrounding the industrial relations activities at WRA. In particular, the employees at WRA perceived the climate dimensions of fairness (WRA had the highest score among the six cases) and union–management consultation as being relatively high. The overall outcomes of industrial relations at WRA was noticeably higher than other organizations in our study. This reinforced the general positive view held by the industrial relations actors, absence of any major industrial action, low employee turnover and absenteeism, and an expressed satisfaction with the negotiations by the union representative.

The situation in 1989

Eighteen months later the situation with regard to the workplace industrial relations climate at WRA, as well as the outcomes of the industrial relations, had changed. The overall climate had deteriorated slightly, and the outcomes indicated a drastic fall. A comparison of the overall climate scores and the various climate dimensions over this period is shown in figure 6.2.

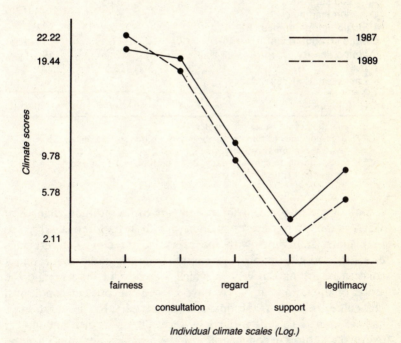

Figure 6.2 A comparison of climate scores for WRA (1987 to 1989)

It can be seen from figure 6.2 that the overall decline in the favourability of the climate reflects a decrease in the employees' perceptions of union support, union legitimacy, and, to a weaker extent, mutual regard. The overall outcomes decreased from a score of 7 in 1987 to 1 in 1989. In an attempt to understand these changes, we have used our model to analyze the changes occurring in the 'input' factors at WRA, which may help to explain the changes in climate and outcomes in this organization. A comparison of a selected list of factors between 1987 and 1989 is shown in table 6.1.

Table 6.1 A comparison of selected factors in Western Recreational Association (1987 and 1989)[a]

	1987	*1989*
1 Number of people employed	100	63
2 Structural flexibility	106	90
3 Overall climate (WIRC)*	60.46	59.33
fairness	21.86	22.22
consultation	19.47	19.44
mutual regard	9.91	9.78
union support	3.05	2.11
union legitimacy	6.17	5.78
4 Single-union dominance	2	3
5 Union Commitment	6	8
6 Union density	12%	19%
7 ILM	16.5	14.5
8 Labour market dependency	7	6.25
9 Training	16	12
10 IR outcomes	7	1

[a] For explanation of measures see chapter 4
* 1987: 20 respondents to climate survey, mean position = 1.55, mean age = 32.6 years, mean tenure = 4.3 years
  1989: 9 respondents to climate survey, mean position = 1.56, mean age = 37.1 years, mean tenure = 5.9 years

One of the major contributing factors to the attitude changes at WRA is the after-effects of sudden growth in the previous three to four years. Interviews with the executive director, the residence director, and the union representative clearly indicated a major concern regarding the way in which increases in the size and the scope of operations at WRA have caused the present conditions. Difficulties relating to the financial aspects of WRA's operation (it had accumulated a substantial debt since 1987) were attributed to the over-expenditures in connection with the new facilities, and a general drop in community participation (membership rates).

An immediate reaction of WRA to this situation had been to cut down on staff. This was accomplished through planned lay-offs as well as staff volunteering to leave. The overall number of people employed by WRA in 1989 was sixty-three (compared to 100 in 1987). The internal organization and the reporting relationships at WRA also underwent some changes. The position of assistant executive director was eliminated and a new position of finance director was created, reporting directly to the executive director. The departments were rearranged to fit under two broad functional units of service department (day care, residence, and building operations), and programme department (aquatics, adult fitness, preschool, and personal/professional development). The number of people reporting directly to the executive director had increased from seven to ten, and the organization had become more flat.

Reflecting these changes, our analysis of decision-making central-ization indicated that the levels at which authority is vested to make various operational decisions had been pushed down (i.e. WRA had become more decentralized in terms of levels at which decisions were being made). However, our examination of the extent of decision sharing and participation clearly indicates that there was *less* participation in 1989 than in 1987. This might have been partly due to the current economic problems facing WRA, and partly a result of a general streamlining of internal structure, the introduction of clearer lines of authority, and increased formalization (despite a decrease in the size of organization). Therefore, there appears to have been a decline in what we have termed 'structural flexibility' at WRA, brought about by decreases in decision-making participation and the extent of functional specialization. Due mostly to reductions in the number of departments and hierarchical levels (i.e. complexity) and a slight increase in hierarchical decentralization, our analysis has also shown a slight decrease in 'structural bureaucracy'.

However, the union representative and the departmental managers expressed concerns over the felt 'tension' at WRA regarding labour relations matters. Respondents also commented on the decline of positive attitudes towards labour relations: 'people looking out more for themselves rather than their neighbours', and 'there is an atmosphere of "us" versus "them" around here that never existed before'. The last round of negotiations took much longer to finalize than usual. The issues of shift work and salary were at the top of the agenda and the outcome, from the union's perspective, was not as favourable as they had expected. There was a distinct decline in members' interest in, and commitment to, union activities. Resorting to 'formal' mechanisms to settle complaints and grievances had become the norm (given the size of the organization, most of the complaints and disagreements between the supervisors and the staff had previously been handled informally). Thus, compared with 1987 the rate of grievances and the frequency of minor conflicts between management and the employees had substantially increased.

In summary, a comparison of the 1987 and 1989 situations shows that in WRA there has been a reduction in the extent of structural flexibility, a slight deterioration of the overall workplace industrial relations climate, and a substantial decrease in the extent of positive IR outcomes. The reduction in climate score appears to be related to a decline in people's perceptions of union support and legitimacy. Management and union ratings of the IR situation have dropped. The size of WRA had decreased, but it had been coupled with an increase in the level of formalization. This has coincided with a significant decrease in the extent of participation and consultation in decision making regarding operational matters. Also, due to the structural changes, the hierarchical level at which some decisions were made had been pushed down. Thus WRA represents a situation where a decline in one key input variable (flexibility) is associated with a decrease in the favourability of workplace industrial relations climate and in turn a deterioration of positive IR outcomes.

The City Library

The City Library was created over seventy-five years ago in a major city in western Canada. It has received funding both from city and provincial governments. Since the 1960s it has been governed by a board of trustees formed in accordance with the provincial Public Libraries Act.

Its main activities include acquiring and organizing book and non-book materials and providing guidance in their use. It also offers information and research services to the community and organizes lectures, workshops, and other programmes in an attempt to foster continued learning. The philosophy of the City Library is consistent with the general principles adopted by the Canadian Library Association in 1966. The following excerpt illustrates the basic organizational philosophy of the City Library:

> Libraries have a basic responsibility for the development and maintenance of intellectual freedom ... to guarantee and facilitate access to all expressions of knowledge ... [and] to guarantee the

right of free expression by making available all the library's public facilities . . . to all individuals and groups who need them. . . . Both employees and employers in the libraries have a duty . . . to uphold these principles.

(City Library's Board Policy 1966: 2)

In 1987 the City Library employed 101 permanent staff and had an equivalent of eight part-time positions (105 permanent positions in total). This comprised eighty-three unionized jobs, twelve supervisors, and seven managers. In addition to its central location, it had five centres or branches, as well as three mobile units, providing general and specialized services to the community.

The operations and organizational structure

Figure 6.3 shows the organization chart of the City Library. The formal reporting relationships, the nature of the departments and their basic duties had not changed significantly since 1986. The only major changes had been the addition of branches (from five branches in 1987 to seven in 1989) and the amalgamation of three suburban branches under the same supervisor in 1989. Prior to 1989 each of the assistant librarians responsible for the different branches reported directly to the assistant chief librarian. Also, as indicated on the chart, the number of people employed in each unit and department had changed between 1987 and 1989.

The adult services unit, the suburban branches unit, adult programming, booktrailers/small branches, children's services, and technical services were reporting directly to the assistant chief librarian, who in turn reported to the chief librarian. The gallery, administrative office, and the maintenance group all reported directly to the chief librarian.

Over the period 1987 to 1989 the size and scope of operations increased substantially. The number of people employed rose from a full-time equivalent of 105 to 159. The number of part-time employees had grown from eight in 1987 to about eighty in 1989. This growth had been in response to community demand caused by the high rate of population growth in the city. Two new major branches had been added and the range of the facilities offered in other branches had substantially increased. There had been a major increase in the demand for children's services in the new areas of the city, causing the children's unit of the library to almost double in size in these two years.

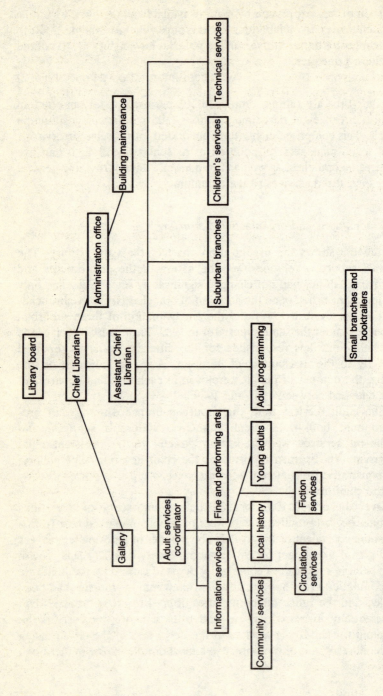

Figure 6.3 The City Library's organization chart (1989)

A comparison of aspects of organizational structure between 1987 and 1989 shows that even though the level of formalization and the hierarchical centralization have not changed, the extent of employee participation (as reflected by our measure of 'distance') has decreased significantly (see table 6.2 for a comparison of scores on key variables between 1987 and 1989). This indicates that the involvement and the participation of staff at different levels in decision processes in the library has been reduced. This was particularly noticeable in areas such as budgeting, organization of the units and departments, and hiring of new staff. Among the other changes in the organizational structure of the library are increased specialization (due to growth and opening new branches) and consequently the greater complexity of the library's structure.

Table 6.2 A comparison of scores on selected variables at City Library (1987 and 1989)*

		1987	1989
1	Number of people employed	105	159
2	Structural flexibility	103	101
3	Overall climate	57.76	54.71
4	Single-union dominance	2	1
5	Union commitment	2	4
6	Union density	79%	66%
7	ILM	20.50	23.75
8	Training	12	13
9	IR outcomes	–1	–4

* For explanation of variable scores, see chapter 4

Computerization has also been a major factor in comparing the operation of the library from 1987 to 1989. During the two years, all the on-line catalogues were computerized (in 1987 they were stored in microfilm projectors). In addition, a major increase in the capital budget of the library had recently been approved, to finance a complete computerization of all the facilities and the setting up of terminals in the central location as well as all the branches.

Human resource practices and consequences

Growth, automation, and an overall increase in demand for library services have put some pressure on the City Library for retaining and developing its staff, particularly the skilled professional librarians. Our analysis has indicated that there was an increase in the extent of the library's dependence on the labour market for skilled personnel.

Despite this, the relatively high rate of employee turnover among the skilled librarians in 1987 (about 20 per cent) had not been contained or reduced, but had increased to 26 per cent among the permanent staff and 33 per cent among the part-time skilled employees.

There appears to have been a slight increase in the library's emphasis on training (both in-house and external). This increase has been primarily for professional librarians and the management group. Our data also show that there had been a considerable increase in the significance of the internal labour market at the City Library. Due to the expansion and possibly in response to the conditions of the external labour markets, professional and clerical staff seem to have been in a fairly upward mobile position compared to the other groups within the library system.

The climate and its outcomes

The library maintenance workers (ten people in 1989) and the professional staff (105 employees in 1989) are represented by two different locals of the same union organization, Canadian Union of Public Employees (CUPE). Our 1987 survey was conducted among twenty-one management and unionized staff. The respondents were all female, mostly professional librarians (over 80 per cent), had an average age of 33, and a large majority had no supervisory responsibility. In 1987, the perception of the overall workplace industrial relations climate of this group was slightly below the average of the thirty-four organizations in our initial sample (57.8 versus the overall average of 58.3).

In 1989 the rate of response to our survey was higher. Forty-five employees responded (over 70 per cent response rate, as opposed to about 40 per cent in 1987). The average age of the respondents was 36, with a mean position that was higher than the 1987 survey; one respondent was male. In many ways the 1989 group was quite similar in its make-up to our earlier group, except that on average the respondents were slightly more senior and, expectedly, about two to three years older (also, mean service years were almost six in 1987, and over eight in 1989).

Figure 6.4 shows the comparison of the climate scales for the two years. The only major change appears to have been a significant drop in the respondents' perception of the climate of fairness. The climate of mutual regard had also decreased, to a lesser extent. In other words, the perception of the average employee in the City Library about the fairness and the co-operative spirit of the union– management relationships shows a considerable decline over the two-year period.

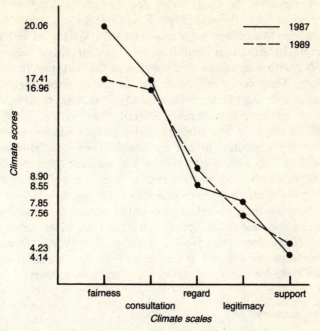

Figure 6.4 A comparison of the climate scores for the City Library (1987 to 1989)

The events described earlier (e.g. growth, increase in part-time employment, limited participation, computerization) may have contributed to the deterioration of the climate. Our interviews with both union and management representatives also unearthed a felt decline in the overall industrial relations climate at the library – the management's rating changed from an unconditional 'fair' to a conditional 'fair' rating. The union's view was 'fairly good' in 1987 and 'tense' in 1989. For the first time in their recent history, they had experienced three grievance cases that had gone to the arbitration stage. They have experienced dismissals, an increase in the number of grievances, and the prolonging of the dispute/grievance settlement periods. While the union density and the context of 'single-union dominance' had decreased, the overall attendance of members at union meetings as well as their general commitment, had increased.

Due to the increase in employee turnover and absenteeism between 1987 and 1989, as well as the features described in the foregoing paragraph, our overall measure of industrial relations outcomes showed a decline.

To summarize, the City Library demonstrates a situation where a reduction in the favourability of workplace industrial relations climate (due to a decline in perceived fairness) is coupled with a slight reduction in structural flexibility (i.e. participation), which have coincided with a significant deterioration in the outcomes of industrial relations. Size, complexity, and the extent of specialization have increased over the two years under study. Industrial relations factors have not changed considerably, except: the union's rating of the overall IR situation has dropped, union density has decreased, and membership commitment has increased. There has also been an increase in the library's provision for training (due possibly to computerization), and an increase in internal promotion and staff mobility (perhaps partly in response to unfavourable external labour market conditions). Therefore, it could be argued that an increase in size and a decrease in the library's structural flexibility, among other factors, have contributed to a drop in the WIRC score. This deteriorating climate had in turn contributed to a decrease in the positive industrial relations outcomes at the City Library.

Merton Brewery

Merton is a branch of a large Canadian brewery. The parent organization is a 200 years old, diversified, Canadian-based company with operations around the world. The overall group employs around 11,600 employees in more than fifty countries.

The Merton plant was founded in 1907 in western Canada. After the end of prohibition, it resumed operations and prospered through a volatile period of changing ownership. It was acquired by the present owning company in 1959. Since then it has improved its operation from a capacity of 150 beer bottles per minute to 700, making it the fastest-producing brewery in the province. In 1987, Merton plant employed 130 full-time permanent employees, ninety-three of which were unionized shop floor employees. Merton plant also employed about thirty part-time employees.

Changes in ownership and structure

Prior to our first contact with Merton Brewery, the owning group had merged with another major brewery. As a result of this merger, a widespread reorganization had just been completed across the many local and regional plants for the two organizations. One key impact in terms of the operation of Merton plant had been its integration with a small brewing plant located in the northern part of the province. The small plant was closed and its facilities and a proportion of its employees were transferred to Merton. For the first time Merton also inherited a Human Resource department, with a manager and two staff members. A partial organization chart of Merton plant in 1987 is shown in figure 6.5.

The operating plant acted fairly independently from the rest of the group, with the president of each plant responsible for the production, sales, human resources, and financial management of the plant. The production, packaging, quality control and maintenance supervisors all reported to the operations manager. Packaging was the largest unit with sixty-two employees, brewing and maintenance the second largest with twenty and twenty-one people respectively, while quality control employed three inspectors and one superintendent.

Between 1987 and 1989 the situation changed to a considerable extent. First, the total number of employees at Merton was reduced to 121. Also, due to shifts in the logic by which the national network of breweries was organized, the operations and responsibilities of the operating plant were altered. The national office implemented a line reporting system with three functional groups (human resource, marketing, and finance). The organization strengthened its regional offices by removing the non-production responsibilities of the once plant presidents and transferring them to the regional offices. In essence the plant presidents became glorified operations managers (i.e. plant managers), with their main duties the production and packaging of beer. New sales managers operated alongside the plant managers, with both reporting to the regional managers. The marketing, finance, and human resource managers reported directly to the national office. A partial illustration of these changes is shown in figure 6.6.

A comparison of our measure of organizational structure shows that the overall structural flexibility has had the highest drop among the six cases reviewed in this chapter. This was primarily due to the significant reductions in participation, that is, less decision sharing and greater decision distance. Understandably, the diminution of the plant president's responsibilities had led to a situation where most of the decisions were taken either at the regional or the national offices. This, predictably, had the consequence of limiting the extent to which plant employees and managers had involvement with operational and/or strategic issues and decisions. At the same time, since the level of the new plant manager is lower in the overall hierarchy of the organization, most of the operational decisions for which he was

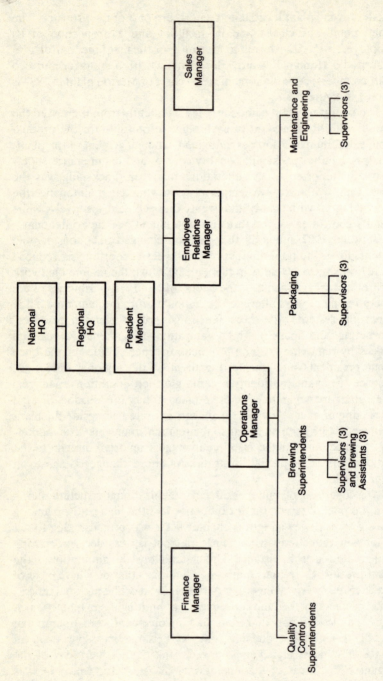

Figure 6.5 Partial organization chart of Merton Brewery Plant (1987)

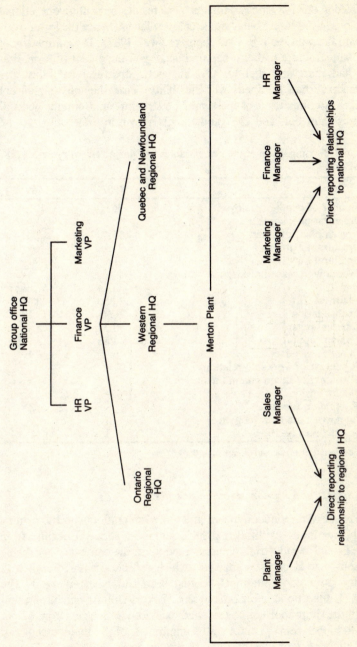

Figure 6.6 Reorganization of Merton Plant in 1989

responsible tended to be made at levels that were lower than had been reflected in our 1987 measurements. As a result, the routine/operational decisions in 1989 were being made at lower levels (hence the lower over-all centralization score in 1989 compared with 1987). The complexity of the plant structure had also been reduced, and the extent of formaliza-tion had increased slightly. Overall, both structural flexibility and bureaucracy had declined, with flexibility being the most significant change. A comparison of the scores on structure and other aspects of Merton plant between 1987 and 1989 is shown in table 6.3.

Table 6.3 A comparison of the key variables for Merton Brewery Plant (1987 and 1989)*

	1987	1989
1 Number of people employed	151	121
2 Organizational context		
(branch plant orientation)	15.40	9.41
3 Structural flexibility	125	66
4 Structural bureaucracy	106	90
5 Overall workplace industrial relations		
climate	63.14	57.66
fairness	20.50	20.41
consultation	20.75	18.19
mutual regard	10.31	8.97
union support	4.88	3.90
union legitimacy	6.70	6.19
6 IR context of workable relations	4	3
7 IR context of union commitment	5	4
8 Union density	62%	69%
9 IR situation (positive)	3	2
10 Employee outcomes (negative)	0	1
11 IR outcomes (9–10)	3	1

* For explanation of measures, see chapter 4

The context and human resource practices

As a result of a reduction in size and more integration with the owning group, our index of 'branch plant orientation' shows a decline from 1987. From the industrial relations standpoint, the context of 'workable relations' had declined somewhat, which reflects a situation where a slightly more confrontational context seems to have emerged. The union (United Food and Commercial Workers Union) which represen-ted all the shop-floor employees, had increased in density (from 62 per cent to 69 per cent). The overall commitment of the membership and their attendance of meetings had, however, declined from 1987.

Partly due to the implementation of a new organizational design philosophy (i.e. more integration with national office) and a more centralized human resource function, it appears that the commitment in the Merton plant to training had considerably improved. Another reason for the increase in provision for training may also have been technological change. The production facility had gone through further automation in the previous eighteen months, which had direct implications for the amount of on-the-job training required for shop-floor employees and supervisory staff. There were no major changes with respect to training for managerial and professional staff, however.

In addition, our data indicated a major increase in the internal mobility of the shop-floor employees. That is, there had been a number of promotions from within in the previous two years, and new policies had been implemented to encourage an internal labour market for all categories of personnel within the larger organization.

Climate and outcomes

In the first round of data collection in 1987, sixteen employees responded to the climate survey. These were mostly employees and supervisory staff from the production/operations unit with an average eight years of service, and an average age of 37. In 1989, the number of respondents rose to twenty-four, who had similar characteristics to the 1987 sample, but were on average rather more senior in terms of their level in the organization. Given the findings of previous climate studies (e.g. Payne and Mansfield 1973), one would expect more favourable climate perceptions in situations where the hierarchical level of the respondents is on average higher. That is, assuming no change in the Merton plant's circumstances, one would expect higher scores on the overall climate in 1989 compared to 1987. However, the overall workplace industrial relations climate score dropped by almost 10 per cent in 1989 (57.66) compared to 1987 (63.14).

Looking more closely at the components of climate, it appears that with the exception of the 'fairness' dimension, all the other climate aspects have decreased. The highest rate of fall belonged to the climate of 'union support' (a drop of about 20 per cent), with climates of 'consultation' and 'mutual regard' having the next-highest rate of decrease (13 per cent drop in both). Figure 6.7 shows a graphical comparison of the climate dimension for the two years.

The above changes indicate that during the two-year period, employees perceived a decline in the extent of communication,

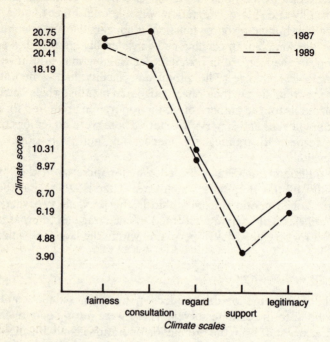

Figure 6.7   A comparison of climate scales for 1987 and 1989 in Merton Plant

openness and consultation between union and management; the extent to which the two parties respect each other's goals and have mutual regard for one another; the degree to which there is an atmosphere of support for unions and union activities; and the extent of union legitimacy in the organization.

The overall positive industrial relations outcomes had also decreased substantially (from a score of 3 in 1987 to 1 in 1989). Even though the rates of employee turnover and absenteeism had not changed, it appears that the general outcome of the negotiations from the union's standpoint in 1989 was much less favourable compared to 1987. In 1987 union attitude to negotiation success was summed up by the comment that they managed to achieve about 85 per cent of their requests. This situation changed in 1989 due to the consolidation of the two companies, lay-offs, and a number of other new elements in the process. Consequently it appears that the union had to make a large number of concessions (e.g. the union forewent the monetary increases in return for major changes in the retirement plans). There seemed, however, to have been a clear awareness on the part of the union representatives interviewed that the organization, and the brewing industry as a whole, was facing threats of increased competition due to the implications of the Free Trade Agreement between the US and Canada. In other words, even though the union had to concede, and even though the nature of the relationships after the merger had become more formal, 'hard-nosed', and more difficult to manage on informal grounds, the overall rating of the union representatives about the industrial relations situation only changed from a generally 'good' relationship to a 'fair' one (rather than 'poor'), reflecting in part the realization of the market and industry changes taking place. In addition, the number of grievances had increased since 1987. Most of the issues centred around the question of benefits (holidays and retirement package) and seniority (development of a national seniority list, as opposed to a local/plant list). Again most of these issues seem to be in direct reaction to change of ownership and the introduction of new policies for the two merged breweries. One observation was that the employees and the union representatives seemed to view the formalization of the industrial relations function as counter-productive, and in many instances implied that the formal ways in which the new unit dealt with issues such as grievances, may have played a part in the deterioration of some of the industrial relations outcomes.

Overall, a review of the situation at the Merton plant indicates that a major drop in structural flexibility has coincided with a fall in the workplace industrial relations climate score, and a decline in more positive outcomes of industrial relations. However, a number of questions relating to the application of our model have been raised. For example, despite a major improvement in the provisions for training, the climate had deteriorated; further, despite a reduction in the organizational context of branch plant orientation, the climate had declined. The present case illustrates the importance of taking into account the interaction among the host of factors affecting climate, and more broadly, the wider context within which workplace changes and transitions are taking place. Here, for example, one has to evaluate the applicability of the model by considering the pervasive influences of the 'consolidation' of the two companies, implications of the potential deregulation in the industry, and the important issue of automation and technological change. It is only by taking full account of these broader changes that we can understand the expected relationship between change in organizational flexibility and certain dimensions of climate and outcomes; likewise these wider changes are relevant to understanding why climate fell despite improvements in training provision and the plant's 'standing' *vis-à-vis* its parent organization.

Clark Brewery

Clark Brewery began operations in 1892 as an independent brewing company. It became part of a larger group of breweries in the 1950s, but maintained its position as a major regional producer of bottled beer. In the 1980s it went through two major ownership changes: one in 1987 involving a change of ownership to a major international group; and a more recent change involving a merger between two of Canada's major brewing organizations.

The Clark plant employed 154 shop-floor employees and fifty staff in 1986. In 1987, twenty of the production employees were laid off, and at the time of our first round of interviews it had an equivalent of 183 full-time employees, of which 134 were unionized. Since 1985 it had gone through major renovations involving the installation of a new bottling facility and a computerized brew shop, at a cost of 35 million dollars. In 1987, Clark was the fourth largest plant within the organization in terms of its market share, supplying one province in western Canada.

The plant was organized in a fairly traditional, functional fashion, with four major departments (production, human resources, sales, and accounting). The managers of each department reported to the plant's general manager, who was answerable to a general manger for the province. The lines of authority from here upward included a president for the western Canada region, and the headquarters in Toronto. In 1987 the production department employed 153 people, the sales department twenty, accounting five, personnel three, and the plant manager's office four people. Due mostly to the implications of the merger in 1988–89, and the utilization of the new plant and computerized facilities, the total number of employees in 1989 was reduced to a total of 153. Almost all the reduction was from the production unit, which maintained 108 hourly workers and eighteen supervisory staff (total of 126 compared to 153 in 1987).

Changes in the structure and context

Even though the formal departmental structure at Clark plant did not change noticeably between 1987 and 1989, there had been a considerable change in the dimensions of organizational structure. Our interviews with the human resource and general managers indicated that the authority and responsibility of the superintendents (the supervisory positions reporting to the department heads) had in fact increased to the extent that decisions such as modifications or minor changes in existing products, budgeting, purchasing, promotions and training were all being made at such levels, rather than at the level of the department heads. Therefore, our measure of decision making decentralization showed a decrease from 78 to 59 (i.e. greater centralization). As a consequence of the increased responsibility of the superintendents, the foremen were also more involved in decision making and their opinion in matters such as training, purchasing, and hiring were being sought on a more regular basis. These changes resulted in our measures of decision sharing and decision distance (i.e. both are aspects of participation) showing fairly sizeable increases. Thus, overall there appeared to be a change in the decision making structure and processes towards more decentralization and more involvement and participation. Due to the integration into the new owning group, there was also evidence of increased formalization of roles (i.e. more written documents pertaining to people's roles and responsibilities; more emphasis on written rules and policies; and so on). The extent of functional specialization did not change significantly, despite the reduction in size. Based on these observations, we calculated the extent of increase in structural flexibility. The degree of structural bureaucracy had at the same time diminished. A comparison of these and other scores on key variables in our study between 1987 and 1989 is shown in table 6.4.

In terms of the context and environment, one issue to emerge was the availability of skilled employees in local labour markets. For skilled manual employees and trained clerical staff, there appears to have been a change from high availability, to a situation where for certain positions the organization had not, on occasions, been able to fill positions for some time. Thus, the extent of labour market dependency of the Clark plant had increased over the two-year period. The impact of this dependency was clearly reflected in the overall increase in provisions for in-house and external training for all categories of employees. Also, there was clear evidence that the internal mobility of shop-floor and clerical employees had improved significantly.

In addition, the extent of Clark's dependency on its parent organization had decreased relative to 1987. This reflects a streamlining of the national organization's structure after the merger, and the general improvement of the Clark plant to become a major

Table 6.4 A comparison of the key variables for Clark Brewery plant (1987 and 1989)*

	1987	1989
1 Number of people employed	183	153
2 Organizational context		
(branch plant orientation)	10.23	2.99
3 Overall training	9.25	10.50
4 ILM		
for manual employees	17	21
for clerical employees	19	23
5 Labour market dependency	6.75	10
6 Structural flexibility	83	100
7 Structural bureaucracy	107	96
8 Workplace industrial relations		
climate	43.43	44.27
fairness	13.82	15.35
consultation	13.74	14.50
mutual regard	5.73	6.31
union support	3.51	2.23
union legitimacy	6.64	5.88
9 Union density	84%	71%
10 IR situation (positive)	–3	–1
11 Employees outcomes (negative)	4	1
12 IR outcomes (10–11)	–7	–2

* For explanation of measures, see chapter 4

branch of the new organization in western Canada (the number of levels in the overall hierarchy of the parent organization had decreased and the hierarchical status of the plant had moved up). Due to the increase in labour market dependency and a decrease in owner's dependency, our overall context measure of branch plant orientation had decreased quite significantly. Thus the organizational context of Clark compared to two years earlier can be characterized as having higher skill requirements and being closer in terms of levels to the policy-making bodies of the parent organization. We have argued earlier in chapter 5 that a decrease in the context of branch plant orientation has the potential of impacting on the climate within the plant in a positive manner (i.e. in terms of the interactions between management and employees and their unions).

In relation to the context of industrial relations, our information shows that there was very little change in the aspects we examined. The context of 'workable relations' has improved only slightly. The union representing the shop-floor employees is a local of the Western Union of Brewery, Beverage, Winery and Distillery Workers. It represents 100 per cent of the workers, and its membership is 100 per cent male. The structure of bargaining has not changed, and is a process involving industry/province bargaining between Beverage Employers Industrial Relations Association (representing the employers in the province) and the central union organization. In addition, local bargaining takes place alongside separate and more plant-specific issues involving the employers and the union locals. The method of handling grievances is formal with no emphasis on or willingness to resolve issues on a more informal basis. The only change in terms of variables under the context of workable relations has been an improvement in the previous round of negotiations. In 1987 the response was clearly a 'poor' rating. In 1989, the responses to the same questions gave a 'fair' rating, which reflected the ongoing process taking place at the plant regarding issues such as job classification, lay-offs, holidays, long-term disability, and plant rationalization. The union representatives, despite being fairly un-satisfied with the current agreement, indicated a degree of improve-ments in administering some aspects of the agreement. Union commitment, single-union dominance, and age, as other aspects of industrial relations context did not change over the period. Union density, however, had decreased from 84 per cent in 1987 to 71 per cent in 1989.

Climate and outcomes

In 1987, forty-five employees responded to our climate question-naire. These were mostly employees from the production unit with average age of 38 and average length of service of almost nine years. The respondents were mainly from positions below the management level and had on average at least high school education. In 1989, the number of respondents was twenty-six. However, in terms of level, department, length of service (average by now about eleven years), and education, they were similar to the 1987 group. The age of the 1989 group was younger on average than the previous respondents (average age 37 in 1989). Overall then, the two groups are reasonably comparable. The overall climate rating in 1989 shows a slight improvement of about 2 per cent in the average ratings. However, a closer look at the various dimensions of climate, as shown graphically in figure 6.8, reveals a more complex picture.

The climate of 'fairness' in the union–management relationship has improved by about 10 per cent, union–management consultation by approximately 7 per cent, and mutual regard by 10 per cent. These indicate that from the standpoint of employees, the positive aspects

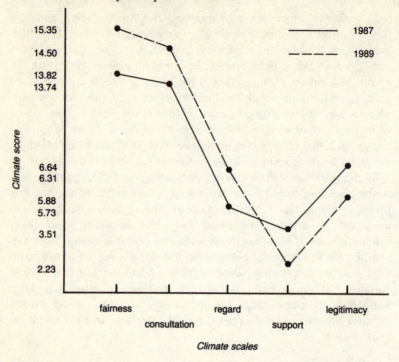

Figure 6.8 A comparison of climate scales for 1987 and 1989 in Clark Brewery Plant

of interactions between the union and management had increased. Other aspects of climate, however, point to areas of potential difficulty. For example, the climate of union support has markedly declined (by 35 per cent), and the climate of union legitimacy has also decreased by 11 per cent. That is, despite the fact that employees perceived the general climate of co-operation to have improved (due possibly to increased structural flexibility and decentralization, as well as improvements in the contextual factors described earlier), the atmosphere characterizing the support for union activities and the legitimacy of the union had deteriorated significantly. Perhaps the frustrations expressed by various employees and union representatives in relation to new management approaches, and a more formal and hard-nosed manner in which the labour relations issues were being dealt with are reflected in these dimensions of climate.

Overall, our measure shows that between 1987 and 1989 the outcomes of industrial relations had improved. In terms of a comparison with the other five organizations discussed in this chapter,

Clark had moved up from the worst performer in 1987 to the second-worst in 1989. Looking at the components of the outcomes variable, it is apparent that there has been an improvement in employee-related outcomes. The rate of employee turnover among shop-floor personnel had declined from about 5 per cent in 1987 to about 1 per cent, and the rate of absenteeism among the same group changed from 7 per cent in 1987 to about 3 per cent in 1989 (the only caveat here is that thirty-seven positions were eliminated in 1987–88 without being replaced). The rating of the union representatives of the success in negotiations changed from a rating of 'poor' in 1987 to 'fair' in 1989. The ratings of the human resource manager and the union representative about the IR situation at Clark had, however, not changed (all the ratings in 1987 and 1989 were classified as 'poor/tense' relationships). The ratings on major industrial relations events, though, improved from those involving a strike and a lock-out situation in 1987 to major and unresolved grievances in 1989. Therefore, overall the index of industrial relations outcomes showed a slight improvement over the two years of study.

Therefore, despite the fact that the Clark plant represents a case where there is ample evidence of frustration, and to an extent hostility, between union and management, concentrating on the changes between 1987 and 1989 suggests a different conclusion. That is, at least in part, increases in structural flexibility and aspects of human resource practices (training and ILM), and a decrease in branch plant orientation have coincided with an improvement in climate (particularly the co-operative aspects of climate), and may have contributed to an improvement in the outcomes of industrial relations.

Canadian Co-operative Services (CCS) Ltd

Canadian Co-operative Services (CCS) is a large co-operative organization involved in the agricultural business and related activities. It began operations in the mid 1920s in western Canada, and since then has grown to be one of Canada's largest corporations and one of the world's more successful co-operatives. It is owned entirely by its 65,000 members, and as a co-operative it has a democratic control structure which ensures that the organization is run in accordance with the needs of the members.

CCS currently employs over 2,800 people, and its main line of service involves collecting, storing, transporting, and selling agricultural produce. In addition, CCS has a printing and publishing division which publishes one of western Canada's major weekly newspapers, with a circulation of over 130,000. In association with other co-operatives, CCS also owns and operates a food processing plant, a fertilizer manufacturing operation, and a marketing organization.

The Chief Executive Officer of CCS is responsible to the Board of Directors for all the operating and commercial divisions. These divisions include food processing, publishing, and three farm and agricultural divisions. The managers of these divisions report to a general manager of operations who reports to the CEO. The staff functions such as finance, human resources, information systems, and planning report directly to the CEO (see figure 6.9 for a partial organization chart).

In 1989, CCS employed over 2,800 people, of which 384 were non-unionized management and supervisory personnel, 1,677 were unionized salaried employees, 694 hourly labour, and 138 part-time employees. Despite a rationalization programme in one of the locations involving over 350 redundancies, CCS's size in terms of the number of employees since 1987 had increased by 8 per cent (in 1987 it employed 2,600 people). This growth has been in the salaried group and in the number of part-time and casual employees. The overall revenue of the organization also showed a 3 per cent growth to $1.8 billion in 1988.

In our discussions with the managers of CCS, they viewed the modest rate of growth of the organization as running counter to certain trends in the agriculture industry in Canada. Faced with reduced demand and a decrease in prices of major agricultural products, the sector in general has been facing some difficult challenges. Despite this, CCS has managed to maintain its position in the market and has achieved growth. This has primarily been as a result of growth in the non-agricultural activities of the organization (such as food processing) and developing its staff functions, such as financial services, to provide assistance to the membership.

There had been relatively little change in the availability of skilled manual workers and clerical staff in the external labour markets between 1987 and 1989. For professional and managerial categories, however, there had been a considerable shift in the labour market, and by 1989 CCS found itself in a much more dependent position with regard to acquiring and retaining skilled professional and managerial personnel.

In terms of the organizational structure, our data shows that CCS had become more formalized, and the extent of decision-making centralization had increased considerably. The latter partly reflects

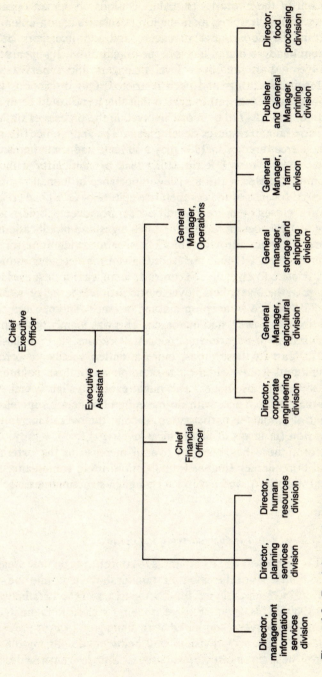

Figure 6.9 Partial organization chart for CCS (1989)

the removal of the authority to make decisions on human resource issues (e.g. hiring, training, manning levels, salaries of non-unionized staff) from the department managers and the managers below department heads to higher levels in the organization. It appears that the involvement of the lower level managers and supervisors in human resource matters had been restricted. Our discussions with both management and staff indicated that this trend could be due to the desire of the CEO to be more involved in the process of staffing, training, and human resource development. The appearance of a new human resource director in 1987 may also have had some impact on this. That is, the new HR director's lack of familiarity with the organization, coupled with the rising importance of human resource development (as part of the co-operative culture of CCS) had created a desire for closer or more centralized control over people issues. Similarly in 1989, decisions relating to changes and modifications in the nature of services provided by CCS were receiving more serious treatment by the CEO and the Board, given the declining industry and CCS's desire to diversify. In contrast, there was no clear evidence of a change in the level of employee participation in terms of decision sharing. The degree of decision making distance (another aspect of participation), however, had increased. This was mainly in the areas of reorganization of departments, budget allocations, and purchasing. That is, at least in these areas, more attention was being paid to collecting inputs from a wider range of employees before making the final decisions on these issues. This might explain a slight increase in decision-making distance, with no meaningful impact on increasing the extent of employee participation, despite the overall increase in centralization (in terms of hierarchical levels).

Therefore, there has been an overall increase in the extent of structural bureaucracy (higher formalization, more complexity, and more centralization), and not much change in structural flexibility at CCS.

Human resource and industrial relations context

Despite CCS's growth and its attempts to concentrate on new areas of activity, our analysis of the extent of training shows a decline over the two-year period (see table 6.5 for a comparison of the data between 1987 and 1989). This decline is more evident for clerical, manual, and professional employees compared with managerial personnel. For example, by 1989 no provision was being made for on-the-job training for these three categories. Also, CCS no longer provides any formal orientation programme, or training prior to new employees taking up their positions. This may indicate a change of approach to their human resource practices compared with 1987, where at least a comprehensive orientation programme was being offered to all new employees, and on-the-job training for certain divisions (e.g. printing) was being clearly emphasized. In terms of chances of promotion and internal mobility of the employees, there was an overall decline compared with 1987. This is particularly evident in the case of managers and professional employees for whom the chances of internal advancement had become much more limited than before. It is interesting to note that this overall decline in the internal labour market is despite the fact that since 1987 about 40 per cent of the manual employees had received promotions and reclassification to higher levels.

CCS had three unions representing its employees. Our concentration is primarily on one of these unions (Grains Services Union). The union had been representing its 1,800 members for over forty years. Over 85 per cent of the membership was male. The bargaining structure was primarily local, as opposed to industry-wide. Since 1987, the union density at CCS has declined from 87 per cent to 64 per cent. Over the 1987–89 period, the context of IR at CCS changed in that it became more 'workable' in our terms, and the overall commitment of the membership improved. The comments of the union representatives conveyed a feeling that the management had made sufficient efforts to protect the interests of the members and the employees. Also, the union representatives indicated that, generally, employee commitment to the union issues was fairly high to the extent that having over 70 per cent attendance at union meetings was not unusual. Due mainly to a reduction in union density, the IR context of single-union dominance had also declined. However, it does appear that the context within which the industrial relations activities take place had become to a certain extent more workable with increased membership commitment.

Climate and the consequences

In our climate survey conducted in 1987, there were fifty-two non-union respondents with an average age of 44, mean position of 2.96 (indicating relatively higher levels – supervisory and management levels below department heads) and average length of service of seventeen years. In 1989, 131 people, of whom ninety were union members, responded to our questionnaire. These had an average age

Table 6.5 A comparison of key variables for CCS (1987 and 1989)

	1987	1989			t-test (significant levels)
1 Number of employees	2600	2824			
2 Organizational context (branch plant orientation)	5.05	-2.17			
3 Labour market dependency	6.75	9.00			
4 IR context					
workable relations	2	5			
commitment	4	5			
single-union dominance	2	0			
5 Structural bureaucracy	71	106			
6 HR practices:					
training	12	8.75			
ILM	22.50	21.75			
7 Workplace industrial relations climate					
	1987	*1989*			
	(N=52)	(N=131) all	(N=41) non-union	(N=90) union	
overall	61.55	57.44	59.28	56.73	NS>
fairness	21.37	19.08	20.46	17.56	0.00
consultation	20.02	18.01	18.92	17.56	0.05
mutual regard	10.28	9.18	9.70	8.95	0.06
union support	3.67	4.27	3.42	4.67	0.00
union legitimacy	6.22	6.89	6.56	7.04	0.05
8 Union density	87%	64%			
9 IR situation (positive)	1	1			
10 Employee outcomes (negative)	3	2			
11 IR outcomes	-2	-1			

of thirty-eight, an average level of 2.50 (slightly lower-level respondents compared with 1987), and with a mean length of service of about fourteen years. Due to these differences in the composition of the two groups of respondents (1987 and 1989), we have shown in table 6.5 a further breakdown of the 1989 data for union and non-union respondents. In making the comparisons, we have also attempted to compare similar groups (i.e. non-union respondents) for more accurate estimation of the change in climate.

The overall climate rating in 1987 was above the average for the sample (61.55). This rating for the comparable group in 1989 (i.e. non-union respondents) changed to 59.28, indicating a drop of about 3 per cent in the favourability of the overall climate. Comparing the overall responses (N=131) showed a 7 per cent reduction in climate rating. The 3 per cent reduction for the comparable groups was mainly related to an average of 4 to 5 per cent drops in perceptions of fairness, consultation, and mutual regard. The climate of union support showed a 6 per cent decline, whilst union legitimacy increased by 5 per cent. In other words, the climate of co-operation in general and support for union activities in particular have deteriorated, whilst the perception of people considering unions as legitimate organizations to represent employees has become stronger.

The increase in the climate of union legitimacy is perhaps an indication of the beliefs of members of a co-operative organization in the basic support for democratic processes and mechanisms such as unionization (even though they were non-unionized employees and managers). This may have strengthened perhaps due to the actions of management and changes in the processes introduced by them since 1987 (e.g. more formality and bureaucracy), reinforcing the feeling that members have the right to join the unions and that unions are legitimate organizations. On a more practical level, it is possible that the evidence observed by the respondents in terms of general co-operation and support for union activities, caused by a host of organizational and IR factors (e.g. decrease in participation), may have affected the drop in the ratings of these climate aspects.[1]

In terms of the outcomes of industrial relations, there is a marginal improvement in the overall outcomes between the two dates. This has been primarily due to reductions in both employee turnover and absenteeism, as well as to improvements in handling grievances and complaints. No major industrial relations incidents emerged over the intervening two years. However, in 1988 there was a strike vote by the membership and 89 per cent voted in favour of strike over new salary plans. This was dealt with satisfactorily by the negotiating parties, however, and the matter was resolved.

In reviewing the situation, there seems to be a concern expressed by the employees and their representatives that excessive formality at CCS (both in terms of formalization of work and the negotiation process) has proved to be counter-productive. For example, constant use of outsiders and lawyers, which has brought with it increased formalization of negotiations, has not helped the process. In this light, the critical role of the human resource department was stressed, and there was a general agreement among the union representatives that the HR department could play a role in bringing things back to a level where formalization and bureaucracy could actually be used to facilitate the union–management interaction rather than being an obstacle in developing a better relationship. Here, an increase in formalization and bureaucracy, and a decrease in human resource practices (e.g. training) have coincided with an overall decrease in climate of the workplace industrial relations. It is possible to argue that union and management's attempts to create more positive organizational and IR contexts (e.g. the context of workable relations) may have been responsible for the improvements in outcomes, despite the deterioration of the overall climate.

Graphica

Graphica is a printing and publishing company operating in three locations in western Canada. It began operations in 1911 as a small partnership. In 1952 it became a limited company owned by one family. In the early 1970s it acquired another small printing operation and continued to prosper throughout the 1980s. In 1987 Graphica employed about sixty people with annual sales of five million dollars. At that time, Graphica specialized in a variety of printed materials, cookbooks, brochures, and print advertising. At that time its major client was the provincial government.

In 1988, Graphica merged with another printing organization. This printing firm, Preston Printing Company, was owned by a large co-operative corporation. As a result of this merger, the family-owned nature of Graphica became a thing of the past. The co-operative members now owned over 80 per cent of the company, and the owning family retained 20 per cent ownership of the new organization. The number of employees in 1989, therefore, increased to 169 with a projected sales revenue of over $20 million. The nature of products and services of Graphica have also changed with the merger. The company now produces a major weekly newspaper, is capable of printing larger volumes, and has gained expertise in catalogues, magazines, and products such as telephone directories.

Changes in organization and operation

The effects of the merger on Graphica have so far been quite substantial. The size of the organization in terms of the number of people employed has increased by more than 200 per cent, and its revenue has quadrupled. The merger also meant acquiring new technologies that Graphica's employees were not familiar with (e.g. a computerized newspaper production system, and a unique technology involving heat-set web processes for larger volume products).

In terms of the organizational arrangements and departmentation, Graphica had moved from a fairly simple, functional organization involving two basic units, to a more complex arrangement based on a mixture of functional (sales/marketing, finance, and production) and geographical (southern and northern facilities) organization. The three vice-presidents, of marketing, finance, and manufacturing, reported to the president/chief executive officer, who in turn reported to the Board of Directors.

Due to the merger, Graphica had become more functionally specialized, and considerably more formalized. This is partly due to the influence of Preston Printing, which had always belonged to a larger and more bureaucractic group, and therefore had developed a fairly formalized work system. The extent of decision-making centralization at Graphica had also increased compared to 1987. Despite the increase in size, which is often related to attempts to decentralize, our data indicates that most decisions were being made at higher levels (e.g. purchasing, budgeting, and product change decisions). Even though the extent of decision sharing, particularly between top management and the new middle management groups, had increased, there had been a sharp reduction in the decision distance (an aspect of decision making participation which reflects the involvement of people lower in the organization in the decision process). Therefore, the overall structural flexibility (specialization, sharing, and distance) had not changed to any noticeable extent, whilst structural bureaucracy (formalization, centralization, and complexity) had increased considerably.

The availability of required skilled employees seems to have diminished compared to 1987, thus the extent of Graphica's dependence on the external labour market (particularly regarding production workers) had increased. There had been no change in the extent of training, and the use of internal labour markets had substantially reduced. This latter factor, limiting the internal mobility of employees, might have been an indication of the market conditions (despite the increase in sales, many of the interviewees indicated a general tightening of the market opportunities in western Canada) and the cautious approach adopted by the Board in stabilizing the company's operations and manpower policies after the merger. Despite this, in early 1989 the company hired a consulting company to study the possibility of introducing a gainsharing (profit-sharing) plan, and the management was hopeful that it would be introduced in the few months following our interviews.

In terms of the number of unions representing the employees, the situation changed markedly, from having one main bargaining unit in 1987, to three unions and a total of seven locals in 1989. The three main unions were Graphics and Communication International Union, Allied Printers and Lithographers Union, and Print Media Union. This increase in the number of unions representing the employees is despite an overall reduction in union density (Preston Printing had a relatively high proportion of non-unionized administrative and supervisory staff, which Graphica inherited, thus reducing the union density). Regarding our measures of industrial relations context, the single-union dominance had clearly declined, and the context of workable relations had also declined.

Climate and its consequences

In 1987, eleven people from Graphica responded to our survey. Four (35 per cent) were managers, while the remainder were from skilled and semi-skilled grades. The average age of respondents was 38, with an average length of service of ten years. In 1989, there were ten respondents, of which two were managers (20 per cent), the rest mostly from the semi-skilled grades (thus, on average, the 1989 survey respondents were from lower levels in the company). Their average age was 42, and the average length of service was about thirteen years. Both groups were from the old Graphica company, rather than from the newly acquired Preston Printing.

The overall workplace industrial relations climate had decreased in terms of its favourability by a relatively large extent (by almost 10 per cent in terms of the ratings). Given the lower levels of the respondents in the second survey, we may have expected slightly lower

Table 6.6 A comparison of organizational and IR factors for Graphica (1987 and 1989)*

		1987	1989
1	Number of employees	60	169
2	Organizational context (branch plant orientation)	2.63	−1.11
3	Labour market dependency	8.25	9.00
	Labour market for production workers	9.00	12.00
4	Structural flexibility	62	61
5	Structural bureaucracy	41	61
6	Training	7	7
7	ILM	18.75	14.50
8	IR context		
	single-union dominance	3	−1
	commitment	2	2
	workable relations	7	6
9	Number of unions	1	3
10	Union density	75%	58%
11	Workplace IR climate	64.76	58.50
	fairness	22.36	19.80
	consultation	20.64	19.00
	mutual regard	11.09	10.10
	union support	4.27	3.20
	union legitimacy	6.40	6.40
12	IR situation (positive)	5	6
13	Employee outcomes (negative)	3	0
14	IR outcomes (11–12)	2	6

* For explanation of measures, see chapter 4

ratings. However, the drop in climate proved to be the highest among the six cases reviewed in this chapter. In this sense, we consider the decline in climate as quite significant. Climates of fairness and consultation declined by 11 per cent and 8 per cent respectively. Mutual regard, however, dropped by over 15 per cent in rating, and union support by a considerable 25 per cent. There was no change in the rating of union legitimacy. Such drops in climate perceptions such as mutual regard and union support reflect the turbulent conditions the company was going through as far as labour relations issues were concerned. A decrease in union density, despite the increase in the number of unions, is quite telling in this situation. Given this, and the introduction of new organizational and human resource policies (e.g. gainsharing plans), it is not unreasonable to assume that the general influence or power of the major union was in the process of decline. One comment made by a number of union officials interviewed was that the company has by and large convinced the major union (the union representing the employees prior to the merger) to accept a 'no seniority' clause, similar to the one that existed in the case of the incoming unions. The predominant reaction of the union representatives was a feeling of relief after the merger, in the sense that job security was no longer an issue (merging with a large successful organization reassured the unions of no lay-off programmes in the foreseeable future). Despite these feelings, and the reduction in employee turnover and absenteeism, the tensions and uncertainties created by (i) the merger, (ii) the rapid merging of the cultures among the management of the two companies (Graphica with an entrepreneurial spirit without a major concern for improving union–management relations, and Preston Printing with a co-operative ideology and concern for fairness and democracy), and (iii) the declining role of the unions in the light of the new company policies, have caused the biggest drop in climate in our longitudinal study. One can also argue that as a by-product of the merger and responding to the market conditions, the increases in formalization and structural bureaucracy, as well as reductions in human resource practices such as ILM and training, may have contributed to climate deterioration. However, similar to the previous case (Canadian Co-operative Services), the connection between climate and our view of IR outcomes has been weak in this case due mainly to other influences (e.g. size, merger, labour market conditions, unions' goals and strategies, and declining power of the unions).

THE CROSS-SECTIONAL CASE-STUDIES

To provide a richer account of the cross-sectional study reported in chapter 5, three illustrative cases have been prepared. A summary of the main characteristics of these three firms is shown in table 6.7. In the present section we discuss briefly the main points arising from these cases; a fuller description of the cases is given in appendix 2.

The three organizations are all subsidiaries or plants belonging to larger (usually US) owners. They are small- to medium-sized firms operating in southern Ontario. Base Industries, a manufacturer of automobile parts and materials, faces high competition in the industry which has fuelled management's concern for efficiency and cost consciousness. This is exemplified by investment in state-of-the-art technologies for manufacturing, and a lack of structural arrangements encouraging lateral communication and employee involvement. In our study this resulted in organizational design characteristics of low flexibility and high formality and bureaucracy. Climate at Base Industries was found to be low on management-related dimensions (fairness, consultation, mutual regard), and high on union support and legitimacy. Despite a considerable emphasis on training at Base (mostly technical on-the-job training for production staff), the industrial relations outcomes, as predicted by our model, are less than favourable: a recent strike, high absenteeism and turnover, and a significant increase in grievance rates.

Table 6.7 Characteristics of the three case examples from the cross-sectional study[1]

Variables	Sample mean	Base Industries	Richmond Furniture	Denman Industries
I Organizational context				
1 Size	725	222	407	190
2 Ownership		subsidiary	plant	subsidiary
3 Production Technology		large batch (auto parts)	large batch (upholstery)	large batch (textile)
II IR context				
1 Facilitative	5.9	6	5	5
2 Commitment	3.7	4	2	2
3 Union Dominance	1.5	3	4	3
4 Union Age	3.6	4	3	2
III Organizational structure				
1 Flexibility	79.3	58	52	41
2 Bureaucracy	86.2	82	85	77
IV Workplace IR climate				
1 Overall	58.2	55.5	56.9	56.6
2 Fairness		low	low	low
3 Consultation		low	–[2]	high
4 Mutual Regard		low	–	–
5 Union Support		high	low	low
6 Union Legitimacy		high	–	–
V Human resource practices				
1 Training	11.95	13.25 (high)	7 (low)	13 (high)
2 ILM	20.07	18.25 (med.)	15 (low)	14 (low)
3 HR Changes	4.65	4 (med.)	6 (high)	3 (low)
VI IR outcomes				
1 Overall	0.13	–5	–1	n.a.
2 IR Events		strike	warnings	no strike
3 Absenteeism		high (10%)	med. (5%)	low (3%)
4 Turnover		high (4% up)	low (1% up)	stable
5 Grievances		100% increase	40% increase	low

1 Case descriptions of these three organizations are provided in Appendix 2
2 Indicates no major difference to sample mean.

Richmond Furniture, a medium-size company, and one of the leading, upholstered furniture manufacturers in Canada, demonstrates some of the similar characteristics to Base Industries. It could be argued, however, that the market conditions are quite different – in some ways considerably less competitive, and the nature of technological requirements are quite dissimilar to Base. Even though Richmond is a mass producer, it has to rely heavily on the craftsmanship of its skilled employees for certain aspects of production. Flexibility of organizational structure is comparatively low, formality and bureaucracy are relatively high, and there is clear evidence to suggest that the management has a strong desire to maintain a very tight control over operations. Training and internal mobility are comparatively low. All these factors according to our model help to explain the below average workplace IR climate at Richmond. In particular, there is a low perception on the part of the employees of 'fairness' in union–management relationships. The company also demonstrated a low score on 'union support'. Given that the union is an in-house organization, and there have been talks of a take-over by a major union in the industry, this low climate of support is not quite so surprising. Given the above situation, a low to moderate IR outcome could be expected (particularly in comparison to Base Industries), and our data confirms this.

Denman Industries, on the other hand, demonstrates a situation of a small-town textile company with a long history in the community. No major competitive forces are evident. Due to technological demands, and the low skill requirements of the organization, a low score on structural flexibility was expected and was indeed evident. This, however, despite the above average emphasis at Denman on training, could have contributed to the slightly below average overall climate score – particularly in terms of fairness. The climate of consultation is high, but union support is low. The history and the prevailing culture at Denman may have been partly responsible for the high score achieved on consultation (as well as factors such as lower formality and higher training), and the relatively low support for the union as indicated by the union representative. The industrial relations outcomes, possibly due to the highly consultative atmosphere prevailing at Denman, are reported to be fairly favourable, and neither the management nor the union had any major concerns in this regard.

CONCLUSION

In this chapter a number of cases have been described; most attention has been paid to the results of a longitudinal study of six organizations, with additional descriptions of three further cases on which we gathered data at a single period. Our objective in discussing these cases has been, first, to expand the results reported in chapter 5, and second, to elaborate on the dynamics of workplace industrial relations climate over time, within the boundaries of our model.

A summary of the six longitudinal cases is presented in table 6.8. Four of the longitudinal studies have shown that changes in some of the key aspects of the 'input' factors (i.e. organizational context and structure, the context of IR, and human resource practices) can have significant impact on the formation of climates at the workplace level, which in turn can affect the overall outcomes of labour–management relationships.

In many ways, the four cases (i.e. WRA, City Library, Merton and Clark Breweries) confirm the findings of our quantitative analysis in chapter 5. That is, the influence of changes in input factors on IR outcomes can better be understood through their potential effects on climate perceptions, than by examining their direct impact on IR outcomes. In three of these cases, decline in participation and the overall flexibility of organizational design, coupled with other input factor changes such as growth in size, increase in what we have described as 'branch plant orientation', decline in training and other positive HR practices, have been associated with climate deterioration (in terms of general co-operation and trust), and have possibly led to decreases in the favourability of IR outcomes. In one case (Clark Brewery), increases in flexibility of the organization's structure, coupled with greater emphasis on training, have contributed to an improvement in climate, and in outcomes.

In the remaining two cases (Graphica and CCS) the complexity of the issues surrounding climate are more evident. Input factors interact with one another to produce impacts that our model in its most simple form can not predict. For example, the merger of the printing establishment with another firm, coupled with the changing role of the main unions, have caused the climate in Graphica to demonstrate the highest rate of decline,and yet at the same time a substantial improvement in the outcomes. The selling and the labour markets, as well as the general prosperity of the business, have apparently contributed to the disassociation between climate and

Table 6.8 A summary of the six longitudinal case-studies

Cases	Change in key input variables	Change in workplace IR climate	Change in outcome variables
1 WRA	1 A sharp decline in structural *flexibility* 2 Declines in *training* and *ILM*	Climate deteriorated (particularly *union support* and *legitimacy*)	An increase in conflictual outcomes
2 City Library	1 An increase in *size* 2 A decrease in structural *flexibility* 3 Moderate increase in *ILM* and technical *training*	Climate deteriorated (particularly *fairness* and *mutual regard*)	An increase in conflictual outcomes, and decrease in actors' ratings of IR situation
3 Merton Brewery	1 A substantial drop in structural *flexibility* 2 A reduction in *size* 3 An increase in technical *training* 4 Change in ownership structure (merger)	Climate deteriorated (*consultation*, *mutual regard*, and *union support*)	A decrease in favourability of negotiation outcomes from union's view
4 Clark Brewery	1 An increase in structural *flexibility* and slight decrease in *bureaucracy* 2 An increase in HR-related practices (*training* and *ILM*) 3 A decrease in branch plant orientation	Improvement in climate (*fairness*, *consultation* and *mutual regard*	Overall decrease in conflictual outcomes
5 CCS	1 An increase in structural *bureaucracy* 2 A decrease in HR practices (*training*)	Deterioration of climate (*fairness*, *consultation*, and *mutual regard*)	A slight improvement in positive aspects of outcomes (reductions in absenteeism and turnover)
6 Graphica	1 Ownership changes (merger) 2 Increases in structural *bureaucracy* and *size* 3 Reduction in emphasis on HR practices (ILM and training)	Deterioration of climate (*fairness*, *consultation* and *union support*)	Improvement in positive aspects of outcomes (turnover, grievances, and absenteeism)

outcomes here. CCS also shows an improvement in outcomes despite a drop in climate favourability. In both cases we have attributed the drop in climate to increases in bureaucratic aspects of the organizations and a decline in resources devoted to HR practices. For CCS, however, management's attempts to create a more favourable IR context (more facilitative relations) may have been responsible for the unprecedented increase in the outcomes.

Therefore, it is possible to begin to examine the interactions among the input variables, and attempt to understand the complexity of the issue in its entirety by taking the two latter examples.

NOTE

1 Including the climate data from the ninety unionized employees in 1989 would cause the differences in climate scales of fairness, consultation, and mutual regard to widen (10–11 per cent vs. 4–5 per cent rates of decline). Also, this inclusion would cause the climates of union support and legitimacy to increase (15 per cent and 6 per cent respectively). However, in order to maintain comparability, our analysis has taken into account the comparison of the two non-union groups only.

7 Conclusions and future inquiry

In embarking on a study of workplace industrial relations climate, we had a number of objectives in mind. In previous field-work experiences we had often found ourselves discussing the 'atmosphere' of plant or departmental industrial relations with managers and employee representatives. While this atmosphere was seen by different groups to comprise marious elements and be influenced by a range of factors, there was a broad consensus that by understanding this atmosphere one could gain a closer insight into the character of industrial relations at a particular location. To us at the time (the early 1980s) it seemed that while certain writers (notably Alan Fox) had highlighted certain aspects of this atmosphere – in particular the levels of trust and discretion in relations between management and the work-force – overall, this area of industrial relations had evaded detailed attention. Though organization theorists had built up a corpus of knowledge relating to organizational climate, this had not been reflected in the work of industrial relations' specialists. Moreover, while a number of previous studies had sought to employ industrial relations climate as an explanatory variable, it was apparent that none had approached the measurement of climate in a way which made us content simply to adopt their measures.

Against this background, then, the aims of the study were: to establish an initial model which expressed the potential for climate to influence the relationship between inputs and outcomes of industrial relations systems; to create and validate a measure of climate which was capable of being used in a diverse set of work organizations; and to collect data which would enable us to test the relationships between inputs, climate and outcomes, both at an aggregate level and within individual work settings.

Looking back over our findings, we are reasonably happy with our creation of a valid and reliable measure. That the measure was subsequently usable in a wide range of organizations was particularly satisfying. As the range of economic activity expands (through, for example, the growth of new service and professional activities), it is becoming progressively more important for organizational researchers to take this into account when establishing appropriate samples and characterizing 'typical' organizations. In the same way, changes in the average size of establishments (in terms of the number of people employed) and the growth of small- and medium-sized enterprises, means that it is increasingly necessary for those same researchers to recognize the significance and value of studying smaller as well as large-scale organizations. In industrial relations inquiry, the study of smaller organizations has been neglected. This has begun to change (see, for example, Rainnie and Scott 1986). The present study demonstrates further possibilities for using a common approach to the study of small, medium and large-scale organizations. Climate as a feature of industrial relations was as readily identifiable in the smaller establishments as in the larger ones.

Following the discussion of how the climate measure was created and tested, the aggregate data reported in chapter 5 confirmed many of the general assumptions underpinning the model and indicated that including a measure of climate improved the overall ability to predict the nature of industrial relations' outcomes. More specifically, different configurations of organizational and industrial relations' inputs were associated with different kinds of industrial relations climates. Further, the outcomes of the different industrial relations' systems were more adequately explained when data on the workplace industrial relations climate variable was included, than when reliance for explanation was placed solely on the nature of the organizational and industrial relations inputs. Moreover, by analyzing the data from different starting points, the identification of climate as an 'intervening' variable between inputs and industrial relations' outcomes was confirmed.

It is one thing to achieve a general confirmation of a model using aggregate data; it is another to witness that model in operation within individual workplaces. At a general level we are dealing in overall tendencies which may be relatively slight but takes on an added significance by their replication in different contexts. In the individual workplace, however, such a model is exposed to the full force of particular circumstances. In examining the relationships more closely within individual workplaces we were aided by the continued co-operation of a sub-sample of organizations, which allowed us to return at a later date and repeat many of the measures and follow up the events which had occurred during the intervening period. These were not organizations which were hand-picked because they reflected the overall findings (these findings were not known to us when we approached the organizations for further access). What these more in-depth studies revealed was that the relationships between inputs, climate, and outcomes are more complex than the overall pattern of relationships would suggest.

Our analysis of six organizations over a period of two years indicated that changes in what we regarded as key input variables to our model have, without exception, related to corresponding changes in workplace industrial relations climates. In four of the cases (WRA, City Library, Merton and Clark Breweries), changes in the extent of structural flexibility tended to be associated with corresponding overall changes in the climate scores of each organization. In addition, changes in flexibility tended to go hand in hand with changes (usually in the same direction) in human resource practices and policies, such as provision for training and the establishment of internal labour markets (ILM). In the case of WRA, reductions in flexibility and in HR practices tended to produce a less positive climate, leading to a decrease in favourability of outcomes. At Clark Brewery these relationships were reversed; that is, an increase in flexibility and an increase in HR practices, among other things, have been associated with improvements in workplace industrial relations climate and, in turn, the improvement in outcomes over the two-year period.

For City Library and Merton Brewery, again reductions in structural flexibility were related to climate deteriorations, as well as to a lessening in the favourability of outcomes. However, these two cases show slight increases in training and ILM which go against the predictions of our model. Yet, closer examination of the two organizations showed that due to computerization in the case of the library and technological changes (automation) as well as ownership changes in the case of Merton, increases in training have been with regard to technical, and mostly on-the-job, programmes for the employees.

The remaining longitudinal cases, CCS and Graphica, demonstrate a predicted pattern of relationships between input variables and climate, but the influence of these on outcomes is less clear and is subject to a more complex set of influences. In both of these cases, an increase in formalization and bureaucracy as well as a decrease in emphasis on human resource practices (training and ILM) were related to a worsening of the overall climate over the two years of the study. Despite this, CCS showed a slight improvement in terms of employee-related outcomes such as absenteeism and turnover, and Graphica showed a marked increase in positive outcomes, including the rate of grievances and employee-related measures of absence and turnover. Our analysis of these organizations led to the realization of the impact of a range of factors that our model in its present form has not taken into account. These include the influence of mergers and merging two opposing cultures over a short period of time, as well as the changing role and the power position of the unions involved (in the case of Graphica). And, in the case of CCS, it appears that the reliance on excessive formalization as a means of managing union–management interactions, as well as the clash between the basic philosophy of the organization (i.e. being a co-operative organization) and its current approaches in dealing with human resource issues and industrial relations, have been instrumental in bringing about improvements in outcomes despite a decline in the favourability of the workplace industrial relations climate.

Therefore, our case-studies as well as our quantitative analysis have shown the value of the general framework proposed in this volume for understanding the determinants of workplace industrial relations climate and its possible consequences at the level of the organization. The longitudinal case analyses have also brought to our attention a series of external and internal factors that can have a substantial influence on the process of climate formation and transition. These include: mergers and aquisitions, industry deregulation, changes in industrial relations strategies, and technological change. Overall, however, climate appears to provide a good vehicle for identifying some of the significant changes taking place within organizations and their impact both on the atmosphere of industrial relations and on the outcomes of those relations. With a potentially bewildering range of possible influences on the attitudinal and behavioural aspects of industrial relations, it is increasingly important to be able to utilize concepts such as climate both to evaluate the significance of individual inputs and to compare across diverse settings.

The case-studies further indicate that there is more work to do on understanding the particular circumstances in which climate operates in the way we have generally pictured it, and where it appears to contradict or at least not support our general model. However, before we consider other ways in which we might improve our model and our approach in future investigations, it is worth noting here that overall the climate study has reinforced two related arguments that were noted earlier in connection with the study of industrial relations.

First, the value of looking for influences and explanations beyond a narrow industrial relations sphere has been demonstrated. This has been increasingly recognized in recent years, with more and more researchers identifying various ways in which patterns of industrial relations are influenced and constrained by a wide range of intra- and extra-organizational factors. Our particular attention here has been on dimensions of organizational structure and context, including certain more external features such as the nature of the organization's labour requirements and its degree of dependence on the external labour market.

Second, this interaction of various facets of the organization reinforces our belief in the value of greater cross-fertilization between industrial relations enquiry and different branches of organizational analysis. The present study has highlighted not only empirical relationships between variables normally treated within the separate domains of organizational behaviour and industrial relations, but also the conceptual value of seeking to apply ideas developed in one discipline within the other. The growing acceptance that patterns of industrial relations are crucially influenced by a range of non-industrial relations variables will encourage this widening of perspectives.

Different commentators have recently argued in much the same way regarding other fields of business studies. Armstrong (1989) for example, persuasively makes the point of a need for a greater awareness of the influence of management accountancy on the practice of human resource management. Similarly, Marchington and Parker (1990) have provided further evidence of how the nature of product markets and customers can influence the character of employee relations. The present study has identified the importance of organizational features such as size, degree of bureaucracy, and level of organizational flexibility, as well as the nature of the organization's labour market, as further influences on the process of industrial relations.

REFINING THE MEASURES

Lest we seem too satisfied with the present study, let us identify some of the major shortcomings which we feel need to be rectified in subsequent studies on this topic. The shortcomings relate to the climate measure itself, the inputs and the industrial relations outcomes used. First, in terms of our climate measure, it is arguable that as we applied it in the main study, it does not fully measure the degree of conflict or hostile attitudes which may be present within the organization. It will be recalled that when sample organizations were initially approached to take part in the study, there was considerable managerial resistance to a small number of items in the measure explicitly referring to hostility and conflict. Compromises were necessary which resulted in modifications to the measure, involving the dropping of two of the original attitude statement scales. The result was that while negative climate could be judged from many of the other items (both through agreement with negatively worded statements and disagreement with positively worded ones), this remained a less than ideal position. While such concessions are often the *realpolitik* of field research, future investigations will need to address this and seek the degree of co-operation needed for a more comprehensive study of hostility as an aspect of workplace industrial relations climate.

Turning to the omissions from, and improvements to, our input variables, the difficulties here are more evident but ways of resolving them more complicated. We discussed in chapter 3 the problem of the vast range of potential influences on the nature of plant-level industrial relations, ranging from the weather to the policies of incumbent governments. Our own initial conceptualization had led us to a long list of potential influences (Blyton *et al.* 1987). At the stage of operationalizing the model, however, it was necessary to give priority to some of the variables rather than others. Our particular interest was to include a number of organizational aspects in the measure, together with aspects of the industrial relations context and human resource practices. Though sufficient for our present purposes, it remains the case that identifying relevant input factors is a considerable conceptual and empirical study in its own right. By dwelling particularly on organizational variables, we have sought to strengthen further the bridge between organizational and industrial relations research, but this has been at some cost. For example, some readers will no doubt feel that the findings are 'de-personalized' to too great an extent. There is no doubt that the nature of industrial relations in some settings will owe much to the character and approach of past and present individuals involved in those relations (just as the origins of distinctive cultures in some organizations such as IBM and Marks and Spencer can be traced back partly to the philosophies and practices of their founders). The importance of personalities does show up in a number of the case-studies reported in chapter 6, and of course the way the principal actors in workplace industrial relations behave is likely to affect attitudes towards those relations and thus the measures of climate as reported in chapter 5. Future refinements of the model, however, could usefully address this issue; indeed it represents an area which could usefully be explored more extensively by organizational psychologists among others: to date the explicit contribution of psychology to industrial relations has been more restricted and less recognized than its relevance to the subject merits.

As well as individual factors, some readers may feel that the influence of management and trade union strategies towards industrial relations have not been fully investigated in the present account. We too recognize this, though judging from many of the interviews we conducted (and have conducted in the course of other investigations recently) we would concur with the argument that in practice the development of such strategies occurs considerably more rarely than the frequency with which they are discussed would suggest. In the present study, a much more typical situation was the continuation of more *ad hoc*, short-term, and unco-ordinated approaches to industrial relations. In some contexts, longer-term objectives on the part of both management and unions were evident, but rarely had these been formalized into a co-ordinated and coherent strategy.

Nevertheless, greater exploration of industrial relations policies and objectives at workplace level could yield further insight into the different influences of parent organizations and central union policies at local level. In the present investigation, some sensitivity to the importance of higher levels of the organization was gained through examining issues such as degrees of centralization of authority in the organizations. Moreover, throughout the study, our focus of discussion of industrial relations issues was firmly on those areas which were bargained locally. Nevertheless, we recognize that this approach will tend to underestimate the co-ordinated aspects of bargaining in multi-plant enterprises; also that the attitudes of those at plant level towards industrial relations are likely to be affected not only by what takes place locally but also the outcome of supra-workplace industrial relations.

Besides the relevance of individual variables and broader union and management policies towards industrial relations as inputs into the workplace industrial relations system, a third area not as well represented here as some would wish is a greater consideration of the market conditions in which the organizations operated. Whilst collecting information on the nature of markets and extent to which these were changing, our principal focus was on labour market, rather than product market, dependency. Various studies in recent years have emphasized the extent to which the nature of product market competition can influence the amount of 'room for manoeuvre' which managers have within industrial relations. In the chemical plant studied by Marchington and Parker, for example, a less intensely competitive market provided the managers with scope to devote more time and resources to employee development and workplace communications. The intensely competitive market of a retail store, on the other hand, was seen to contribute to a more 'fire-fighting' approach by management, with little time devoted to improving industrial relations (Marchington and Parker 1990). Other studies have similarly identified a link between product market competitiveness and industrial relations 'style' (Purcell and Sisson 1983; Kochan, *et al.* 1984; see Marchington and Parker 1990: 84–96 for a review of studies in this area).

In the present study our consideration of market conditions was restricted by the obvious difficulties of comparing conditions facing organizations as diverse as breweries, meat-packing plants, libraries, hospitals, hotels, and prisons (the last raises particularly thorny questions concerning their market!). Nevertheless, in future extensions of this work, more consideration could usefully be given to integrating measures of product markets, customer and client bases more fully into the research design.

In the same way that the measure of climate and the list of relevant input variables may benefit from further refining and extension, the measure of industrial relations outcomes that we employed may also benefit. In an earlier chapter we noted that many studies of industrial relations fail to take sufficient account of the subjective outcomes of the union–management relationship. In the present account we found it not only possible but also highly advantageous to have a broad view of the industrial relations outcomes, not only containing subjective and objective outcomes, but also identifying conflict as a possible *outcome*, rather than classifying it simply as part of the *process* of industrial relations.

In reviewing our measure of outcomes, however, one omission which would have proved beneficial is more objective information on pay settlements. Again our reasoning for omitting this from the measure was that we were focusing on workplace-level negotiations and in many of the sample organizations (e.g. hospitals, public libraries, and prisons) the pay negotiations were handled at a higher level. Nevertheless, following the argument above, attitudes toward workplace industrial relations are likely to be influenced, to a greater or lesser extent, by the outcomes of negotiations occurring at higher levels. Thus in future studies of climate we would seek more detailed information on the economic aspects of industrial relations, and in particular on pay settlements.

Besides these specific issues which need to be addressed, the present study has raised a number of more general questions about the further development of this line of enquiry. In particular, only the first steps have been taken here to assign weights to the various input factors impacting upon industrial relations processes, climate and outcomes. The correlation and regression data discussed in chapter 5 offers some suggestions as to the relative significance of particular input variables in the present sample. However, in various ways these insights can only be tentative. First, with a relatively small sample of organizations, an ever-present difficulty is establishing a broad enough range on individual variables to adequately test their significance. While a number of the variables in the study had such a range – for example, the variables relating to organizational structure – others contained a much narrower variability.

To establish whether the weightings indicated in the present study are sustained in a broader population, two strategies are available (and both are expensive in time, effort and resources). First, conducting a similar enquiry using a much larger sample would provide a greater variability range across not only the input factors but also the industrial relations outcomes. For completeness, this would entail not simply a bigger sample in a single country, but in addition matching that sample with others in different national contexts in order to evaluate the peculiarities of country-specific variables on the model. A second approach would be to adopt a longitudinal design but with a significantly larger sample than in the present case, to track the relative importance of different associations over time. If this latter course was followed (and in the knowledge that an over-time design would inevitably reduce the size of the sample), consideration would have to be given to choosing organizations which exhibited (or over the time period would be likely to exhibit) change in the main variables under investigation. Another important consideration is the timescale of changes, and identifying when is the appropriate time to measure the impact of the change on areas such as climate. This is a highly complex area, however, not least because the instances of change, their timescales and the extent of any time-lag between the change occurring and its effect on other aspects of the organization, are generally very difficult to predict. Such problems notwithstanding, even on the basis of the small longitudinal study reported here, this type of investigation could yield much additional insight into the implications of particular changes and events for the character of both industrial relations climate and outcomes.

INDUSTRIAL RELATIONS AND EMPLOYEE RELATIONS

A further question relates to the measuring of industrial relations climate at a time when there is a good deal of speculation and some evidence that at least in certain sectors the model of industrial relations based on trade unions and collective bargaining is partially giving way to a system which has been described as 'employee relations'. Here the approach is more explicitly unitary than pluralist in character, with management utilizing mechanisms such as direct involvement and communication with employees, together with more individualized, performance-related pay. There is relatively little evidence (particularly outside the United States and certain industries in Canada such as construction) that companies are pursuing explicit de-unionization policies. However, there is more evidence of employee relations policies being progressed alongside existing industrial relations machinery. In these situations, there will be a tendency for trade unions to become more marginalized, with collective bargaining representing only one, rather than the sole, method of regulating pay, conditions, and work practices (Guest 1989).

We do not wish to exaggerate these trends away from more traditional industrial relations, partly because for a considerable period in many organizations different channels of communication and representation (e.g. joint consultation and workplace bargaining) have co-existed with little apparent effect on the status of the union or the bargaining institutions. However, what we have developed here is a measure of climate focused explicitly on local *union–management* relations, which would not be directly applicable to non-union plants, and would be misleading where the conduct of relations between workforce and management was structured as much through non-union as through union channels. Future refinements of the measure could profitably address this, either by extending the scope of the climate measure, or by establishing different measures for contexts where unions are not present or have a limited role and impact.

A FINAL WORD

Much of the discussion in this concluding chapter has addressed the academic issues relating to refining and extending the climate concept. However, while it has not been our prime concern in this monograph, we would not wish to leave this discussion without pointing to some of the possible uses of climate for practitioners. Following the various stages of the climate measure, what we have ended up with is a reasonably good measure of climate which can easily be used by managers, consultants and academics alike as a more detailed guide to the perceived atmosphere of workplace industrial relations, than has typically been used hitherto. Hopefully the study also indicates the areas which need to be examined in seeking explanations for changes in climate over time, or between one workplace and another. Extended use of the climate measure in this way would further sensitize managers to the different facets of climate within their organizations and the ways the atmosphere of relations can influence outcomes. Given the current importance being placed on such attributes as organizational culture, employee commitment, positive employee attitudes, quality consciousness and so on, it seems highly appropriate for managers to be increasingly aware of their workplace industrial relations climate and its potential impact on the outcomes of those relations.

Appendix 1 The interview schedule and climate questionnaire

INTERVIEW SCHEDULE

I Background information

1 Could you tell me something about this organization's history? When it began? Have there been any major changes?

2 (a) Explain the nature of this organization's ownership. (Who owns it? What percentage?)

(b) Is this organization a branch, subsidiary, HQ ...? If it is a principal unit (HQ), does it have branches or subsidiaries? Explain.

3 How many people work here? Part-time? Full-time? Total assets (approx)? (Or budget, for public organizations)? Total sales?

4 Explain your products/services. Your markets. What is your market share for your main products?

II Operations and structure

5 Explain the facilities/functional units of this organization. Explain the nature of technology (if appropriate).

6 Do you have a written organizational chart? Can I have a copy? Who normally receives this? (If chart is not available, sketch one in the space below.)

7 (a) Do you have a list of various positions/job titles? Could I have a copy?

(b) Functional specialization. Do you have employees dealing exclusively with each of the following activities (an activity is specialized when at least one person performs that activity, and no other activities):

General

1 Sales, service or customer complaint:
2 Advertising or public relations:
3 Transportation or distribution:
4 Purchasing or materials control:
5 Maintenance:
6 Accounting:
7 Planning:
8 Quality control:
9 Work study, operations research:
10 New product development:
11 Administrative procedures (statistics, filing):
12 Legal and insurance matters:
13 Market research:

Human resources

14 Recruitment:
15 Other personnel and employment matters (benefits, files, placement):
16 Staff training/education:
17 Industrial/employee relations:
18 Health and safety:
19 Wage administration/job evaluation:
20 Organization development:
21 Others (specify):

8 Do people normally receive written job descriptions here? Who does? Who does not (i.e., senior managers, middle level managers, supervisors, others)?

9 Do you have written procedures for various job categories? Explain. Do some people receive written operating instructions? Explain.

10 Are organizational policies written? Do you have a copy I can have?

11 Do you normally give information booklets or pamphlets to new employees? How many of these booklets do you have? Could I have a copy (e.g. anything from booklets on the firm to pension, insurance, benefits, etc.)?

12 How many senior managers work here?
   How many supervisory personnel?
   How many administrative personnel?
   How many clerical personnel?
   How many support personnel?
   How many qualified technical personnel?

13 In this section I am interested in the way in which some of the important decisions are made in your organization. Could you tell me (i) who gets involved in the following decisions, and (ii) who is the most junior person on whose decision action is normally taken regarding these decisions (even though it may be ratified later at some higher level).
   (If a *committee* is in charge, consider the level of the chair of the committee.)

(For a list of the decision items and the scale used see p. 75).

III Personnel related and employment

14 Would a typical (or average) newly hired employee have:

   *Mgt./Admin. Profess. Manual Clerical**
   1 No prior work experience
   2 Little work experience
   3 Some work experience
   4 Considerable work experience

15 What proportion of your vacancies is normally filled by your current employees?

   1 1–10%
   2 11–40%
   3 41–70%
   4 More than 70%

(*Use this scale for questions 15, 16, 18, 26, 27*, or use actual figures)

16 What proportion of vacancies that are open to external persons is normally filled by people:
   In your community?
   In your province?
   From outside the province?

---

* For questions 14 to 32, data for the four categories were collected separately.

17 In your opinion, what are the chances of promotion for a new employee with limited prior work experience over five years in your employ?

1 None/poor
2 Fair
3 Good
4 Excellent

18 What proportion of your employees over the past five years has been promoted?

19 What are the chances of an unskilled position to be promoted to a semi-skilled one?

1 None/poor
2 Fair
3 Good
4 Excellent

20 What about a semi-skilled to a skilled position?

21 Would you say that for each category, your organization has a ladder or a hierarchy of promotion in place?

1 No
2 Yes: only for few positions
3 Yes: for many positions
4 Yes: for all positions

22 Do you provide training before employees assume their duties?

1 No
2 Yes: for few positions
3 Yes: for many positions
4 Yes: for all positions

23 Do you provide in-house educational programmes to improve employee skills?

1 No
2 Yes: for few positions
3 Yes: for many positions
4 Yes: for all positions

24 Do you provide formal on-the-job training with your financial support?

1 No

2 Yes: for few positions
3 Yes: for many positions
4 Yes: for all positions

25 Do you support education/training outside this establishment?

1 No
2 Yes: for few positions
3 Yes: for many positions
4 Yes: for all positions

26 What proportion of your employees are unionized?

27 What proportion of your employees are part-time?

28 Current rate of employee turnover (and how they define it)?

29 Current rate of absenteeism

30 How frequently do you find that you are unable to fill a position within a reasonable time?

1 Never
2 Rarely
3 Sometimes
4 Almost always

31 How often have you had to undertake training or other special programmes because there were not enough available qualified people for the job?

32 Overall, how do you rate the availability of required skilled personnel externally?
(In the Province)
(In Canada)

1 Virtually non-existent
2 Poor
3 Moderately available
4 Very available

33 Have you had any positions vacant that you have been unable to fill? How many over the past five years?

34 Has the number of employed increased or decreased over the past few years? By how much?
Overall:

35 Over the past few years, how would you characterize the staff situation in your organization (check as many as applicable)?
Significant changes in job descriptions
New skills
Whole new skill areas
New and different equipment
Whole new jobs
Higher job qualifications
Increased legal or technical requirements

36 Over the past few years, has your organization:
Undertaken a building or expansion programme
Become more specialized as to the type of services/products
Offered new products/services

IV Industrial relations

37 What are your views on IR/labour relations in this organization?

38 Describe some of the major IR events, if any? (Disputes, agreements, what was the last agreement for each union like ...?)

39 Explain the IR situation regarding different unions (bargaining units).

40 What are the most pressing *local* issues?

V Questions for union representatives

41 Descriptive information: membership (number and sex, kinds of professions/positions); age; level of influence.

42 Detailed information on the bargaining structure, i.e. level at which the bargaining takes place (local, industry, provincial).

43 What are the issues that are normally raised in the negotiations?

44 How successful have you been in the negotiations (what happened *last year*)?

45 How do you describe the IR scene in this organization? Who are the key people on both sides?

46 How are the grievances handled? Any comment about absenteeism, turnover, and strike actions?

47 How do you describe the relationship between management and unions?

48 What would you like to see changed?

49 Comments on membership commitment and participation in unions?

50 Any additional 'organization-specific' issues that you may want to add?

CLIMATE QUESTIONNAIRE

This questionnaire is designed to gain an understanding of the work environment in your organization.

Please complete this section before starting with the questions on the next page:

Name of your organization

Your position/title

Your department/unit

Years of service in this organization

Your age

Are you male   or female

Your level of education: University
                         High school
                         others

Are you a member of an employee's association/union? Yes   No

If yes, name of employee's association/union?

Questionnaire

For your organization please indicate your degree of agreement with the following statements. In responding to these statements, please write a number in the left-hand margin based on the following scale:

        5 Strongly Agree
        4 Agree
        3 Undecided
        2 Disagree
        1 Strongly Disagree

1 Unions and management work together to make this organization a better place to work.

2 Unions and management have respect for each other's goals.

3 The parties in this organization keep their word.

4 Unions make a positive contribution to this organization.

5 In this organization, joint management–union committees achieve definite results.

6 There is a great deal of concern for the other party's point of view in the union–management relationship.

7 Informal consultation takes place frequently between unions and management.

8 In this organization negotiations take place in an atmosphere of good faith.

9 Employees have a positive view on joint union–management committees here.

10 The collective agreement is regarded as fair by employees in this organization.

11 Generally, employees here do not have much interest in the quality of the union–management relationship.

12 Joint union–management committees are a common means of implementing important changes in conditions.

13 Grievances are normally settled promptly in this organization.

14 Employees generally view the conditions of their employment here as fair.

15 In this organization unions have the strong support of their members.

16 The parties exchange information freely in this organization.

17 Management and unions co-operate to settle disputes in this organization.

18 Shop stewards are treated with respect here.

19 A sense of fairness is associated with union–management dealings in this place.

20 Management often opposes the changes advocated by unions here.

21 Shop stewards in this organization generally play a helpful role.

22 People are encouraged to get involved in union activities here.

23 Management often seeks input from the unions before initiating changes.

24 Unions and management in this organization make sincere efforts to solve common problems.

Appendix 2 Three cross-sectional case studies*

BASE INDUSTRIES

Base Industries began operations in Chicago in 1903 making radiators for the first production line automobiles. It moved to Detroit in 1910 in order to get closer to its major customers at the time and eventually moved into Canada in 1932 when the automotive market was becoming established there. The current operations are centred in south-western Ontario with the major production facility in the city of Cambridge. Here the company manufactures its three major product lines: radiators, oil coolers and evaporators.

The major growth of Base Industries in Canada occurred in 1973. It was stimulated by a booming automotive industry that resulted in doubled employment and revenues. Following this burst of activity, it experienced an unsettling series of fluctuations related to the automotive business cycle, which prompted the search for a diversification strategy. This search took the company into the heavy equipment market which eventually helped to steady product demand. Unfortunately the US owners were never satisfied with the division's business results. Consequently in 1983 it was sold to a group of private investors which included the local management team: a group which currently runs the three-facility operation as equal partners. The focal operation for this study is the Cambridge plant which houses the main production facilities of the company. It is a largely autonomous entity operating with little interference from the Oakville head office.

The critical strategic issue throughout Base's history has been its reliance on the North American automotive industry. Since its major spurt of growth in 1973, it has experienced three major industry

* See chapter 6.

cycles in which operations and profits were significantly curtailed. Its recent initiatives in the heavy equipment market have dampened the effect of major slow-downs in automotive activity but it is still strongly dependent on this market.

From the perspective of the workplace climate model the market, and particularly its uncertain nature, exerts a significant influence on Base's operations. Important input factors would be matters of foreign competition, ecological concerns regarding pollution, increasing regulatory activity, and mounting social concern about car safety. For the past twenty years in Canada the domestic automotive market has been strongly challenged by foreign imports. This has caused the normal cyclical fluctuations to amplify in a rather unsettling manner. While the market has now largely adjusted to the competition it remains a recurring uncertainty for everyone, including parts suppliers such as Base. Adding pressure to these economic conditions has been the rather strong ecological focus that has come to centre on the industry. Governments have become increasingly zealous regarding emission-control and gasoline consumption. In addition, highway safety has emerged as an important social issue with significant regulatory implications.

A host of other concerns and developments tend to keep this industry unsettled. Automotive traffic tends to be choking the highways and Canadians are being chided for their dependence on this mode of transportation. More automobile traffic means more accidents and, with this, the costs of repairs have skyrocketed. Related insurance costs and coverage has reached a crisis stage across the country.

Import competition continues to plague domestic producers but this has been somewhat ameliorated by government requirements that large import-producers establish domestic facilities. Such facilities for most of these firms merely means assembly plants and this has not created any major markets for most Canadian automotive parts producers.

To place the company itself in perspective regarding the model inputs, a number of factors should be noted. The company is small by current study standards. It has only 270 plant employees, but it nevertheless dominates the Canadian Market with an average 60 per cent market share in its major lines. It also appears to enjoy a good reputation in the market.

The management team has recently assumed ownership, making it a private and wholly-Canadian owned company. This team operates as equal partners and forms an executive committee for managing the operation. The technology at Base is not regarded as particularly complex in that the products fit into a well-established and quite stable technical field. The critical technical issue is to have 'state of the art' equipment and run it efficiently. This places a distinct focus on the technical production function as the main principle of viability for this operation. The sales and marketing function, while important, is constrained by the small customer base and the focus on meeting product specifications as a condition for getting and holding customers.

The labour force at Base is predominantly that of a non-skilled variety. Three-quarters of the employees are women assembly workers and one-quarter are males – mostly machinists. The average seniority is fifteen years – employees tend to stay. There is, in these terms, a fairly strong internal labour market operating. Up to 70 per cent of the new-hires for shop and clerical are internal promotions. There is frequent and well-established progression from unskilled to skilled ranks, and both in-house education and on-job training to support this promotional system. Positions are filled almost exclusively from within the community with little difficulty, except for the positions of tool-and-die makers. The major trend within the work-force is toward the development of new skills and the resultant creation of higher job classifications.

The organization structure at Base could be characterized as one of medium-to-high formality, depending on the department being considered. The strongest hierarchy occurs in the manufacturing area, which has six management levels. This is a key part of the operation and probably creates an overall impression of rather high formality. The rest of the functions operate with either three or four levels and would be perceived as less formal. These functions, however, involve a very small portion of employees. There are twenty-two management personnel in the plant, or just less than a 1:10 ratio to non-management. Eighty per cent of the management staff are connected directly with manufacturing.

On the other hand, this plant exhibits a fairly high degree of functional differentiation for such a small operation. There are seven distinct departments in the plant, although this may be more form than substance. Many of these functions do not contain much vertical depth as noted above, so that job-holders tend to do multiple tasks – only purchasing, maintenance, accounting and hiring are the subject of exclusive individual specialization.

Because of the predominant size of the manufacturing department and its strategic ascendency, this group is perceived as a power unto themselves. This is reported to restrict lateral relations with other functions, but the hierarchical range of decision making within the manufacturing function appears to be reasonably great.

The industrial relations environment at Base is described by both management and labour as better than average, but still adversarial. The situation appears to have deteriorated of late with the new union president who took office in 1985, and has pursued a much more militant stance than previous incumbents. The shop is totally unionized and represented by the Union of Machinists and Aerospace International. This union allows a large degree of local autonomy in the bargaining process.

The bargaining structure consists of a four-member union group headed by the international representative and a three-member management group headed by the plant manager. However, the major discussions go on between the union president and the personnel manager, who apparently personally dislike each other.

The important local issues for union and management are primarily wages, followed by the benefits package. Historically, agreements have been achieved with reasonable dispatch and have been fairly quickly ratified. Similarly, in the past there have been few disagreements and little time has been spent on the actual wording of the contract. This situation implied a certain level of trust between the parties. In the recent past, bargaining had been centred almost exclusively on monetary issues since the sides basically accommodated each other on the non-monetary matters if and when they surfaced. Most recently, that co-operation has become somewhat strained.

There seems to be no particular imbalance of power or significant difference of objectives that arise in the management-employee relationship. The parties appear to recognize their reciprocal reliance in the interest of running the operation in an efficient manner. Management reportedly tries to involve employees in the decision process and employee response has been largely favourable.

The input factors discussed above are structural, human relations, and workable relations variables. From a structural point of view, Base is just slightly above average on the 'bureaucratic' dimension but far below the study average on the measure of 'flexibility'. The component measures of 'flexibility', the sharing of decisions, the hierarchical range of decision making, and the degree of functional specialization seem to be relatively restricted at Base. Functional specialization was rather extensive within several departments but the predominant power of the manufacturing department reportedly restricted lateral networks outside this central function. The effect is that decision making is departmentally, if not hierarchically, confined.

The flexibility measure is the only input variable that departs significantly from the study averages. Because this is only one of five measures one would not expect it to impact on the workplace climate to any great degree. Other input factors yielding about average results would tend to create an average effect. This turns out to be the case and interestingly the results are in the right direction. The workplace climate measure comes out just below the study average (55.5 vs. 58.2).

Referencing the workplace industrial relations climate factors directly, three of them fall below average and two are above. The factors of fairness, consultation and mutual regard fulfil the former condition, union support and union legitimacy, the latter. This would indicate that plant people are supportive of the union but have some reservations about the management. This is not just a disenchantment with negotiations, because there is strong union support. The dissatisfaction must rest on the firm's management.

Conceptually speaking, the lower climate scores, according to the model, should result in a less favourable set of system outcomes. These outcomes cover a profile of different factors, only some of which appear to be operable in this case. The outcome related to industrial action and strikes does not not appear to be affected by the lower than average climate. The only strike was in 1978 and there has been no other significant industrial action. It may be that there is not a big enough difference between Base and the average score to trigger critical action of this kind.

Turnover and absenteeism as output factors do tend to suggest some negative impact. The company measures turnover as an increase from year to year and the four per cent figure, while not high in absolute terms, is higher than expected in somewhat depressed employment conditions. The absenteeism figure at ten per cent is also historically high and somewhat unexpected for the same reason.

The one output factor that may have the most significant bearing on these results is the question of grievance handling. Interviews with the union suggested that they were quite unhappy with management's legalistic and obstructionist approach to the grievance process. This was partly historical and more recently due to the two major participants adopting very adversarial postures. This development had come to be widely known in the plant and given the evident union support would likely be surfacing as a negative influence.

The model seems to be reasonably explanatory in the case of Base Industries. Critical economic, ecological and social development issues have created a very competitive and difficult environment for the automotive industry. Base's response has been to adjust by adopting state of the art technology and a strictly controlled manufacturing function with high vertical differentiation. They appear to have sacrificed lateral differentiation to this critical issue of manufacturing control and efficiency. Because they produce a limited product line, using well-established technology, they can apparently get the efficiency they desire without the need for strong lateral relationships. The result of this arrangement in model terms is an organizational characteristic of low 'flexibility'. This indicates that decision-making is not widely shared, that decision making does not span many levels in the hierarchy, and that there is rather limited functional specialization. In the latter case this does not appear to be true for Base but when one considers the interview evidence it is clear that only the manufacturing department, because of its size and centrality, had much decision-making authority.

The low 'flexibility' generated as a major input factor in the system can then be related to the intervening variable of the workplace industrial relations climate. Because decision making is not shared and enough management levels are not involved there is a workplace climate perception about low 'fairness', low 'consultation', and low 'mutual regard'. The workplace climate perception does not deteriorate further because it is bolstered by better-than-average perceptions about union legitimacy and union support.

The lower than average workplace climate scores then relate to similar system output scores. Perceptions regarding low fairness and consultation could trigger the historically high turnover and absenteeism results. Low consultation perceptions and strong union support may well result in the bitter feelings about the grievance process that combined with the former output factors, yield a predictably less than average industrial relations outcome result.

RICHMOND FURNITURE LTD

It is a blatantly obvious observation that industrial relations managers seldom look forward to contract negotiations. Notwithstanding this assertion, Bill Butler was particularly apprehensive about the impending bargaining at Richmond Furniture Ltd. Things had reached a peak last Friday when Jim Thompson, the operators' Vice-President, had informed him that the US owners, previously noninterfering, were making noises about shutting the plant if the impending settlement was as generous as the last one. It was clearly no empty threat because the Canadian plant was losing money and, although the red ink was largely attributable to a major expansion, this would not be likely to alter the head office position. The US owners had given their blessing to the expansion plan but had apparently become disenchanted as the anticipated pay-back was slower than expected. Canadian management, Butler included, thought that the big increase in Canadian market share to the current 40 per cent, and a little patience waiting for the market to improve, would get the operation back on track with the five-year business plan. However, the latest message from Canadian VP Thompson was that US patience was wearing thin and that Canadian negotiations were going to be a high profile issue at US head office. Butler was told to expect a telephone call shortly from his US counterpart which in turn was expected to reveal a more definitive picture of the parent company position.

The call was more than Butler had bargained for. After the usual pleasantries, Evert Floyd, the parent IR Manager, steered the conversation to contract negotiations and his tone began to change. Floyd expressed a very strong concern about the outcome of negotiations and then quietly dropped a bomb. The parent company wanted two of their own executives to sit on the Canadian bargaining team. Never before had this been attempted or even suggested and Floyd's protestations that it was not interference but just a new and more active interest rang a rather false and ominous note. Butler quickly concluded that the traditional and largely autonomous relationship with the US had taken a significant turn and so, he feared, would the relationship with the union.

The Richmond Furniture Ltd union was an in-house organization that had experienced substantial growing pains from a 30 per cent per annum growth in its membership over the past three years. Things in general were pretty upbeat. The contract of two years ago stood as a pretty clear union victory: management had yielded far more on the issues than had the union, and Butler expected that the rumours about a new sense of union clout were probably true. There was already some confirmation of this in the significant increase of union grievances; a development far more noticeable than the typical posturing expected prior to negotiations. In fact, it was not only the increasing incidence of grievances but the emerging militant and legalistic attitude that concerned Butler. There had been no change in the union executive; its strategies were still orchestrated and clearly dominated by its president Joe Miller. Butler, on good evidence, believed that most of the union members – now consisting of 85 per cent of the work-force – were rather docile and content to let Miller and the union executive be 'the union'. Miller's attitude, and particularly any impending change, would have to surface in the next few weeks.

The flexing of the union's new muscle came as no particular surprise and it did not appear to be the new blood in the membership that had made it more militant. The arousal factor seemed to originate with the overtures of the United Auto Workers International at the last contract time who wanted to become the new bargaining agent at Richmond. Management was adamant in its resistance to the UAW as a replacement for the in-house union.

In retrospect, the last settlement seemed to reflect a fear of the potential influence of the UAW although, at the time, Butler felt management had not been that transparent in the negotiations. Evidence had mounted to the contrary, and now Butler suspected that the union sensed a rather sensitive management pressure point for the impending bargaining. It would remain to be seen how hard they pressed. A meeting with Miller was on the morning agenda and Butler hoped that some clue to the union strategy might be revealed.

Miller was somewhat stereotypical of the union boss in his forceful and unyielding manner. Nevertheless he was very knowledgeable and articulate in labour matters. He also had a reputation for enjoying power, which he definitely possessed at Richmond; it was for this very reason that Butler expected he wanted to keep the in-house union.

At the meeting, Miller appeared particularly buoyant, and even somewhat smug. Though the two men interacted quite compatibly, Butler felt the urge to prick the Miller 'balloon', and the Floyd bombshell of this morning would probably do the trick. Butler could easily rationalize that management would have to reveal changes in its bargaining team at some point anyway. Butler decided to wait for a good opportunity.

Miller was in an expansive mood at the meeting and began by recounting recent union developments. Membership, he noted, had doubled to 400 people and ninety per cent representation in a short three-year period. Notwithstanding this growth and the associated growing pains, plant productivity had improved substantially. The union had also helped to bring a new plant location on stream and was enjoying the attendant improvement in working conditions. Miller suggested, in an oblique way, that these developments were largely union accomplishments, conveniently forgetting the significant company investment in new equipment during this same period. However, in concluding his piece, Miller suggested that things could be better. In particular he mentioned that improvement in employee benefits had developed into a very important issue in union discussions since the last contract. The topic of improvement in employee benefits had been introduced by the union in the last contract discussions but the distance that needed breaching at that time was so great that its current mention made Butler apprehensive. To make matters worse, the major item in the benefit package, it seemed, was going to be pension improvements.

It seemed a good time to pull in the reins so Butler interjected with his announcement about the two head office members of the management bargaining team. The effect on Miller was immediate; head office was known for its resistance to the encroachment of benefits, particularly pensions, into the contract negotiations. The threat hung almost palpably in the room. Miller seemed to ponder quietly, and then quietly erupted. His well-controlled voice had an almost lethal edge. Canadian management, he said, had been exposed and this proved they hadn't the balls to stand up to the Yankee owners. It was a big sell-out and management could expect their wimpy behaviour to have a serious effect on the impending bargaining. Would Miller let the US union president come and negotiate a Canadian contract? Miller suggested that the union team should go to the States and bargain where the real decisions were made.

Butler, his ploy of deflating Miller having gone somewhat astray, attempted to retrench by minimizing the US influence at the bargaining table. Miller was unconvinced. He reminded Butler that relations with management had been quite amicable in the past and that management had the relatively easy task of facing an in-house union. Negotiations, he pointed out, were never very lengthy or heated and, until the last contract, management had been the perpetual winner. Now when the union was trying to regain some lost ground and particularly to get more benefits for its membership, management called in the hard-liners from the south. Miller knew them, he said. Snot-nosed kids with MBAs, who knew nothing of the company and union history and cared even less was his description of them. Well, the union would wait and see but Miller could operate his team without any imports and if it came to that the union would show the Yanks that somebody in Canada had a backbone.

Butler tried, without success, to defuse Miller's anger, although he found he could be only half-hearted because he somehow felt there was the glow of truth in Miller's reaction. He reminded Miller that Richmond Furniture Ltd was a family-controlled company in the US; that it was concerned about its employees, and had a pretty high ranking on benefit provision as US firms went. It sounded apologetic; Butler and Miller both seemed to know it and Butler was further disappointed in himself for playing so obviously into Miller's hands.

Miller rose to go and summarized his view of the situation quite bluntly as he left. Management had had it good but if they were calling in the big guns the union could also play that game. This was obviously Miller's counter to Butler's threat of head office interference; he asked if Miller meant the UAW. Miller left the office without replying.

Butler was thoroughly disconsolate following the meeting, and though he knew he had to report to VP Thompson he wanted a little time to reflect. Butler thought about the Richmond Furniture Ltd organization and its management. The management structure was relatively flat and accessible from the bottom. Only three management layers were encountered getting from the shop floor to the top plant management. Nor were these hierarchical barriers considered very rigid, with the possible exception of the VP of production, Butler felt that a rather easy familiarity permeated employee relations in the plant. This atmosphere seemed to have contributed to a state of mutual respect and had paved the way for relatively smooth negotiations in the past. The fact that there had never been a strike, and little other industrial action, seemed to reinforce this conclusion.

Most of the plant-operating decisions involved the lower supervisory group and this in turn kept the non-salaried employees reasonably well informed. Planning decisions, on the other hand, were quite centralized, involving only the VP of Operations and various diad relations between himself and other functions. There was no management committee and therefore no strong sense of team involvement in planning endeavours.

Thompson maintained clear control of company activities. He knew the business in all its major aspects, technical, financial, and marketing. Producing upholstered furniture was not a highly technical process, but having state of the art equipment was essential to competing in this price-sensitive market. Thompson knew enough to ensure that Richmond Furniture Ltd got this equipment. From a market standpoint the few major products had changed very little over the companies' history and Canadian preference for it remained strong. There was continued high demand, with only two other competitors and largely unchanging conditions. In this environment

Thompson ran a tight ship. The recent three-year growth spurt had put his powers of control to the test, and from two unexpected sources – the US management, and the plant union. Thompson had maintained his directive approach throughout the difficult period, and while Butler thought it was time for more team-type activity, involving both managers and the union, he had found it difficult to convince his boss. Butler felt that Thompson's relationship with the union was coloured by the chief executive officer's belief that they were only interested in money. The last contract had reinforced this opinion and, strangely enough, it was bolstered by similar comments even from some of the union executive.

Butler found the parallels between the management and union operations rather interesting. Both embraced a philosophy of top-level control. The effect was more apparent on the management side and certainly Miller gave the constant public impression that he was expressing the wishes of the membership in his dealings with management. In reality, Butler knew that Miller and his three union executives initiated and sold most of the ideas that had come forward in Miller's eight-year tenure. The union itself had existed for only fifteen years. This time period had been difficult in many ways for the union. Unemployment had been high not only in the area but throughout the country since the early 1980s and apart from positions for skilled workers, which applied to only 10 per cent of the Richmond Furniture Ltd work-force, jobs were very scarce. It was consequently difficult to push wage demands, and only the threat of a raiding attempt by the UAW had strengthened the union position.

The company's employment practices tended to emphasize work experience, and the internal filling of vacancies. Seniority was established as the primary criterion for filling new job openings, although the average seniority had declined from almost ten to two years. Management had not taken advantage of the soft labour market to push merit criteria in job postings. Whether in response to the latter situation or not, the union had exhibited a low absentee rate of 5 per cent, which was comparable to the management rate. Turnover had been extremely low – less than one person per week on average for the past five years.

Management acceptance of seniority as a promotion principal had created a difficulty in the supervision ranks where many were getting rather long in the tooth. This was not conducive to the development of the new techniques and procedures that were necessary to make the new equipment effective. Management and union members both complained about this situation.

The union membership at Richmond Furniture Ltd was reported to be rather inactive. It trusted its executive to get what it could get and that appeared to be mostly wage concessions. Since negotiations only occurred once every two years there was little to do in the mean time. Other than money, only grievances seemed to attact member attention, and recently the union had been very busy at this activity. This development, combined with a new appetite for benefits, and the lurking threat of the UAW suggested that negotiations with the union might be working up a more strongly adversarial position.

The foregoing description of the situation at Richmond Furniture Ltd translated into some rather distinctive conditions as related to the workplace industrial relations climate model. The most dramatic of these features was the very low score registered on structural 'flexibility'. Basically this measure indicates the amount of sharing, laterally and vertically, that occurs in the decision-making process. This low score would reflect the fact that the management did not tend to share the more important decisions with others in the organization. True, the structure was rather flat and reasonably informal but there was not much functional specialization and management clearly attempted to maintain tight control.

The 'bureaucratic' structure, which assessed vertical and horizontal complexity, the extent of rules and regulations, and the true level of decision-making, was about average (at 85 vs the sample average of 86.2).

Also diverging significantly from the sample was the result measuring the human resource practices; in effect the extent of total training and initiatives in this area. This would impact negatively on the workplace climate results, and also presumably on the output of the system or the industrial relations output. Other system input elements did not appear important since they were all in the 'average' range.

The workplace climate results turn out to be below average at Richmond – but only slightly so (56.9 vs 58.2). Thus the low scores on 'flexibility' and 'human resource' practices appeared to have had only a very small negative impact. The workplace climate results therefore appear to support the model in being negative, but the relationship in this case is clearly weak.

The industrial relations outcomes as applied to the Richmond data are also below average, but again not dramatically so. The slightly negative workplace climate data could be perceived as creating corresponding negative industrial relations outcomes. The absence of any recent industrial action, strikes, or high rates of turnover and absenteeism, tended to keep the outcomes score within the average range.

DENMAN LTD

Denman Ltd is a small textile firm that has operated quietly but profitably in the same small-town location for nearly forty years. It is rather unique on all three counts; its survival as a threatened textile species, its past and current profitability, and its successful adaptation to life in Martinville.

The town of Martinville is an anachronism. It lies within easy commuting distance of metropolitan Toronto but its way of life is far removed from that of a typical modern city. Martinville is predominantly Mennonite and it maintains a traditional way of life as a bulwark against the frenzied pace and shifting mores of the modern urban society that surrounds it. This devotion to an ancestral religious heritage, to its ways, and to its values, pervades the town and much of the surrounding rural area which is also predominantly Mennonite. Set within this old-world order there is also a modern commercial world. This includes a number of well-known Canadian enterprises with substantial investments in the town, and whose operations provide an economic base for Martinville's prosperity.

In a sense, these cultures form two solitudes since the old-order traditions are essentially hostile to modern commerce. Nevertheless they have arrived at an accommodation where the Mennonites, on their own terms, provide services and labour to the business community. The Mennonites will not integrate; they tend to import and export from a closed society according to stringent roles of propriety. Mennonite labour is highly sought after because of the strongly associated work ethic and a resistance to any kind of labour protest. Since this ethnic group is a significant part of the available work-force, its influence is felt throughout the commercial sector in terms of employment conditions, policies, and treatment of employees, and in general affects the state of industrial peace in Martinville.

In this context Denman is one of Martinville's better known and more prosperous industries. It was founded in 1951 by a local family and maintained this family ownership until 1985. Since then, it has gone through two ownership changes. The first was an unhappy, but fortunately short, interlude with an American owner who reportedly did not understand, and quickly grew disenchanted with, the textile business. The second and now current owners, also American, entered with a more understanding and commodious approach toward both the Denman operation and the business itself. Most notably, the new owners have indicated through their planning and investment programmes that they are committed to the business for the long haul.

Apart from the recent changes in ownership, Denman's history has been without significant incident. It has established a reputation as a good employer in the town and receives high grades on corporate citizenship. Few differences have arisen regarding the town's and the company's interests and this happy state of affairs is reinforced by the company's unblemished record for maintaining industrial peace.

If there is a dominant theme in Denman's history it is one of relative prosperity. The company has a limited product range of knitted and pile fabrics but it dominates the market with a significant two-thirds market share. Its focal products are neither fashion-driven nor high profile so it is protected from fashion swings on the one hand and the attention of potential competitors on the other. Also advantageous is the fact that market entry is rather costly which, combined with a relatively small market, tends to deter new entrants. Not least important, the product also demands considerable technical expertise in order to maintain acceptable quality standards, and this capability takes time to develop. For all these reasons, Denman tends to be largely unchallenged in its market niche. Consequently one senses an atmosphere of success at Denman. There is a perceptible confidence at the management level which is probably grounded in its ability to generate consistent profits in a difficult industry.

Reinforcing these favourable market and technical factors are some similarly favourable conditions on the input side. Martinville has had comparatively high unemployment conditions for almost a decade, a situation that has included a fairly substantial pool of skilled workers. Consequently, Denman has found it relatively easy to hire both the workers and the skills it needs for its operations.

For Denman the dominant theme of prosperity has been reinforced with another theme – productivity. It is this latter focus that is credited with gaining Denman both market share and profitability. While the production technology related to knitting and finishing processes is generally characterized as stable it is nevertheless considered vitally important to have the latest in reliable high speed equipment in order to sustain low production costs. Quality is a key success factor as well and it, too, depends on utilization of the best equipment. Quality further relies on process expertise which Denman has developed in its highly skilled and experienced workforce. A craft approach to the finished product goes hand-in-hand with good technical equipment and Denman can access labour with craft-type attitudes quite easily in Martinville.

The new owners tend to appreciate the critical aspect of getting the best technical equipment and matching this with quality-minded workers in the production process. They have actively followed this approach while giving Denman's management virtual autonomy in achieving the targeted results. Because the characteristics of the product do not change much, Denman has been able to concentrate its efforts on a high quality, high production strategy.

The Denman strategy noted above has tended to focus management attention more on the production process than on the product markets. A significant issue arises here as to how fully management and plant workers share the productivity and quality objectives of the firm. This congruence will be reflected in their relations both past and present and in the workplace climate that has developed.

The workplace industrial relations climate at Denman can be characterized as quite co-operative. This can be attributed to a number of reasons, including the small-town environment, high area unemployment, non-confrontational attitudes in the work-force, and consistently successful operations. Added to this is the effect of ownership over the first thirty-five years of existence by a family that had developed a reputation of sincere concern for the worker's welfare. In return, or by ethnic persuasion, or both, the employees generally seem to exhibit a commitment to the company and to its objectives. These overlapping interests are specifically expressed by both management and worker groups.

The workplace climate is also affected by the structure of the organization. It is an important influence in that it impacts upon the interests, autonomy, and ability of the focal parties to achieve their goals. Methods of characterizing the structure of the workplace are rather varied, but the current model identifies certain specific structural elements for consideration. One such element is the matter of structural 'flexibility' and is defined as the degree of lateral and vertical sharing in the decision-making process, combined with a measure of functional specialization. The hypothetical effect would be that of a positive correlation between flexibility and workplace climate.

In addition to 'flexibility', the model identifies an element referred to as 'bureaucratic structure'. This variable includes three other sub-elements of 'structural complexity', 'formality', and the decision-making 'centralization'. A negative correlation would be expected with 'bureaucratic' structure.

Specific indicators of 'flexibility' at Denman show that decisions do not tend to span many levels in the organization. This is particularly true of major policy and strategic decisions, which are largely confined to a small management group. These types of decisions do not usually involve participants below the director or fifth level of management. Functional specialization, which completes the measure of 'flexibility', was not highly developed at Denman except in the plant.

The foregoing factors taken in combination would suggest a low degree of flexibility which, in fact, occurred. Denman registered the second-lowest score in the sample and was far below the average (41 vs 79.3).

The result for bureaucratic structure was also well below average (77 vs. 86.2). This would suggest a tendency to exhibit a less complex structure in terms of total vertical and horizontal differentiation, less formalization with respect to rules and procedures, and real decision-making taking place at lower organization levels. The two former conditions fit the pattern at Denman, whereas the latter seems to contradict the flexibility data. However, the measure attempts to identify the lowest level at which decisions are made, not the number and importance of these decisions. Many day-to-day operational decisions could be made at lower levels, contributing to a lower result on the bureaucratic nature. The types and incidence of these decisions may not increase the organizational flexibility.

When 'flexibility' and bureaucratic structure are considered together, the impact on the workplace climate would be negative but not significantly so since they would operate in different directions. However, other model input factors such as union history and union–management relations must be considered before assessing the final effects.

The union structure at Denman was less formal and less centralized than management. Procedures for decision making called for membership input, with all-important issues subject to membership vote. In addition, most individuals were reported to have ready access to the union executive. Denman is a small union which covers primarily the plant workers – all of whom belong to it. The union influence and power is probably best indicated by its strong control of the job-manning process. It is a union shop and membership is mandatory. Along with this there is strong emphasis on seniority for both promotions and newly created jobs.

The union at Denman is an international – the Amalgamated Clothing and Textile Workers. All plant workers belong and this covers 73 per cent of the employees. The structure of the local is quite typical, being fairly flat and having only four rather informal levels of authority between the plant steward and the international office. This structure includes the chief steward, the union vice-president, and the union president. Access by members to the union president is apparently unencumbered.

The international office provides a representative to assist in the local bargaining process who, with the local's president, vice-president, and chief steward form the bargaining team. There is only one union at the Denman plant and it covers all employee groups. The local union reports minimal to non-existent interference from the international body. The role of the international is predominantly advisory and mostly confined to bargaining strategies. This support, however, often includes explicit assistance in the event of a new local union executive. The international role, even in this case, has typically been to help achieve previously-set local objectives. The determination of local bargaining objectives at Denman is also rather typical in that the local executive, with somewhat sporadic member input, develops a slate of issues which are vetted at periodic union meetings. However, active individual members or groups can reportedly have a significant impact on the content of the bargaining slate. Nevertheless member interest in the union is reported to be lukewarm in the interval between contract negotiations and is apparently triggered more by individual grievance issues than group bargaining issues.

Contract negotiations typically centre on local issues and these have not changed for some period of time – at least within the recall of the current negotiators. Productivity, as discussed earlier, has dominated negotiations at least since the mid-1970s; a time when Canadian industry received a general scare from foreign competition. As a result, it became fashionable to parade the productivity issue into collective bargaining negotiations.

Interestingly, the local at Denman had long accepted productivity as a mutual problem and entered discussions willing to shoulder its share of the responsibility. Consequently, since the mid-1970s, and even more so in the 1980s, the union has co-operated in management productivity efforts by accepting new equipment changes, revised output standards, overtime work, and a number of retraining programmes. Management in turn has been very pleased with the union's attitude of relatively open co-operation in this area and regards this as a key factor in what they describe as open and generally peaceful negotiations.

The other major negotiating issue continues, not surprisingly, to be the matter of wage rates. The union sees the wage issue clearly tied to that of productivity in that it wants to get its share of the improvement that it helps to create. The arguments apparently shift back and forth in fairly predictable fashion regarding who is responsible for what improvement and therefore entitled to what compensation.

More important than the specific arguments here is to note that this issue generates most of the tension that does exist during bargaining.

Management, for its part, feels it has been too generous with wages in the past, and in the last two contract settlements has argued for industry-based settlements. The union counters with its preference for a geographical base but, even more importantly, presses the principle of monetary participation in productivity gains. Since Denman has maintained generally strong profitability through most of its history, discussions on sharing are usually rather protracted. No strike has ever occurred at Denman, but the last contract (1984) rather narrowly avoided a strike over wage rates. Interviews with central members of the negotiating parties indicate that, while relations are quite amicable, the issue of wages and particularly their productivity component will gain even more prominence as a potential strike issue in the future.

Non-management personnel, according to both union and management officials, harbour quite positive feelings toward the Denman organization. The union is certainly non-militant in the generally accepted sense of the word; however, it believes it has done well in getting wage increases, benefits and better working conditions for the membership. Indeed, management's well-known dissatisfaction with the high wage rates is often used to illustrate the union's success and may contribute to the current upbeat union attitude.

Union success at Denman has not been an unmixed blessing, having created some degree of complacency in the membership. Union representatives report low interest in union activities and little commitment to it other than occasional situations involving worker rights. If events affect someone personally, such as rights grievances, the membership reacts with a strong and united front; otherwise there seems little interest in its activities or aims. Additionally, at contract time interest is predictably piqued and the membership becomes increasingly involved and more confrontational.

Grievances, according to union opinion, are handled by management with reasonable dispatch. The union's only consistent complaint is that the management tends to involve itself too early in the grievance procedure. No particular explanation is given for this except that management appears over-zealous in its efforts to demonstrate its concern with any contractual problems. The membership would prefer to solve more of the problems at lower levels and feels that this would contribute to a more effective grievance process.

The foregoing conditions describe what the model generally refers to as 'workable relations' in the firm. It assesses, among others, factors like the favourable outcome of negotiations and the informality of the grievance process. For Denman, the results on this factor are below but relatively close to the average. The general tenor of relationships here seemed to be quite positive and, though below average, was still in the top range for the thirteen firms in the manufacturing category. Furthermore, from the viewpoint of affecting the average position, this result on 'workable relations' would have only minimal impact.

The data on workplace industrial relations climate itself shows Denman slightly below the sample average (56.6 vs. 58.2). Three specific measures receive lower-than-average rating; fairness, mutual regard and union support. The divergence from the average is, however, quite minimal, nor would much difference be expected from interview data covering these matters. The largest percentage difference was in the low score on member-support for the union.

It would appear that the major input factors that showed any large variability were working in opposing directions at Denman and the result was a slightly less than average workplace climate score.

The output of the system would tend to comply with this average result. The total industrial relation outcome score was slightly below the average. This reflects fairly average turnover rates (4.2 per cent) and absenteeism rates (3.2 per cent). Also keeping this 'output' score low would be the fact that Denman has never experienced a strike. The slightly negative direction of the score may be reflecting the slightly lower-than-average climate scores noted earlier.

References

Abbey, A. and Dickson, J. W. (1983) 'Work climate and innovation in semiconductors', *Academy of Management Journal* 26: 362–8.

Academy of Management Review (1989) 'Special forum on theory building', *Academy of Management Review* 14 (4).

Adams, W. and Mueller, H. (1986) 'The steel industry', in W. Adams (ed.) *The Structure of American Industry*, 7th edition: 74–125, New York: Macmillan.

Althauser, R. P. and Kalleberg, A. L. (1981) 'Firms, occupations and the structure of labour markets: a conceptual analysis', in I. Berg (ed.) *Sociological Perspectives on Labor Markets*, 119–49, New York: Academic Press.

Anderson, J. C., Gunderson, M., and Ponak, A. (1989) 'Frameworks for the study of industrial relations', in J. C. Anderson *et al.* (eds) *Union–Management Relations in Canada*, 2nd edition: 1–22, Don Mills, Ontario: Addison-Wesley.

Angle, H. L. and Perry, J. L. (1986) 'Dual commitment and labor–management relationship climates', *Academy of Management Journal* 29: 31–50.

Ansari, M. A., Baumgartel, H., and Sullivan, G. (1982) 'The personal orientation – organizational climate *fit* and managerial success', *Human Relations* 35: 1159–78.

Appelbaum, E. and Albin, P. (1989) 'Computer rationalization and the transformation of work: lessons from the insurance industry', in S. Wood (ed.) *The Transformation of Work?* 247–65, London: Unwin Hyman.

Argyris, C. (1958) 'Some problems in conceptualising organizational climate: a case study of a bank', *Administrative Science Quarterly* 2: 501–20.

Armstrong, P. (1989) 'Limits and possibilities for HRM in an age of management accountancy', in J. Storey (ed.) *New Perspectives on Human Resource Management*, 154–66, London: Routledge.

Ashforth, B. E. (1985) 'Climate formation: issues and extensions', *Academy of Management Review* 10: 837–47.

Atkinson, J. (1984) 'Manpower strategies for flexible organizations', *Personnel Management*, August: 28–31.

Bain, G. (1970) *The Growth of White-Collar Unionism*, Oxford: Clarendon Press.

Bain, G. (1986) 'Introduction to a symposium on the role and influence of trade unions in a recession', *British Journal of Industrial Relations* 24: 157–9.

Bamber, G. (1989) 'Flexibility of work organization: an international comparison', paper presented at a conference 'A Flexible Future', Cardiff Business School, September.

Barbash, J. (1975) 'The unions as a bargaining organization: some implications to organizational behaviour', *Proceedings of Industrial Relations Research Association*.

Barkin, S. (1987) 'The flexibility debate in western Europe', *Relations Industrielles* 42: 12–45.

Bassett, P. (1986) *Strike Free*, London: Macmillan.

Beaumont, P. B. (1990) *Change in Industrial Relations: The Organization and Environment*, London: Routledge.

Billings, R. S. and Wroten, S. P. (1978) 'Use of path analysis of industrial/ organization psychology: criticisms and suggestions', *Journal of Applied Psychology* 63: 677–88.

Blauner, R. (1964) *Alienation and Freedom*, Chicago: University of Chicago Press.

Blyton, P. (1989a) 'Hours of work', in R. Bean (ed.) *International Labour Statistics*, 127–45, London: Routledge.

Blyton, P. (1989b) 'Working population and employment', in R. Bean (ed.) *International Labour Statistics*, 18–49, London: Routledge.

Blyton, P. (1991) 'Flexibility' in B. Towers (ed.) *The HRM Handbook*, Oxford: Basil Blackwell.

Blyton, P., Dastmalchian, A., and Adamson, R. (1987) 'The concept of industrial relations climate', *Journal of Industrial Relations* 29: 207–16.

Blyton, P. and Morris, J. (1991) (eds) *A Flexible Future?* Berlin: De Gruyter.

Boyer, R. (ed.) (1988) *The Search for Labour Market Flexibility: The European Economies in Transition*, Oxford: Clarendon Press.

Brass, D. J. (1981) 'Structural relationships, job characteristics, and worker satisfaction and performance', *Administrative Science Quarterly* 26: 331–48.

Brett, J. M. (1980) 'Behavioural research on unions and union–management systems', in B. M. Staw and L. L. Cummings (eds) *Research in Organizational Behaviour* 2: 177–213, Greenwich CT: JAI Press.

Brett, J. M. and Goldberg, S. D. (1979) 'Wildcat strikes in bituminous coal mining', *Industrial and Labor Relations Review* 32: 465–83.

Brogden, P. M. (1949) 'A new coefficient: application to biserial correlation and to estimation of selective efficiency', *Psychometrika* 14: 169–82.

Buchan, J. (1989) 'A hard won but fragile prosperity', *Financial Times*, 19 May.

Burns, T. and Stalker, G. (1961) *The Management of Innovation*, London: Tavistock.

Carter, N. M. and Cullen, J. B. (1984) 'A comparison of centralization/ decentralization of decision-making concepts and measures', *Journal of Management* 10: 259–68.

Casey, B. (1988) *Temporary Employment Practices and Policies in Britain*, London: Policy Studies Institute.

Child, J. (1972) 'Organizational structure and strategies of control: a replication of the Aston study', *Administrative Science Quarterly* 17: 163–77.

Child, J. (1984a) *Organizations: Guide to Problems and Practice*, 2nd edition, London: Chapman.

Child, J. (1984b) 'New technology and developments in management organization', *Omega* 12: 211–23.

Child, J. (1985) 'Managerial strategies, new technology and the labour process' in D. Knights, H. Willmott, and D. Collinson (eds) *Job Redesign: Critical Perspectives on the Labour Process*, 107–41, Aldershot: Gower.

Clegg, H. A. (1979) *The System of Industrial Relations in Great Britain*, Oxford: Basil Blackwell.

Collard, R. and Dale, B. (1989) 'Quality circles', in K. Sisson (ed.) *Personnel Management in Britain*, 356–77, Oxford: Basil Blackwell.

Cooke, W. N. (1989) 'Improving productivity through collaboration', *Industrial Relations* 28: 299–319.

Coombs, R. and Green, K. (1989) 'Work organization and product change in the service sector: the case of the U.K. National Health Service', in S. Wood (ed.) *The Transformation of Work?* 279–94, London: Unwin Hyman.

Coser, L. A. (1956) *The Functions of Social Conflict*, London: Routledge & Kegan Paul.

Craig, A. W. J. (1983) *The System of Industrial Relations in Canada*, Scarborough, Ont.: Prentice–Hall.

Cronbach, L. J. (1951) 'Coefficient alpha and the internal structure of tests', *Psychometrika* 16: 297–334.

Cross, M. (1988) 'Changes in working practices in UK manufacturing 1981–1988', *Industrial Relations Review and Report* 415: 2–10.

Crowther, S. and Garrahan, P. (1988) 'Invitation to Sunderland: corporate power and the local economy', *Industrial Relations Journal* 19: 51–9.

Daft, R. L. (1988) *Organization Theory and Design*, St Paul MN: West.

Daniel, W. W. and Millward, N. (1983) *Workplace Industrial Relations in Britain*, London: Heinemann.

Dastmalchian, A. (1984) 'Environmental dependencies and company structure in Britain', *Organization Studies* 5: 227–41.

Dastmalchian, A. (1986) 'Environmental characteristics and organizational climate: an exploratory study', *Journal of Management Studies* 23: 609–33.

Dastmalchian, A. and Adamson, R. (1984) 'Organizational climate and labour–management relationship: exploring the concept of industrial relations climate', in H. Abravel (ed.) *Organizational Behaviour* 5: 53–60, Guelph: Administrative Sciences Association of Canada.

Dastmalchian, A., Adamson, R., and Blyton, P. (1985) 'Measuring industrial relations climate: key actor opinions', *Proceedings of the National Conference of the Association of Human Resource Management and Organizational Behaviour*, 647–51, Boston.

Dastmalchian, A., Adamson, R., and Blyton, P. (1986) 'Developing a measure of industrial relations climate', *Relations Industrielles* 41: 851–9.

Dastmalchian, A. and Blyton, P. (1989) 'Organizational structure, human resource practices and company industrial relations', Paper presented at European Group on Organization Studies (EGOS) Conference, Berlin, July.

Dastmalchian, A., Blyton, P., and Abdollahyan, R. (1982) 'Industrial relations climate and company effectiveness', *Personnel Review* 11: 35–9.

Dastmalchian, A., Blyton, P., and Adamson, R. (1989) 'Industrial relations climate: testing a construct', *Journal of Occupational Psychology* 62: 21–32.

Dastmalchian, A. and Javidan, M. (1987) 'Centralization and organizational context: an analysis of Canadian public enterprises', *Canadian Journal of Administrative Sciences* 4: 302–19.

Dastmalchian, A. and Ng, I. (1990) 'Examining the relationship between industrial relations climate and grievance outcomes', *Relations Industrielles* 45.

Derber, M., Chalmers, W. E., and Stagner, R. (1985) 'Environmental variables and union–management accommodation', *Industrial and Labor Relations Review* 11: 413–28.

Dion, G. and Hebert, G. (1989) 'L'avenir du syndicalisme au Canada', *Relations Industrielles* 44: 5–24.

Doeringer, P. B. and Piore, M. J. (1971) *Internal Labour Markets and Manpower Analysis*, Lexington, Mass.: Heath.

Donaldson, L. (1985) *In Defence of Organization Theory*, Cambridge: Cambridge University Press.

Drexler, J. A. (1977) 'Organizational climate: its homogeneity within organizations', *Journal of Applied Psychology* 62: 38–42.

Duncan, O. D. (1966) 'Path analysis: sociological examples', *American Journal of Sociology* 72: 1–16.

Dunlop, J. T. (1958) *Industrial Relations Systems*, New York: Holt.

Eisele, C. F. (1974) 'Organization size, technology and frequency of strikes', *Industrial and Labor Relations Review* 27: 566–71.

Ekvall, G. (1987) 'The climate metaphor in organization theory', in B. M. Bass and P. D. J. Drenth (eds) *Advances in Organizational Psychology: An International Review*, 177–90, Beverly Hills: Sage.

Emerson, R. M. (1962) 'Power dependence relations', *American Sociological Review* 27: 31–41.

Enderwick, P. (1985) 'Ownership nationality and industrial relations practices in British non-manufacturing industries', *Industrial Relations Journal* 16: 50–59.

Fox, A. (1974) *Beyond Contract: Work, Power and Trust Relations*, London: Faber.

Freeman, R. B. (1989) 'What does the future hold for U.S. unionism?', *Relations Industrielles* 44: 25–46.

Glick, W. H. (1985) 'Conceptualizing and measuring organizational and psychological climate', *Academy of Management Review* 10: 601–16.

Glick, W. H. (1988) 'Organizations are not central tendencies: shadowboxing in the dark, round 2', *Academy of Management Review* 13: 133–7.

Gouldner, A. (1954) *Wildcat Strike*, Yellow Springs: Antioch College.

Guest, D. 'Human resource management: its implications for industrial relations and trade unions', in J. Storey (ed.) *New Perspectives on Human Resource Management*, 41–55, London: Routledge.

Hage, J. (1980) *Theories of Organizations: Forms, Process and Transformation*, New York: Wiley.

Hakim, C. (1987) 'Trends in the flexible workforce', *Employment Gazette*, 95: 549–60.

Hakim, C. (1988) 'Homeworking in Britain', in R. Pahl (ed.) *On Work: Historical, Comparative and Theoretical Approaches*, 609–22, Oxford: Basil Blackwell.

Harris, C. W. (1967) 'On factors and factor scores', *Psychometrika* 32: 363–79.

Hoerr, J. P. (1988) *And The Wolf Finally Came: The Decline of the American Steel Industry*, Pittsburgh: University of Pittsburgh Press.

Hudson, R. and Sadler, D. (1989) *The International Steel Industry: Restructuring, State Policies and Localities*, London: Routledge.

Hughes, J. J. (1989) 'Unemployment', in R. Bean (ed.) *International Labour Statistics*, 50–76, London: Routledge.

Hutchins, D. (1988) *Just In Time*, Aldershot: Gower.

Hyman, R. (1972) *Strikes*, London: Fontana.

Hyman, R. (1975) *Industrial Relations: A Marxist Introduction*, London: Macmillan.

Hyman, R. (1989) *The Political Economy of Industrial Relations: Theory and Practice in a Cold Climate*, London: Macmillan.

Inkson, J. H. K., Pugh, D. S., and Hickson, D. J. (1970) 'Organization context and structure: an abbreviated replication', *Administrative Science Quarterly* 15: 318–29.

Institute of Social Research (1975) *Michigan Organizational Assessment Package: Progress Report II*, Ann Arbor, Mich.: Survey Research Centre, ISR.

International Labour Organization (1986) *Economically Active Population: Estimates and Projections 1950–2025*, 1, Geneva: ILO.

Jacobs, D. (1974) 'Dependence and vulnerability: an exchange approach to the control of organizations', *Administrative Science Quarterly* 19: 45–59.

James, L. R. (1982) 'Aggregation bias in estimates of perceptual agreement', *Journal of Applied Psychology* 67: 219–29.

James, L. R., Demaree, R. G., and Wolf, G. (1984) 'Estimating within-group interrater reliability with and without response bias', *Journal of Applied Psychology* 69: 85–90.

James, L. R. and Jones, A. P. (1974) 'Organizational climate: a review of theory and research', *Psychological Bulletin* 84: 1,096–112.

James, L. R., Joyce, W. F., and Slocum, J. W. jun. (1988) 'Comment: organizations do not cognize', *Academy of Management Review* 13: 129–32.

Joyce, W. F. and Slocum, J. W. (1979) 'Climates in organizations', in S. Kerr (ed.) *Organizational Behaviour*, 317–33, Columbus, Ohio: Grid.

Joyce, W. F. and Slocum, J. W. (1984) 'Collective climate: agreement as a basis for defining aggregate climates in organizations', *Academy of Management Journal* 27: 721–42.

Katz, H. C., Kochan, T. A., and Gobeille, K. R. (1983) 'Industrial relations performance, economic performance and QWL programs: an interplant analysis', *Industrial and Labor Relations Review* 37: 3–17.

Kelly, J. (1988) *Trade Unions and Socialist Politics*, London: Verso.

Kelly, J. E. and Nicholson, N. (1980) 'The causation of strikes: review of theoretical approaches and potential contribution of social psychology', *Human Relations* 33: 853–83.

Knights, D. and Willmott, H. (eds) (1990) *Labour Process Theory*, London: Macmillan.

Kochan, T. A. (1980) *Collective Bargaining and Industrial Relations: From Theory to Policy and Practice*, Homewood, IL: Irwin.

Kochan, T., Katz, H., and McKersie, R. B. (1986) *The Transformation of American Industrial Relations*, New York: Basic Books.

Kochan, T., McKersie, R., and Cappelli, P. (1984) 'Strategic choice and industrial relations theory', *Industrial Relations* 23: 16–39.

Kozlowski, S. W. J. and Hults, B. M. (1987) 'An exploration of climates for technical updating and performance', *Personnel Psychology* 40: 539–67.

Levy, P. and Pugh, D. S. (1969) 'Scaling and multivariate analysis in the study of organizational variables', *Sociology* 3: 193–231.

Lewin, D. and Feuille, P. (1983) 'Behavioural research in industrial relations', *Industrial and Labor Relations Review* 36: 341–60.

Lewin, D. and Strauss, G. (1988) 'Introduction to symposium on behavioural research in industrial relations', *Industrial Relations* 27: 1–6.

Lincoln, J. R. and Zeitz, G. (1980) 'Organizational properties from aggregate data: separating individual and structural effects', *American Sociological Review* 45: 391–408.

Litwin, G. H. and Stringer, R. A. (1968) *Motivation and Organizational Climate*, Cambridge, MA: Harvard University Press.

Lockwood, D. (1966) 'Sources of variation in working class images of society', *Sociological Review* 14: 249–67.

McCarthy, W. E. J. (1966) *The Role of Shop Stewards in British Industrial Relations*, Research Paper 1, Royal Commission on Trade Unions and Employers' Associations, London: HMSO.

McKinlay, A. and Starkey, K. (1991) 'Between control and consent: corporate strategy and employee involvement in Ford UK', in P. Blyton and J. Morris (eds) *A Flexible Future?* Berlin: De Gruyter.

McNally, L. (1989) 'An analysis of joint consultation in Saskatchewan organizations', unpublished M.Sc. thesis, College of Commerce, University of Saskatchewan, Saskatoon, Canada.

Mansfield, R. and Payne, R. L. (1977) 'Correlates of variance in perceptions of organizational climate', in D. S. Pugh and R. L. Payne (eds) *Organizational Behaviour in its Context: The Aston Programme III*, 149–59, Farnborough, Hants: Saxon House.

Marchington, M. (1989) 'Joint consultation in practice', in K. Sisson (ed.) *Personnel Management in Britain*, 378–402, Oxford: Basil Blackwell.

Marchington, M. and Parker, P. (1990) *Changing Patterns of Employment Relations*, Brighton: Wheatsheaf.

Marginson, P., Edwards, P. K., Martin, R., Purcell, J., and Sisson, K. (1988) *Beyond the Workplace: Managing Industrial Relations in the Multi-Establishment Enterprise'*, Oxford: Basil Blackwell.

Martin, J. E. (1976) 'Union–management problems in the federal government: an exploratory analysis', *Public Personnel Management* 5: 353–62.

Martin, J. E. and Biasatti, L. L. (1979) 'A hierachy of important elements in union–management relations', *Journal of Management* 5: 229–40.

Massey, D. (1988) 'What's happening to UK manufacturing', in J. Allen and D. Massey (eds) *The Economy in Question*, 45–90, London: Sage.

Meltz, N. (1988) 'A Canadian perspective on a new era of industrial relations', in *New Departures in Industrial Relations: Developments in the U.S., the U.K. and Canada*, Washington D.C.: British–North American Committee.

Meulders, D. and Wilkin, L. (1987) 'Labour market flexibility: critical introduction to the analysis of a concept', *Labour and Society* 12: 3–17.

Micelli, M. P. and Near, J. P. (1985) 'Characteristics of organizational climate and perceived wrongdoing associated with whistleblowing', *Personnel Psychology* 38: 525–44.

Morey, N. C. and Luthans, F. (1985) 'Refining the displacement of culture and the use of senses and themes in organizational studies', *Academy of Management Review* 10: 219–29.

Ng, I. and Dastmalchian, A. (1989) 'Determinants of grievance outcomes: a case study', *Industrial and Labor Relations Review* 42: 393–403.

Nicholson, N. (1976) 'The role of the shop steward', *Industrial Relations Journal* 7: 15–26.

Nicholson, N. (1979) 'Industrial relations climate: a case study approach', *Personnel Review* 8: 20–25.

Nie, N. H., Hull, C. H., Jenkins, J. G., Steinbrenner, K., and Bent, D. H. (1975) *Statistical Package for the Social Sciences*, 2nd edition, New York: McGraw Hill.

Nunnally, J. C. (1978) *Psychometric Theory*, 2nd edition, New York: McGraw–Hill.

Oliver, N. and Wilkinson, B. (1988) *The Japanisation of British Industry*, Oxford: Basil Blackwell.

Organization Studies (1988) special issue: 'Current Trends', *Organization Studies* 9: 1.

Osborne, D. and Blyton, P. (1985) 'Contrasting perspectives on productivity bargaining', *Journal of General Management* 10: 65–78.

Parsons, T. (1964) *Essays in Sociology Theory*, New York: Collier-Macmillan.

Payne, R. L. (1971) 'Organizational climate: the concept and some research findings', *Prakseologia* 39/40, ROK: 143–58.

Payne, R. and Mansfield, R. (1973) 'Relationships of perceptions of organizational climate to organizational structure, context and hierarchical position', *Administrative Science Quarterly* 18: 515–26.

Payne, R. L. and Pugh, D. S. (1976) 'Organizational structure and climate', in M. D. Dunnette (ed.) *Handbook of Industrial and Organizational Psychology*, 1125–73, Chicago: Rand McNally.

Peterson, R. B. (1975) 'The interaction of technological process and perceived organizational climate in Norwegian firms', *Academy of Management Journal* 18: 288–99.

Pfeffer, J. and Cohen, Y. (1984) 'Determinants of internal labor markets in organizations', *Administrative Science Quarterly* 29: 550–72.

Piore, M. and Sabel, C. (1984) *The Second Industrial Divide: Possibilities for Prosperity*, New York: Basic Books.

Pondy, L. R. and Mitroff, I. I. (1979) 'Beyond open system models of organization', in L. L. Cummings and B. M. Staw (eds) *Research in Organizational Behaviour* 1: 3–29, Greenwich, CT: JAI Press.

Poole, M. and Jenkins, G. (1990) *The Impact of Economic Democracy: Profit-Sharing and Employee Shareholding Schemes*, London: Routledge.

Powell, G. N. and Butterfield, D. A. (1978) 'The case for sub-system climate in organizations', *Academy of Management Review* 3: 151–7.

Price, R. (1989) 'Trade union membership', in R. Bean (ed.) *International Labour Statistics*, 146–81, London: Routledge.

Pugh, D. S. and Hickson, D. J. (eds) (1976) *Organizational Structure in Its Context: The Aston Programme 1*, Farnborough: Gower.

Pugh, D. S., Hickson, D. J., Hinings, C. R., and Turner, C. (1968) 'Dimensions of organizational structure', *Administrative Science Quarterly* 13: 65–105.

Pugh, D. S. and Payne, R. (1977) *Organizational Behaviour in its Context: The Aston Programme III*, Farnborough: Saxon House.

Purcell, J. and Sisson, K. (1983) 'Strategies and practice in the management of industrial relations', in G. Bain (ed.) *Industrial Relations in Britain*, 95–120, Oxford: Basil Blackwell.

Rainnie, A. F. and Scott, M. G. (1986) 'Industrial relations in the small firm', in J. Curran *et al.* (eds) *The Survival of The Small Firm, Volume 2*, Aldershot: Gower.

Roberts, K. H., Hulin, C. L., and Rousseau, D. M. (1978) *Developing an Interdisciplinary Science of Organizations*, San Francisco: Jossey Bass.

Ross, A. and Hartman, P. (1960) *Changing Patterns of Industrial Conflict*, New York: Wiley.

Rousseau, D. (1978) 'Characteristics of departments, positions and individuals: contexts for attitudes and behaviour', *Administrative Science Quarterly* 23: 521–40.

Rousseau, D. M. (1988) 'The construction of climate in organizational research', in C. L. Cooper and I. Robertson (eds) *International Review of Industrial and Organizational Pychology*, Chichester: Wiley.

Rubery, J. (1986) 'Trade unions in the 1980s: the case of the United Kingdom', in R. Edwards *et al.* (eds) *Unions in Crisis and Beyond: Perspectives from Six Countries*, Dover, Mass.: Auburn House.

Rutherford, T. (1990) 'The Canadian automobile industry: work reorganization and industrial relations change', *Employee Relations* 12: 27–32.

Sabel, C. (1982) *Work and Politics: The Division of Labour in Industry*, Cambridge: Cambridge University Press.

Sack, J. and Lee, T. (1989) 'The role of the State in Canadian labour relations', *Relations Industrielles* 44: 195–223.

Schneider, B., Parkinson, J. J., and Buxton, V. M. (1980) 'Employee and customer perception of services in banks', *Administrative Science Quarterly* 25: 252–67.

Schneider, B. and Reichers, A. E. (1983) 'On the etiology of climates', *Personnel Psychology* 36: 19–39.

Shimada, H. and Hayami, H. (1986) 'Working hours and the revision of the labour standards law in Japan', Proceedings of the International Industrial Relations Association, 7th World Congress, 3: 211–22 (*New Trends in Working Time Arrangements*), Hamburg.

Shrout, P. E. and Fleiss, J. L. (1979) 'Interclass correlation: uses in assessing rater reliability', *Psychological Bulletin* 88: 420–28.

Sisson, K. (1989) 'Personnel management in transition?' in K. Sisson (ed.) *Personnel Management in Britain*, 22–52, Oxford: Basil Blackwell.

Smircich, L. (1983) 'Concepts of culture and organizational analysis', *Administrative Science Quarterly* 28: 339–76.

Starkey, K. and McKinlay, A. (1989) 'Beyond Fordism? strategic choice and labour relations in Ford U.K.', *Industrial Relations Journal* 20: 93–100.

Storey, J. (ed.) (1989) *New Perspectives on Human Resource Management*, London: Routledge.

Strauss, G. (1987) 'The future of human resource management', in D. J. B. Michell (ed.) *The Future of Industrial Relations*, Los Angeles: Institute of Industrial Relations, University of California.

Strauss, G. and Feuille, P. (1978) 'IR research: a critical analysis', *Industrial Relations* 17: 259–77.

Swamidass, P. M. and Newell, W. T. (1987) 'Manufacturing strategy, environmental uncertainty and performance: a path analytic model', *Management Science* 33: 509–24.

Tagiuri, R. and Litwin, G. H. (1968) *Organizational Climate: Exploration of a Concept*, Boston: Harvard University Press.

Terry, M. (1986) 'How do we know if shop stewards are getting weaker?', *British Journal of Industrial Relations* 24: 169–79.

Thompson, J. D. (1967) *Organizations in Action*, New York: Wiley.

Thomson, A. and Warner, M. (1981) *The Behavioural Sciences and Industrial Relations*, Aldershot: Gower.

Turnbull, P. (1988) 'The limits to Japanisation: just-in-time, labour relations and the U.K. automotive industry', *New Technology, Work and Employment* 3: 7–20.

Turner, H. A., Roberts, G., and Roberts, D. (1977) *Management Characteristics and Labour Conflict*, Cambridge: Cambridge University Press.

Ursell, G. (1991) 'Human resource management and labour flexibility: some reflections based on cross national and sectoral studies in Canada and the U.K.', in P. Blyton and J. Morris (eds) *A Flexible Future?* Berlin: De Gruyter.

Ursell, G. and Blyton, P. (1988) *State, Capital and Labour: Changing Patterns of Power and Dependence*, London: Macmillan.

Warr, P. B., Fineman, S., Nicholson, N., and Payne, R. L. (1978) *Developing Employee Relations*, Farnborough: Teakfield.

Watson, D. (1988) *Managers of Discontent*, London: Routledge.

Wheeler, J., Mansfield, R., and Todd, D. (1980) 'Structural implications of organizational dependence upon customers and owners: similarities and differences', *Organization Studies* 1: 327–48.

Whetton, D. A. (1980) 'Organizational decline: a neglected topic in organizational science', *Academy of Management Review* 5: 577–88.

Wickens, P. (1987) *The Road to Nissan*, London: Macmillan.

Wilkinson, B. and Oliver, N. (1990) 'Obstacles to Japanisation: the case of Ford UK', *Employee Relations* 12: 17–21.

Wood, S. (1988) 'Between Fordism and flexibility? the US car industry', in R. Hyman and W. Streeck (eds) *New Technology and Industrial Relations*, 101–27, Oxford: Basil Blackwell.

Wood, S. (1989) 'The transformation of work', in S. Wood (ed.) *The Transformation of Work? Skill, Flexibility and the Labour Process*, 1–43, London: Unwin Hyman.

Woodward, J. (1965) *Industrial Organizations: Theory and Practice*, London: Oxford University Press.

Wright, S. (1960) 'Path coefficients and path regressions: alternative or complementary concepts?' *Biometrics* 16: 189–202.

Zammuto, R. F. and Cameron, K. (1985) 'Environmental decline and organizational responses', in L. L. Cummings and B. M. Staw (eds) *Research in Organizational Behaviour* 7: 223–62, Greenwich CT: JAI Press.

Zeffane, R. M. (1989) 'Centralization or formalization? indifference curves for strategies of control', *Organization Studies* 10: 327–52.

Zeffane, R., Dastmalchian, A., and Adamson, R. (1990) 'The effects of demographic factors on group climate: evidence from an Australian study', Working Paper, Division of Administration, Griffith University, Brisbane, Australia.

Zohar, D. (1980) 'Safety climate in industrial organizations: theoretical and applied implications', *Journal of Applied Psychology* 65: 96–102.

Index